SKINNY TAN & RICH

When nothing is sure,
everything is possible.
— MARGARET DRABBLE

SKINNY TAN & RICH

A MEMOIR

UNVEILING THE MYTH

Maryanne Comaroto

BRIDGE THE GAP PUBLISHING
CLARITY OF VISION
SAN FRANCISCO, CALIFORNIA

PUBLISHED BY
BRIDGE THE GAP PUBLISHING
CLARITY OF VISION
336 BON AIR CENTER, STE 124
GREENBRAE, CA 94904
www.bridgethegap.com

PRINTED IN THE UNITED STATES OF AMERICA

FIRST EDITION

LIBRARY OF CONGRESS CONTROL NUMBER: 2003107425
ISBN 0-9716712-9-X

BOOK AND COVER DESIGN: DOTTI ALBERTINE
EDITED BY: ELIANNE OBADIA AND MARILYN SCHWADER
BACKUP COPYEDITING AND PROOFREADING: GEORGE MARSH AND HEIDI GARFIELD

FOR MY SON

I love you more than the world.

My parents on their wedding day

Me at age five

CONTENTS

ACKNOWLEDGEMENTS

Finishing this manuscript took me six and a half years. It felt like twenty. Thank you all for your relentless support and encouragement. It was like being pregnant for almost seven years and then—OH MY GOD, it's a book!

To my son, whom I love more than the world, the absolute greatest joy I have ever known. To Shakti, catalyst supreme, my stylist—God knows I needed one—and my Ed McMahon. Without your deafening cheerleading I would have never finished this book. You have been my best friend (even when I didn't want one), something only you could get away with. To Maxi—my rock, my family: Our love will harbor always. I couldn't have done it without you.

Peter, I trusted you when I trusted no one. You're a model for any man. Ron, thank you for being a gentleman; you've become the father we all wish we had. Doug, I didn't even know what a writing coach was until you. Your belief in me was greater than my own when I handed you the first draft of my dream. I can barely comprehend, never mind express, my gratitude for your selfless devotion. Thanks a million, billion apples. To Cynthia Oti, my friend on high. Your priceless tears shed light for me in a place of otherwise grave darkness. This book would have made you laugh. To Karen, for reminding me to play. To Lee, for your generosity of heart. To John and Deborah, for not giving me a bill and for helping me extend my reach. To M.T., for being in the wrong place at the right time and saying yes and no when I needed to hear it.

To my mother, for your courage and for passing me the baton. To my father, for being an ambitious sperm donor. You gave me the gift of life and a great pair of genes. To David, for hearing my call through the ethers, for loving my most ugly parts and helping me fulfill my dreams.

To Palen, my elegant, brilliant, most trusted friend. Yin and yang have got nothing on us, sister. I love who you are. To Marilyn—whew, where did you come from? Oh, right . . . God sent you just in time. You are impeccable and graceful. Your gentle nature is like salve on very old wounds. Elianne, for your love of God and dedication to making a good book great. You truly are the Writer's Midwife. I am grateful we could complete the circle. Thank you for your willingness to let J. transcend your inheritance. To Dawna, publicist extraordinaire, I'm so glad you picked up the phone. You are more proof of the Divine. (P.S. Thank you for getting me and being relentless.) To Robert, my precious friend, you are a huge talent, a gifted photographer, and an even more beautiful soul. I can't thank you enough for all you have done.

Dotti, you were a master at translating the essence of this story into a cover that is a compelling invitation. Thank you for making being naked safe—as it was intended to be. Here's to all your trudging! George, you have plussed this world by just being in it; you should have had a million kids. You're an ace as a backup editor and proofer, to boot—lucky us. To Paul—yellow shorts, lead in your thumb—for suggesting steak instead of pizza and for not getting mad when I projected that real men don't wear tennis shoes with jeans. Your heart is pure and so is your love—thank you for sharing it with me.

To Heidi, for being a speeding bullet and quickly jumping on board—and doing a fine job at the most critical time. To Lisbeth for providing the zig for our zag. Wendy, Wendy . . . all I can say is, "Willie Wonka Lives!" Huge isn't a big enough word for you. To my second home in Beverly Hills, the Four Seasons Hotel, for providing a safe nest so I can soar to greater heights. Gene, you're not last; actually you're next in line to God. Whaddya think Richard's doing right now? Is he still on the phone? To James, David T, Nicole, King Arthur and Lady Guinevere, Barney's, and Trudy—and to myriad wonderful people I've met along my travels while producing this book. You know who you are—thank you with all my heart.

And to God, Divine Master of the Universe, whose unconditional love, sense of humor, and sometimes infuriating sense of timing has shown me the way so that I can be free.

I go forth to do your bidding . . .

PREFACE

It's a sunny morning and I'm sitting in my favorite chair by my kitchen window, watching my eleven-year-old son gyrating in front of me, playing his air guitar. Pretending to be Jimmy Page and then John Bonham, he switches back and forth between guitar and drums. And we laugh as he grinds around inside his imaginary hula hoop (his imitation of me dancing) while we both make funny faces. He is free in his body, mind, and spirit—the way kids are supposed to be—without feeling foolish. Even so, he looks over at me from time to time to make sure I am watching him. I am. What I am "supposed to be" doing is finishing my book. My production team is waiting for the part where I'm supposed to tell you why you should read this book and explain what you will get out of it. But they, and the book, will have to wait. Because I know that look in my son's eyes—that pure, innocent need to be seen, to be adored. And I know that his self-esteem and future hinge on what I choose to do at times like this. And now it dawns on me what I want to say to you—why I wrote this book in the first place.

Each time I can really be here for my son, it becomes less and less likely that he will spend the rest of his life as I did, desperately trying to fill that natural longing we all have, that turns into a gaping hole when that longing is crushed by ignorance, neglect, or abuse. Every time I meet him in this sacred place means one less time he'll have to turn to things that can never give him what he's really looking for.

I am reminded of a saying that I have heard for years: *You can't give what you don't have.* I understand now precisely why I can share this thing with my son and why my parents could not give this thing to me. That is what this book—my story—is about. Finding that thing.

FOREWORD

It is rare that one meets a writer with true insight into the mechanics of how people act and react—a writer who also knows how to artfully verbalize that process. I have known Maryanne Comaroto for many years and in all the meetings I have had with her to discuss strategies and tools for happiness, I have been amazed at her no-nonsense approach. She deftly uses her skills to get to the core of what is going on with people. Most importantly, her genuine demeanor encourages people to listen to, and absorb, her advice rather than just react impulsively to it.

Time and time again, Maryanne's concern for people has put them at ease so that they can really benefit from her knowledge. She is like the perfect teacher—comforting, not authoritarian; empowering, not egotistical. More than anything she has an uncanny way of letting those she counsels see the light by making them feel that she is just a catalyst—that it is they who are achieving the goal. In my years of developing cognitive strategies, I have never come across another person who applies such creativity to the psychological and emotional arenas of counseling.

Maryanne is a refreshing voice and talent whose insights will resonate with readers from all walks of life. *Skinny, Tan & Rich* will inspire you to get closer to what we all really want—happiness and passion in our lives.

— GARY R. GRUBER, PH.D.
   AUTHOR OF 30 BOOKS ON CRITICAL THINKING

NOTES TO THE READER

My family has suffered enough. Causing them further pain is not my intention as I share my story. Most of my family members are firmly and steadily journeying their own path toward wholeness and consciousness. This book recognizes the brave and noble efforts on their part that critically illustrates what happens as we stumble through our lives, trying every which way to fill that hole inside each of us.

The events portrayed in this book are all true. If anything, sometimes I have toned down my stories because I wasn't sure you'd believe me. Only the names have been changed—except for the dog's and the cat's—to shield the innocent and to protect myself from the guilty.

And, as far as God is concerned, please use any name that does it for you—plain old "God" has always worked for me. Spirit, the One, Higher Power, Allah, Hashem, the Divine Master of the Universe—whatever . . . as long as you give God the credit, he, she, or it doesn't care what name you use.

INTRODUCTION

When I was a young girl, I wanted to be Skinny, Tan & Rich. When I grew up, I wanted to be Skinnier, Tanner, and Richer. I believed that then, everything would be okay. Because for most of my life, every-thing was far from okay. Death, drugs, abuse, alcoholism, and the Mob—that was my reality. Being Skinny, Tan & Rich for me trans-lated into living happily ever after—it was the only place I thought I could find immunity from pain.

I don't have to look far to see that I haven't been alone in this struggle. Our culture breeds and then subsidizes the illusion that when we finally get _____ (fill in the blank), everything will be okay: "If I had a different family . . . when I get a better education . . . if I were smarter . . . if I had more money . . . when I get married . . . if I were prettier . . . when I get that Porsche . . . when I get a divorce . . . if I had kids, no kids, fewer kids, more kids . . ." We ache for some-thing—some person, some circumstance, some object—to fill the hole, escape that gaping blankness. Most of us go to our grave with-out even wondering if there is something wrong with this picture. And even if we do, we aren't even asking the right questions: So what is it we are really seeking? And where do we begin to look for it?

This book is the beginning of my story about how things were, how I wanted them to be, and how I sold my soul to bridge that gap. It's about waking up—when all hope is lost, when you have tried over and over again, only to find that the faces in your life have changed but you haven't. When you think you can't take it anymore—you can't read one more self-help book, listen to one more pearl of wisdom, go to one more therapy session or workshop—when you are convinced you have exhausted every possibility. It's about the miracle that hap-pens right at that point . . . when, with your last authentic breath, you reach out and ask to be set free.

MY RESUME´

My background is mayhem and madness
I have mastered insufferable tortuous resolve
This plague of shame and battered innocence
My shattered spirit beyond reproach
The truth
In and between each shallow breath
Apocalyptic excruciating surrender
The end of suffering
I am that

PART ONE

■ *Who They Told Me I Was*

MY FAIRY TALE—call it my childhood—alternated between Disneyland and a war zone. And if I had to pick a war—well, I would have to say Vietnam. The fact that my father's name is Bruno and not Ho Chi Minh is merely a coincidence. I was sent into combat unprepared after my prebirth application for conscientious objector was denied. And just for the record, I did not volunteer. If I'd had a clue, I would have fled to Canada.

What must have looked from the far ethers like an episode of *Father Knows Best* was, up close, in mortal flesh, more like a suicide mission at My Lai. Our shell-shocked cast and crew included my two brothers, four stepmothers, and one actual mother who fell out of an Alfred Hitchcock movie, and landed on her . . . knees.

It's true, we did resemble most of the other two-car-garage, picket-fenced dwellers that lined the streets where we lived. We even had family traditions—only ours involved offensive language and weapons, and were frequently characterized by huddling together like sitting ducks waiting for the next guided missile to land.

Routinely making veins pop out of his neck and forehead before he threw one of us through a wall was my father's idea of intimacy. My father—Benvenuto Adolph DelRiccio, aka Bruno—was a cross between Hitler and Hulk Hogan: a self-appointed evil dictator and bottle blonde on an unholy mission to have whatever he wanted, whenever he wanted it, no matter what it cost the rest of us. With aplomb, panache, and carnivorous zeal, *Daddy Dearest*—a da Vinci of charm, a Picasso of seduction, a minotaur of self-absorbed charisma—seduced the weak by force and had his fill. And if charm and seduction didn't work . . . well, they always did. And I, his reluctant disciple.

He called me his Little Princess, which for all intents and purposes led me to believe I would someday inherit . . . I don't know, a throne, maybe. Well, turns out the only throne I was going to inherit was located in the john and it already had a second mortgage on it.

Enter Daddy Bruno: The Family Values Antichrist

"REPEAT AFTER ME: 'Daddy's handsome, tall, and strong!' Come on. Say it! 'Daddy's handsome, tall, and strong!'" The words are still imprinted like a neon tattoo in my cerebral cortex. Nearly every time my father walked by a mirror, he'd stop, hold up his arms, flex his bulging biceps, flash himself this enormous, seductive smile, exposing his perfect white teeth, and simultaneously pulse his chest muscles rhythmically from left to right: *boom boompa-boom, boompa-boom, boompa-boom.* Not even he could resist his own well-rehearsed, finely honed charm. How could the rest of us? Now if his smooth, airbrushed persona, good looks (an Elvis Presley–Gregory Peck hybrid), and diabolical cunning weren't enough, his demoralizing verse was. My father drank Molotov cocktails and pissed nitroglycerin—gifts he eventually showered on us all. But he used to bring me salami and Mortadella at the end of the day, delivered always with that devastating smile. Grateful for small favors, at one time, I thought he was God.

In truth, my father was a city boy and a third-generation Italian mutt. Instead of sending him to private schools my grandparents spent their money trying to keep him out of jail. And my parents spent part of their honeymoon in court fighting a rape charge from one of his teenage girlfriends.

Enter Mother: The Lamb in Mink Clothing

MY MOTHER WAS EASILY one of the most beautiful women on the planet. She was fit for a king—at least that's what my father always said. Her parents spent their money sending her away to private Catholic "good girl" school, where mean nuns taught her fork etiquette. My grandparents said she had to go because her blood was blue. I wondered if that meant mine was purple. Due to her heavy breeding, Mother was predisposed to falling from the land of make-believe and landing on her random appendages. This lamb had most assuredly married the Big Bad Wolf. But doomed or damned, anyone who could wear a seven-story beehive on her head and still look fabulous was my hero. (I did wonder where all that hair went, come morning. Did it suck back into her head like my new Barbie's? And did bees actually live in it?) Mother's Grace Kelly elegance mixed with Doris Day warmth and a dash of *I Love Lucy* was a self-addressed, stamped invitation to Satan. Her most attractive quality was her naïveté; she thought vanity was a color of lipstick.

Her idea of exercise was a motion faintly resembling a side bend, followed by what she swore was a leg lift, and sometimes two. Afterwards, she'd exhale as if she'd run a marathon and resume her station at the kitchen sink. Yet it must have been exercise, as she never gained weight. When I'd ask why she didn't sweat when she exercised, like Daddy did, she'd purse her lips and reply, "Ladies perspire, they don't sweat." I thought she was just lazy.

My mother rarely missed a beat where her children were concerned. One day my younger brother, Tony, flew out the rear window of our wood-paneled station wagon at twenty miles an hour—just to see if he could (topping his feat the week before of drinking half a bottle of paint thinner and vomiting pink champagne bubbles—or were they Captain Crunch Berry Chunks? I can't remember). When my older brother and I announced at the top of our lungs that Tony had leapt to his latest death, her expression didn't change. In fact, she never said a word. She stopped the car, put it in Park, glanced over her shoulder above the rims of her white Jackie O sunglasses, got out, knelt gracefully, and peered under the first car in the cavalcade now stopped behind us. When she spotted Tony under the car, she stood up. Her expression of mild disapproval seemed to say, "Really now, Tony." She wriggled under the car and disappeared up to her thighs.

Meanwhile, its owners, an old couple who'd unwittingly driven on top of my little brother, had gotten out of their car and stood nearby, clutching each other in horror, while my older brother and I hung out the back window, lapping up the suspense. Mother emerged a moment later, pulling my three-year-old brother's slightly bruised body out like a rabbit out of a hat.

"Not a scratch on him!" said the old man, amazed and relieved. Mother just smiled and put Tony back in his seat. And we drove off with the back window still open.

Enter Me: Maryanne Savannah DelRiccio
Born 9 lb. 10 oz | Hopelessly Female
10.24.1964 | 2:21 p.m. | San Francisco, California

DID I MENTION THAT I WAS BORN? That's when my troubles began. My initial infant gender-bias programming was hardly over when female emasculation boot camp started. I was five and fated to learn the hard way what good girls do—and don't. The guiding "Good Girl" principle was simple: Anything that felt good (like kissing boys and masturbating) was "bad" and everything that felt bad (like eating Brussels sprouts, drinking cod liver oil, or being punished for doing what felt good) was "good." Imagine my confusion. Not to mention my disappointment. I was drawn toward the "bad" things and spent most of my time savoring guilty pleasures with a feeling of impending doom. It didn't help that I was, at least in theory, Catholic. Which engendered my spiritual disorientation.

Every Sunday morning, while my father was still sleeping, Mother would drag the rest of us to church—which smelled like moth balls—so we could listen to some old guy yell at us and she could hit herself in the chest every time he started talking about God's lambs. Stand-up-sit-down, stand-up-sit-down, and then every once in a while, we got to rest while we kneeled on that long leather kickstand thing, which made my back ache. Anyway, I would fold my hands and squeeze my eyes shut and pray, "Please, God, hurry up and make this guy finish so we can go." And even though the priest never

once said, "Eat it or wear it" before he stuck those little white card-
board discs into our mouths (a reprieve from our usual invocation at
the dinner table), I knew somehow that this was all an act because as
soon as we left church to go home, I was reminded that we belonged
to one holy and alcoholic church. And everyone knew that we already
served one God—and his initials were not J.C. They were B.A.D.

In our house we didn't have to wait to see if God would answer
our prayers; we knew the answer as soon as our father came through
the door at the end of the day. Most all personal requests were met
with a proverbial, "What part of 'no' do you not understand?" It was
plain to see that tyrannical rhetoric was one of the things the Catholic
Church and my father had in common.

The "Good Girl Do's and Don'ts" that defined my life were not
only dictated by my father, but also by the random zealots who occupied the pulpit every Sunday. They were reinforced ad nauseam like
Orwellian propaganda by my teachers, neighbors, relatives, strangers,
policemen, TV shows and commercials, magazines, movies, books,
and probably even J. Edgar Hoover (who no one yet knew was a flam-
ing queen). And I was already sufficiently reminded—shamed,
spanked, hit, manipulated, and scolded by these ubiquitous Behavior
Police, and even barked at by stray dogs—that I wasn't "getting it." It
was made perfectly clear that if I was to survive in this world, young
lady, I had better get one thing straight! I never did find out what that
"thing" was. Anyway, I had other fish to fry.

Enter Gypsy Rose: Me, First Grader

MOTHER BOUGHT ME A LITTLE RED MINISKIRT in the first
grade. It was really short, and very red. I loved it. Alas, seeing one's
chubby little buns hanging out of a skirt that wasn't much more than
a cummerbund and thinking, "How cute!" was destined to skip my
generation; already, at six, my father reminded me that that's how
whores dressed. But wearing it for that one brief year gave me that
"good" naughty-girl feeling I already knew was "bad" and loved so
much. The feeling was nothing I could articulate—more like a subtle

film, an ambiance that seemed to surround and accompany me, as it would for years to come.

This is how, at age six, I was inexplicably sucked vacuum-like into my first cultural taboo: the inappropriate display of female sexuality. (It is precisely here where someone switched the word "shame" for "sexuality" in my Good Girl Handbook.)

My taboo revealed its versatility, when I got a crush on two boys at the same time: Mike Smith and David Pirotto. Ohhh, they were both so adorable. Mike more charming; David just plain handsome. And I wanted them both. What dilemma? It never occurred to me this was some either/or situation. Until my so-called friends informed me that I had to pick one or the other. (It apparently had something to do with Valentine's Day. I didn't see the logic.) I felt confused, then suddenly ashamed. I felt like something was wrong with me. But why should I have to pick? Who said I could only like one person at a time? And say, what's the rush here? I'm only six! Besides, Robert Aucci likes me too! And maybe I like him. Three! Maybe I like liking them all. Get me a calculator; I'm going to keep liking them all . . . and I'll just keep it to myself!

So a life of strategizing was born, trying—against all odds—to preserve my authentic self while doing what everybody else wanted me to do. On rainy days during recess I'd orchestrate a game called The Flintstones, which took place in the year ten gazillion B.M. (Before Monogamy). In our "cave" underneath a classroom table, Mike was Fred and David was Barney. A replaceable girlfriend, whose sole function was to stand there and act as cover while I was under the table with the two boys, took the part of Betty. And I, of course, was Wilma, a six-year-old closet polygamist. Ohhh, bad, bad Wilma. Naughty, naughty. How I used to pray for rainy days.

Enter Daddy: Drunk, 3 a.m.—Exit God

PRAYING WAS AS COMFORTING as my mother's presence. Neither provided the barrier of protection necessary to ward off reality, and both were on par with trying to slay a dragon with a tiara.

"Now I lay me down to sleep. I pray the Lord my soul to keep. If I should die before I wake, I pray the Lord my soul to take . . ."

Sometimes at night I can still hear his footsteps coming down the hall. That deliberate walk, the distinct way he cleared his throat. I would hold my breath, lie perfectly still, hoping he was on his way to the kitchen. My body frozen stiff, listening for those extra steps, I prayed to God that my father would walk past my bedroom. But sometimes God didn't want Daddy to go—or couldn't make him go—to the kitchen. Father knows best.

At six years old, I could imagine few things worse than being pressed beneath a 220-pound drunken man. But when it was my father, the contradictions multiplied, and the rules became more complicated. By the time I was seven, my Good Girl Handbook had some astounding revisions, with asterisks and footnotes explaining the murkier paradoxical protocols of filial relations. And being abused by Daddy was the biggest complication of all.

Where's Santa Claus?

"WAKE UP, JOHNNY. GET UP!" I shook my older brother. He was on the top bunk. My little brother woke up first.

"Is Santa here?" Tony asked, rubbing his eyes.

"No, wait, Tony, don't go out there; you stay here. Santa's not here yet. Go back to bed," I commanded. "Johnny, come on," I said, louder.

He pushed me away and turned toward the wall, pulling the covers over his head.

"You have to come out in the living room. Hurry," I said.

"I wanna come too," said Tony.

"Go back to sleep," I said. "I'll come and get you as soon as Santa's here, 'kay?"

"Pwomiss?" he said, with his adorable little lisp.

"I promise. Go back to sleep. Johnny, will you get up!" I said, for the last time.

Brother John threw his pillow at me and muttered, "Okay, okay, I'm coming." He flung his legs over the side of the top bunk, wiping the drool from his mouth.

"Hurry, they're out there," I whispered, as we made our way out into the hall. I pushed him in front of me. "You go first," I said. "They're on the chair."

"Who's on the chair?" he asked.

"Mom and Pedro."

"Who?"

"Mom and Pedro," I repeated. "Look." The two of them were in the living room, sitting right where they were when I left them. Only now they had an audience.

"What is she doing?" Johnny asked.

"What does it look like she's doing?" I snapped. They were wrapped around each other, like Klingons, in the orange swivel loveseat near the Christmas tree.

"She's kissing the gardener. She's making out with the gardener," he said, looking at me in disbelief.

"Good morning, kidz, 'appy Chris-maz," said Pedro, pausing from their face fest and looking up. I waved and gave a courtesy smile. My brother just stood there. My mother was busy looking around for her glass. She hadn't noticed us yet; she was drunk.

Finally she looked up and said, "Gez-wut, kidz? U-git-to opan pressies wiff Pedro." I couldn't understand either one of them. It was like I was still dreaming, only I was in hell and no one spoke English.

"Where's Dad?" asked Johnny, accusation in his voice.

"Your father won't be home for Christmas," she said, suddenly sober. Her eyes filled with tears. She looked like she had already been crying. My mother turned her head away from us. Absolutely flustered, I started to cry.

There were few pauses between absolute frustration and tears during my childhood. If you were going to feel anything in my house, you'd better hurry up or "I'll really give you something to cry about" was waiting for you in your room. Any display of emotion was license to employ punitive measures, sanctioned, of course, by those who owned penises in our family; in this case that meant my brother.

"Stop crying, you baby," said Johnny, punching me in the arm.

"Owww," I whined. "Stop hitting me." He hit me again.

"There's nothing to cry about," he said.

"Stop," I said, and slapped him back. "I'm not crying, you meanie."

"Yes, you are. Baby," he said, pushing me.

"Come on now, open your presents," my mother said, as though we were just having one of our usual arguments. She slopped around, trying to get out of her seat. "Come and give me a hug." My brother, disgusted, stormed off to his bedroom, just having invalidated the entirety of my femininity, which was becoming a habit.

What did I do? I wondered. Did I set Mother up with the gardener? Did I tell Santa to turn me into a human piñata? What the heck is going on? I wasn't sure what I was supposed to do, but I was beginning to see a pattern here: lots of rules being broken, orders being given, and doors slamming. I think they call that the "Do what I say, don't do what I do" syndrome. It was becoming an epidemic in my house—or whoever's house it was; at this point I wasn't really sure.

So far, I had ascertained that anyone taller than me who had a penis (size did not matter) handed down the law and wrote and rewrote the rules as they pleased. The rest of us were advised to calm down, relax, get ahold of ourselves; we were placated or patronized, as the case may be. Until, of course, they needed something. Okay. Got it. Check. Now how do I get one of those penises? Heck, maybe I'd get a bunch of them. I was determined to find a way.

Little did I realize how easy that would turn out to be.

So there I was, frightened and completely weirded out. Christmas was supposed to be all about me and my subplot brothers. Instead, it was like being in the Twilight Zone. Not that I knew what that was, but that didn't stop it from being it. Besides, opening presents with Pedro was definitely not on my Christmas list. As a matter of fact, up to this point, Pedro was just an extra. Like some action figure that lurked around the yard once and a while—you know, like the mailman or the butcher, the baker, the candlestick maker. Like those people that are there, but don't ever come to your house and make out with your mom.

The good news was that my father moved just down the street. The bad news was that my father talked my grandmother, who held our second mortgage, into foreclosing on my mother. So instead of getting the Barbie townhouse that I wanted that Christmas, we moved into one. And instead of having Christmas with my family, I went to my father's new house and spent Christmas with the Addams family: his new girlfriend and her offspring, who were attempting to impersonate children. To say they were creepy was an understatement. And instead of going to Mass on Christmas morning like we usually did, we spent the day with Satan himself.

Right about now is when I stopped believing in the Easter Bunny, the Tooth Fairy, and Santa Claus. My relationship with God would henceforth be scrutinized with the same suspicion I had for all of the above. Our already fragile relationship could not take the added strain of my growing disbelief. I'd about had it up to here, anyway. I just could not understand why, when I prayed and prayed to God, it was the devil who kept answering my prayers.

Being helpless and hopeless, now there's a fine combo! Nothing a whole lot of self-will and a good dose of Darwinism couldn't remedy. But I was only eight. I just wanted my Daddy to come home. A couple of months before he left, my grandfather died. My father and I were taking a shower together; he was crying. I had never seen him cry. He told me he was only taking me to the funeral—not my brothers or even my mother—and that someday I would understand why. I felt special—special because he chose me and special because he had some mysterious message he would deliver to me at some magical moment when I grew up. I could barely wait. There were so many things waiting for me in that future. The secret ingredients to my grandmother's pasta sauce, the secret behind my father's card tricks, and how my grandfather could whistle so loud using his fingers. I just couldn't wait to grow up—because I knew then everything would be okay, just like my dad promised.

Next Stop: Purgatory

AND WHAT OF MISTER ROGERS? Yeah, well, our new neighborhood was like Queens—except there was no queen. And there were also no gardeners named Pedro. That was okay because there was no garden. We had been banished from the kingdom to the other side of the tracks—the place my mother had often referred to as the land where "those people" lived. Now we were those people.

We moved from a castle into a Cracker Jack box, only with no prize at the bottom. Unless you consider being suddenly poor a blessing in disguise. I did not. I had grown quite fond of having whatever I wanted, whenever I wanted it. Being poor was unacceptable. Especially when I was involved.

My mother's new boyfriend, Lance—who only wore white tennis shorts and slicked his hair back with Grecian Formula—joined us downwind. (I wondered, did he ever change his clothes? Did he bathe? Maybe he was European. I just didn't know.)

Incessant reminders from my mother that she was the parent and I was the child, in lieu of some kind of rationale for our recent exile, was getting on my nerves. This was like offering me an ice pick when I had a headache. Her newfound Transactional Analysis perspective, declaring I was the child and she was the adult, would have made sense had she (a) acted like an adult, and (b) not punished me for being a child. So right off the bat her attempt at establishing new rules of engagement was ineffective and obviously contradictory to her own stated values, however passionate her appeal. She did not have a penis and we all knew it.

During my mother's initial attempt to recalibrate our fundamental stimulus-response mechanisms, I was informed that in some parts of the world, kids my age were already working. Why did I need to know that at nine years old? Was this supposed to somehow inspire or motivate me? I didn't care what she said; there was no way she was going to convince me that shopping for anything at Mervyn's, as opposed to Saks Fifth Avenue, was a good thing.

She started repeating herself instead of offering actual explanations for any inquiry. For example, if I said, "Mom, John drank all the milk and Tony ate all the Lucky Charms. What am I supposed to eat for breakfast?"

She'd reply, "When it's gone, it's gone."

I'd try and explain, "Yeah, but . . ."

She'd just repeat, "When it's gone, it's gone."

Gosh. Thanks for your deep insight and understanding, Mother. This is incredibly useful information. I'm starving here! Maybe she thought I was fat and needed to go on a diet. Now we were fat *and* poor—that's just great. I'm sure I'll be very popular at my new school!

Doing dishes, scrubbing toilets, and cleaning out the cat box made me want to barf. This was . . . someone else's job, not mine. What happened to the lady who used to clean our house—why can't she do it? And how is it my mother's duty list seemed to be missing my brothers' names? It must have been that penis thing again . . . although having one of those meant you had to take out the trash. Hardly compensatory. However, it was one less vile task that needed my attention.

For the most part, my brothers and I had always stuck together. (Okay, so occasionally we were traitors.) It used to be that in times of chaos—if, say, we wanted to run away—we did it together. If we wanted to ambush the babysitter, we did it together. All for one and one for . . . me first. It was like being in the Donner party, only we had no teeth.

We were passengers and my mother was the captain. The problem was, she'd never sailed a ship in her life; she'd never even had a job. And I had no idea that my mother had been trying to get away from my father for years; I thought he was the one who left us. So I couldn't understand why we just didn't go back home. Her "picture this" promised-land pitch was starting to get old, and it was about to turn into a real nightmare. My first day at my new school was all the proof I needed to beg the King to take us back. Me, I had no pride. I didn't even know what pride was.

Of course there was the tiny complication of convincing my mother that catching my father in bed with her best friend was, in fact, a figment of her imagination.

Snow White and the Kids at Folsom

I PEERED IN THE DOORWAY of what was to be my new third-grade classroom. I'm not sure if it was the stench of cigarette smoke or the beer stains on the "inmates'" PeeChee folders that troubled me most. Nevertheless, I was absolutely certain that a terrible mistake had been made. This was clearly the holding tank for an adolescent correctional facility. This room full of life forms so closely resembled a scene from *One Flew Over the Cuckoo's Nest* that one could be sure that life does, in fact, imitate art.

It crossed my mind that there was still time to flee, although my patent leather Mary Janes weren't exactly the wheels I needed. Not that my lime-green baby doll dress and the big satin bow perched on top of my head were the ideal gear for my escape plan either. As I contemplated my departure, a bell rang that sounded suspiciously like an air-raid siren. It was clearly signaling lockdown.

Next thing I knew, this girl who resembled Pippi Longstocking on steroids pulled my arm and steered me into the classroom. She wore combat boots, neon-green Ditto jeans, and a T-shirt that read, "Blondes have more fun." She obviously had never met my mother.

"You new?" she asked, wiping something brown that looked like a bit of tobacco off the end of her tongue. Evidently unfiltered cigarettes were third-grade chic here at Cape Fear. She motioned me to follow her by jutting her chin toward the back row.

"Uhhmm. Yes . . . uh . . . I'm . . . My name is—"

She interrupted me. "Nice bow." She pointed at my head as if I didn't know the bow was there. "So do *all* your clothes look like that?" Was I, perhaps, overdressed?

"Uhhmm . . . Well, my Auntie Anne made this dress for me out of a Butterick pattern. I picked it out, though, and . . ."

She didn't care. She studied me up and down for another

moment and said, "Does your Auntie Anne make all your clothes?"

Awkward pause. I was sure there was a proper response, but with indignation, I said, "No! No, she does not. I have other clothes!"

She stared me in the face, leaned over, and said, "That's good! Maybe you should wear those tomorrow."

Sure, you betcha. That is, if tomorrow ever comes. By the looks of things, this may very well be my last day on the planet.

By now my head was swimming and my face was flushed. I tucked my shiny new shoes underneath my chair as far back as my feet could reach. I felt like a meringue pie in a room full of pork rinds.

The truth is, I knew I didn't belong there. My clothes were just an observable difference. Inside me I knew where I belonged, and that place was full of sugar and spice and everything nice. My world was about Barbie dolls and dress up, not a *Real Cops* episode waiting to happen: "Overdressed third grader sporting Halston ready-to-wear being held for ransom at local juvenile correctional facility—scenes at eleven o'clock." And while we're at it, I live in a big house on a big hill and well . . .

"DelRiccio? Maryanne DelRiccio?" Oh God, she was calling my name. Now everyone would see how stupid I looked. Suddenly my big, beautiful, perfectly tied satin bow felt like a billboard that screamed, "Look at me, I am a dork." I felt like a clown in my green getup, and never mind my way-too-shiny shoes, which were the nails in my coffin. Cause of death: socially unacceptable third-grade attire. No, after my imaginary autopsy, I concluded that it wasn't my attire that was wrong. It was worse than that—much worse. I feared that the something that was wrong was me. The acceptance of that truth would prove to be crippling.

"Maryanne dear, are you here?"

Here? Of course I was here. Even the people in the next stratosphere were hip to my arrival! I wanted to die, or at least disintegrate. *Poof.*

"Here," I chirped, listlessly raising my little arm. Alas, I was a day late and an arm short of escaping the firing squad that every new kid has to face.

"Maryanne dear, why don't you stand up so I can introduce you to the class?" 'Oh my God,' I thought, 'please don't make me do this. Why don't you just ask me to grind around in my hula hoop—naked—on *Solid Gold*. Please don't make me do this, please don't make me do this.' Somewhere in there I even managed to pray really hard, a pathetic plea to God for help as a last resort. Although I was pretty sure—evidenced by the fact that he hadn't returned any of my other calls, especially lately—that God had other matters on his plate that were more important than my current fashion emergency.

"Maryanne? Maryanne dear? Stand up so we can see you."

The rest was a blur. I don't think I passed out or threw up or anything. No, I'd say it was the equivalent of having an emotional blackout, because the next thing I remember, school was out and the "Pippi" girl, who had taken some strange liking to me, was trying to download to me some rules of the road. Somehow, Pippi had gotten hold of my Good Girl Handbook—the one my parents had engraved and given me at birth.

Her additions to the Handbook's list of rules: #1. Don't get caught making out in the ball shack. #2. No glass beer bottles on campus, only aluminum cans—or did she say automatic weapons? #3. Don't cover your answers during a test, yadda, yadda, yadda. I ran all the way home after school that day, ate an entire box of Lucky Charms (when they are gone, my ass), and wondered if Charles Manson had any living relatives . . . who went to my school.

Revised Survival Plan: Stay Alive Until Fourth Grade

BEING DEEMED MENTALLY GIFTED seemed comical considering the company I now kept. But that's the story they were telling me. I was summoned to the principal's office one afternoon and spent the rest of the day locked in a little room with a guy who looked like Albert Finney and had really bad breath. I have always had an incredibly heightened sense of smell, so I figured the faster I finished the battery of tests he was giving me, the less likely I was to be asphyxiated by this man's toxic emissions. And as for the accuracy of my answers, well, I knew if I didn't get the test right the first time, I would be doomed to repeat the experience. I may have been naïve, but I was not a masochist.

So there I was, deemed mentally gifted. If Dr. Seuss's *Green Eggs and Ham* can be considered higher learning, I was brilliant. According to this school, "mentally gifted" meant you got to go directly to the head of the class—and in my case that meant all the way to the sixth grade. Not only that, my reading comprehension skills were at college level, so I was immediately catapulted into the status of brain child. Quite a relief for me, too, because until then I thought I might be stupid.

I had only imagined my life was in danger in this place. Now, with my newly certified intelligence, I could trust that it actually was. When one of my new sixth-grade classmates held her steel hair pick to my throat in the girls' bathroom and suggested I give her my lunch money if I knew what was good for me, I was convinced. And of course, without hesitation, I reached into my jeans and emptied out the $1.25 I had in my right pocket. Holding out my sweaty little palm, I inquired whether or not she needed anything else—my jacket, shoes, the keys to our condo in Tahoe? She just stared at me, snatched the money with her grubby hand, and took off. Note to self: Do not use public restrooms. Advice I heed to this day.

My impending fall from the pool of Pulitzer Prize hopefuls brings to mind the conundrum: "If a tree falls in the forest and no one's there to hear it, does it make a sound?" Well, as my father would say, "Who gives a crap?" This may explain, at least in part, the underwhelming amount of grief my parents displayed when I was sent back to third grade after it became clear I was incapable of sustaining my title as mental giant. I vaguely remember my personal attempt to comfort myself. I told myself it is better to be a live fish in any pond. Hence my sudden Academia Dementia. Survival of the skittish, me thinkest.

My father cheered "Atta girl!" when he saw my report card at the end of the school year. But he was more interested to know if I was still a virgin. I wondered exactly what kind of dementia he suffered from and decided it was beyond my scope of understanding. As for my mother, nothing short of burning the house down could break her stride. As long as I wasn't obviously retarded and my accomplishments or failures didn't interfere with her life, I was good to go.

Adding insult to injury was de rigueur for my parents. The two of them were a walking emotional holocaust. And they were always right there to remind me that things could be worse. I could be walking to school barefoot, uphill, in the snow. Wow! I didn't realize this was an option.

The upshot was, if I needed somebody's legs broken or a cement necklace for one of my friends, Bruno was my man. As for my mother, well, let's just say that in the milk-and-cookies department, "When it's gone, it's gone."

Speaking of Gone . . .

JUST WHEN I THOUGHT THINGS could not get worse, of course they did. We moved again, this time into a place that may as well have been a casket because our new accommodations were about the size of one. Okay, the size of a fat man's casket maybe. The bottom line is, I now had to share a room with my mother in this two-bedroom box. This would prove to be unfortunate on many levels.

Bang bang bang, boom, boom, bang, bang bang. Ding-dong, ding-dong.

"Mom, open the door—we can hear you in there." *Bam, bam bam, ding-dong, ding-dong!*

"Ohhhh, uuuuhhhhh, oooooooohhhh, uuuhhh, uuuhhhhh." Tony and I could hear her moaning through the bedroom window.

Bam! Bam! Bam!

"Mother, open . . . the . . . *door!*" I shouted. Nothing, just more moaning, some laughing, and then a man's voice. My little brother and I banged and shouted for ten minutes in front of our apartment door, until it was clear she wasn't going to let us in. "Come on, Tony." I grabbed his arm and headed down the hall to our grandmother's apartment, which was right next door. We knocked and waited. She wasn't home. "Come on," I said, as I headed across the hall, as if I knew where we were going. I didn't.

"Where are we going?" Tony looked up at me, frightened.

"You'll see," I assured him. *Ding-dong*, the bell sounded as I depressed the button on the stranger's door.

After a few seconds a woman with a Southern accent responded, "Yes, who is it?"

"It's . . . My name is Maryanne. I'm, uh . . . we're your neighbors. Hi." I was fighting back the tears of abandonment and fear, trying to act normal. I waved at her through the peephole. The chain rattled as she slid it to one side, and then she opened the door. She was a petite woman, probably in her late fifties, with coiffed blonde hair that looked like cotton candy. She seemed at home in her tidy gray polyester pantsuit.

"Well, hello there," she said.

"Hi," I said. "This is my brother Tony."

"Hello, Tony. You can call me Susie," she said in her heavy drawl.

I started, "Uuhhhmm, well . . . my mother . . . Uuhhhmm, we can't . . . We . . ." I burst into tears.

"What is the mattah? Oh now, come inside, you dear things. Would you like some iced tea?" she offered.

"Thank you," I sniffed. We stood in her kitchen that smelled like she had just baked something with cinnamon and spice, and watched her pour tea into beautiful crystal glasses.

"Now *what* is the mattah, children?"

"Well, my mother locked us out of the house and we have nowhere to go," I said, void of pride. She stood there in silence for a moment, as if she could not comprehend what I had said.

"Well, let's see. Why don't y'all just wait here for a while until she gets home. I'm sure it won't be long." I was too embarrassed to tell her that my mother was inside the apartment.

Unfortunately, a short while turned into a really long one. It was like forever in dog years. We knocked at our door several times, but there was only silence; she must have gone out.

Just shy of eleven o'clock that night, after fifty rounds of Gin Rummy and countless false alarms, we heard the elevator door open once again. Tony and I scrambled to the door and looked out the peephole to see if it might be her. This time the elevator did produce Mommie Dearest. At first, we were excited and relieved, then embarrassed and disgusted. The perfect invocation for shame.

She didn't even recognize us when we opened the door. She muttered something about not being able to find her "f—ing keys" as she rummaged through her purse, which looked as though it had already been emptied that night with the same intention. All that was left in the bag spilled out into the hallway: a pack of Salem cigarettes, some soggy, a few broken; a handful of little white pills, engraved with W-999—which years later I discovered was benzodiazepam, a tranquilizer; some change; a book of matches with "My Cousin's Place" on the cover. But no keys. Which meant we had to wake up the landlord. Well, actually, our new friend Susie did. Perfect! It was the icing on the cake of my familial day.

When Susie finally elected to speak to my mother, her tone was patronizing without being totally condescending, which must have been a Southern thing. She declared, "Well, well, well. You must be their muthah. We were just about to call the police, dear."

My mother threw her arms up in defeat, looked up at none of us in particular, and slurred, "Can't f-fine m' keys."

Susie sighed and said, "Yes, dear, I can see that."

"I don't know where my car is," my mother continued. Then she looked at me and asked, "Where's my car?" Like I knew where it was and was hiding it from her. I just wanted to go to bed. I had to get up and go to school. I hated this; I hated her. But all I could do was nothing. I was just a ten-year-old kid.

I never wondered if other kids had to find their mother's car, or call in sick for their mom, or take care of their little brothers because their mother was too sick to get out of bed. I never wondered if other kids had to pour out their mother's booze so she wouldn't get any drunker and leave and not come home for two days. I never wondered if other kids got locked out of their house and had to make friends with strangers because their mother was having sex and wouldn't let them in. Nope, it never occurred to me.

All I knew was, I was drowning in my mother's drinking and I didn't know how to swim.

Susie finally got my mother into bed that night, which was no easy feat. It involved loud music, food, a tug-of-war, and then my mother passing out—a familiar routine in our family.

Tony and I went to bed in the boys' room, and Johnny never did come home. Susie finally left and we fell asleep, at least for a while.

"Wake up, kids. Shhhhhhhh, it's okay. Don't make any noise," a deep voice said. The room was so dark, I couldn't see a thing.

"Oh God," I blurted out. "Please don't hurt us." The figure had my brother Tony under his arm. I could hear my brother's muffled pleas for help.

"Let's go—quietly. Don't wake up your mother," he whispered.

"Daddy? Is that you?"

"Shhhh," he said. By now we were out in the hallway between the bathroom and my brothers' room. I could see that it was him. All of a sudden my terror turned to joy. My daddy was not only my kidnapper, he was now my savior.

"Shhhhhh," he insisted. I threw my arms around his neck and squeezed him tight. "Come on now, let's find your shoes."

Tony fell asleep as soon as we got in the car. I can remember the shooshing sound the tailpipes made as his new Cadillac sped away into the wee hours of the morning. Me, I couldn't sleep, although I could barely keep my eyes open. We didn't drive for very long, and I couldn't tell you where we were, only that we were in the hills somewhere. We pulled up to a big house where we were greeted by his girlfriend, who brought us inside and tucked us into bed. I could hear them talking as I fell to sleep—something about the police.

Rise and Shine

ALTHOUGH I WAS HAPPY TO BE WITH MY FATHER, I was worried about my mother. Was she in trouble with the police? Was he? Was I ever going home? Did my mother even know where we were? I felt homesick and slightly disoriented.

At the same time, there was a subtle excitement in the air. It was like that feeling you get when you find a hundred-dollar bill on the floor. At first you don't believe it, then you get excited, then you worry that someone is going to take it away from you. Well, sort of like that, except there are no police involved. Unless you were me.

Next thing I knew, the new girlfriend announced that breakfast was on the table and instructed us to get ready for school. "School? What school?" I asked.

"A new one, sweetheart. You're going to a new school. You'll love it there!" she promised.

This meant yet another change, which in my experience could only be a bad thing.

But instead of an institution fraught with hellions and juvenile delinquents, I was welcomed by actual children who played hop-scotch instead of Russian roulette. They wore bobby socks, sneakers, and barrettes and didn't shave or carry weapons. And there was little fear of being held captive for ransom in the girls' bathroom. No, these kids were just like me—afraid of their own shadow.

Finally, I was home! Well, sort of, and actually it was only temporary—six days, to be exact. But for that brief time I knew what it was to breathe again. To be merely self-conscious instead of paranoid—at least at school anyway, since life with Bruno in it in any capacity provoked neurosis beyond definition. But before I knew it, my fantasy of being a normal kid playing foursquare at recess was interrupted by the appearance of my teacher with two clean-cut cops. Back to my mother's, with little explanation. Right from the frying pan into the mire.

The living room in our flat looked like a scene from *America's Most Wanted* when we arrived. One cop on his walkie-talkie, the other one taking notes, my mother crying, her friend Andrew from real estate school on the phone. 'Okay, hold on a minute,' I thought. Something was missing. Where was my brother Johnny? And what was Andrew doing there? Then I heard him giving a description of a dark-haired, thirty-something man of Italian heritage to whoever was on the other end. What the heck was going on around here?

And then Andrew said to me, "Your mother has to go away for a few days. Not to worry, everything is fine," he said, trying to convince himself.

"Go away? Where? What do you mean, 'go away'? We just got here," I said, scrambled by the perpetual drama. He had already walked away to attend to my mother's hysterics; I was talking to myself.

Then I heard: Jail *this,* jail *that;* "the judge said, *blah blah blah* . . ." And then something about five DUIs. Who goes to jail for contraceptives? Did I say jail? Who was going to jail? My mother? My father? All of us? No one would tell me anything. All I knew was that my mother's new best friend was going to take care of us until this whole mess blew over.

Not quite the welcome home committee I was expecting, but hey, aside from jail, kidnappings, and bouts of drunken debauchery, life was grand.

And You Are . . . ?

"MOM!!" I shouted from the bedroom. "Mom!" I yelled loud enough to shatter glass. "God!" I threw off the covers, stormed down the hall into the living room. "Mother! I have to get up for school tomorrow. Go to bed now!" She was lying there almost completely naked in front of the stereo, singing Dionne Warwick's woeful, "One less bell to answer, one less egg to fry." Somehow my brothers hadn't awakened yet; or maybe they didn't want to deal with her.

"Did you hear me, Mother? I said, 'Go to bed.'"

"Hey, it's okay. We're just havin' a good time," the man said from somewhere in the dark. Oh, there he was. Now I saw him. He was sitting behind me at the kitchen table in his briefs, about to light a cigarette. I looked back over at my mother.

"F— you," she slurred, flipping me off with the wrong finger. And then she laughed and started singing again. By now my brothers had stumbled out into the all-too-familiar vista. We looked at each other like a football team in a huddle who knew the play that had to unfold: an 86 left—get the guy out and Mom to bed. That was always the drill. Now, who would get the guy out depended on which one of us—John or me—was playing quarterback. Which boiled down to who was most pissed off. This time it was my brother. I had the fun-filled task of getting my mother away from the stereo and into our bedroom.

I would turn the stereo off, she would turn it on. I would unplug it, she would plug it back in. Eventually I would unhook the speakers, which always threw her for a loop. And at this point she would usually give up and go to bed. Which she finally did. This meant she wouldn't get dressed, go back out, and not come home at all.

Trix Are for Kids

THE NEXT DAY I WAS BACK IN SCHOOL on the other side of the tracks. That night a magician came to our school. I was hoping maybe he could make me disappear, or at least saw my parents in half—six of one, half dozen of the other, the way I saw it. No such luck.

It was standing room only in the auditorium. Everywhere you looked there were doting parents, grandparents, brothers, sisters, aunts, uncles, friends. And then there was my family, whose adoration of me consisted of routinely checking my head for lice and inadvertently noticing that I hadn't lost a limb.

Both my parents were there, but at first I couldn't see where they were sitting. I was in front of the stage, seated on the floor with my class, but I could feel them out there in the expectant sea of kin. Then I saw Bruno leaning against the wall near the exit sign. His eyes were the infrared ones (like when you take a picture and the flash hits that one person just right so they look like the devil when you get the film back). Except he *was* the devil, well, if you asked my mother. If you asked me, I thought he looked more like Elvis. Anyway, he never attended any event that mattered to me, so I thought maybe he was just hiding from the cops. He knew they'd never look for him there. Or maybe one of my classmates owed him some money.

"Ladies and gentlemen," announced our school principal, "may I please have your attention." A hush slowly rippled through the crowd. "I would like to welcome everyone and thank you for coming tonight! As most of you know, we have quite a treat for you this evening. So without any further ado . . ."

You could hear the needle hit the vinyl record as the dusty red velvet curtains parted. The carnival-like music ricocheted through the auditorium while we watched an organ grinder's monkey take a bow and then entertain us with his miniature violin. And then the principal boomed, "And here he is—the Great Zambino!" (What a relief, because for a minute I thought I was going to have to sit Indian-style for an hour and watch some freaky little primate perform *Fiddler on the Roof*.) The audience applauded as the slight, bearded man in an obviously rented black tie and tails appeared in a puff of smoke.

"Thank you. Thank you," he said. And then for about fifteen minutes we watched him as he pulled first a rabbit, then a hamster, then a bird out of a hat, and then dematerialized milk, water, and some man's wallet in it. He extracted dozens of scarves out of the end of a cane and then turned a flower bouquet into a dove. He made playing cards appear out of nowhere and then disappear into thin air. And then it happened: the moment I had been waiting for—only I didn't know it.

"And for my next trick I'm going to need an assistant from the audience," he said.

An assistant? Oh my God, I get to go on stage? Oh my God. I shot my hand up so fast and straight and with such intensity, I just knew he would pick me. The rest of my classmates seemed equally eager for a chance in the spotlight. There were arms flying everywhere, the kids attached to them trying to reach higher than everyone else's.

"Me, me, me! Pick me! Oh, oh, me, me!" we all cried out.

"Pick me, please, oh please, me!" I pleaded, waving my arms like a shipwrecked passenger trying to flag down a plane overhead.

"How about the young lady with the green top," he said, gesturing into the cluster in front of the stage where I was sitting. "You," he said.

"Me?" I asked, pointing at myself. I quickly looked around

to see if anyone else near me was wearing green.

"Come on up," he said cheerfully, and nodded at me. My heart raced. My legs shook as I tried to disentangle them. 'What if I fall off the stage or pass out or something?' I thought as I got up. The audience started clapping. I turned around to share my good fortune, looking down at my classmates with an enormous smile. In what seemed like slow motion, I watched their eyes fill instead with hatred and reproach. Dark little orbs studying me with disdain, punishing me with the glee they withheld, as though I had literally taken something from them. But what? I didn't understand. I stood paralyzed. 'Who do you think you are?' each pair of eyes seemed to scream, crashing into me.

"Come on up here, young lady," the magician blurted out, piercing the silent assassination. I staggered onto the stage. I didn't know what to say when the man congratulated me. "How about that, ladies and gentlemen, let's give her another round of applause." I could hear the audience clap, but it sounded so far away. I didn't dare look down at my classmates because I knew what they were thinking. I could feel it. And for the next ten minutes all I could think about was how I was going to take my next breath. I didn't even want to consider how I was going to face them after it was over.

I vaguely remember being in the box in which the man was going to saw me in half. Enjoying the experience was not an option. I was on fire with self-consciousness. I made a decision that night on that stage, in that box. A decision that would filter my reality for years. A decision that would affect every intimate relationship, friendship, and acquaintance I would ever have. What I told myself was that I need to be small. That when I am big—when I celebrate myself—you don't like me. No, worse, that you will hate me—and that is something I could not live with. That if I want to be loved, who you want me to be is more important than who I really am.

What could have been one of the most empowering moments of my life turned out to be one of the most intensely painful. I felt cut off at the knees. And I didn't have the self-esteem to sustain such a blow.

What's worse is that there was no one to witness my pain. In my world you couldn't talk to anybody about anything real. No one I knew cared enough or was present enough to hear my magician's tale of woe. In "the Family," you didn't talk about how you felt—it was irrelevant. And outside the family, you couldn't either. And not because you didn't want to, believe me. But what would you say? "Hi, my name is Maryanne, and well, uhhm, let's see . . . my mother drinks too much and she just got out of jail, and now she's not allowed to drive. And other stuff: strange guys in my house waking us all up on a school night at all hours. . . Whatever. Don't tell my father, though, because . . . well, I can't actually talk about him because then I'd have to kill you, and well, uuhhmmm—never mind, it's nothing, really; everything is fine. I'm just . . . I'm fine, really; I thought this was the counselor's office. Oh, right, I see—child protective services is in the phone book; that's great, yeah. No, I'm good, really fine. Sorry, I just . . . Do you know where I can get a Band-Aid maybe?"

This is a conversation I actually had with my "counselor" at school one time. She was a real big help. She stared at me blankly while I did my best to tell her what was really going on at home. I worked up a good bout of shame as she tapped her pencil against her notebook a few times and then mentioned that they served toast and peanut butter in pod six before school started, in case I was hungry. In case I was hungry? What the f— was she talking about? I wasn't hungry. I was dying over here. How could she not see what was happening?

I was screaming inside. The problem was, no one could hear me. So I did that which was about to become a signature of my personality. I apologized for bothering her and excused myself. I could tell by the look on her face that she felt sorry for me. But it wasn't pity I needed. I needed her to help me, and she couldn't. I needed a miracle.

Take That . . .

MY MOTHER DID HER BEST to make our lives seem normal. We had pizza night every Tuesday—sometimes. I knew she was trying because she always told me how hard she was working. And I knew she was working because she was never home. And I knew she was never home because I was still crying myself to sleep at night— desperately begging God to please not let her die—or I was busy hurling cutlery at my brother.

"I'm telling Mom!" I screamed after my brother punched me in the breast. My mother had warned my brother not to hit me there, especially since now I wore a bra and everything.

"*Wham!*" My brother drove his fist between my shoulder blades. I spun around, just missing his jaw with my left hook. Tony made a beeline out the front door, screaming down the hall toward our friend Brian Swatchtcas's. I grabbed a butcher knife out of the kitchen drawer and was hot on his trail. I had had enough of this and I was going to put an end to it right then. My brother caught sight of the knife clutched in my fist and frantically jabbed at Brian's doorbell. He escaped into the apartment a half second before the knife plunged mercilessly into the door. I could see the peephole lighten and darken as they took turns looking through it. The knife was still vibrating from the impact. After what I imagine was careful contemplation, the boys opened the door, still hiding behind it. One of them reached around, grabbed on to the knife, and after a few attempts managed to yank it free. They disappeared into the apartment and stayed there the rest of the afternoon.

The truth is, no matter what my mother said or how hard she tried, there was nothing normal about our life. I'll tell you one thing, though, my brother didn't touch me again until he knew he could kick my . . . derrière.

Movin' On Up

THEN THE MIRACLE I was waiting for happened. We moved. Again. But this time to a house—a big house. One with my own room and everything. We even had a cat. His name was Rocky.

Leaving the apartment was like walking away from a train wreck. All you know is you made it out alive—at least you think you did.

For me it was just not-dead. We moved fifteen miles or so to the nou-veau riche side of the tracks. It was the mid- to late seventies; being a hippie was on its way out and being a yuppie was on its way in. My mother started doing phenomenally well at her real estate sales job, and things got much better—at least on the outside. Our new domi-cile was like a palace compared to the sling-blade, downtrodden hovel we'd somehow managed to escape from. Alas, it wasn't a gated community, which would have been much more fitting for a princess. However, the house was a two-story, three-bedroom, three-bath dream come due. It even had an atrium. At least, until I burned the house down, but I'll get to that later.

May I Present . . . ?

"GET THE DOOR. Will somebody get the door!" I wailed from my bedroom on the second floor. Nothing. Just incessant ringing: *ding-dong, ding-dong, ding-dong.* "Juuust a min-ute!" My voice jumped up and down in cadence as I bombed down the stairs.

I could see a shadowy figure through the smoky beveled glass. I opened the door, surprised to see what could best be described as Laverne DeFazio meets Rebecca DeMornay, only this schmaltzy, trampy vixen was barely thirteen years old.

"Hey, I'm Veronica. I live right over there," she said, pointing out a house twice as big as ours at the end of the street. She stood bare-foot, wearing lots of silver jewelry with a ring on practically every finger (I think one was a skull). The lids above her steely blue eyes were caked with frosty blue eye shadow and smudged with black kohl pencil. She had on a short-sleeved T-shirt with a glossy picture of Black Sabbath laminated on the front, and skin-tight, faded 501 jeans—a size too small, by the looks of things. She even had a tattoo, which back then, especially for a girl, wasn't New Age chic—there was no such thing yet. It wasn't hip, and it definitely wasn't a fashion statement. What it meant was: You are truly a scary person.

"Got any cigarettes?" she asked casually, as she brushed past me like I was the toilet attendant in the ladies room.

"Uuhhmm, cigarettes? No . . . I, uhhh, don't . . . sm—"

"How about your folks? I bet they have some stashed around here somewhere."

"Yeah, I guess so, I mean yes! My mother probably has. . . She smokes. Maybe she . . ."

Veronica, ignoring me, walked around the corner into the kitchen. "How about in here?" she asked, opening our junk drawer underneath the phone. Sure enough, she pulled out a pack of Salem Light 100s, plucked one from the opening, and slid it between her lips. She dug around in her pocket and pulled out a shiny silver Zippo lighter. Just as she flicked back the lid of the Zippo and was about to singe the end of the stealth menthol stick dangling from her mouth, I lurched toward the atrium door and abruptly slid the screen open. My subtle suggestion: 'Maybe you should do that out here.' I didn't want my mom to think I was smoking.

She cupped the end of her smoke as she pulled her first drag, walking outside as though she'd intended to all along. She examined the cherry-red ember at the end of her cigarette as she exhaled. I watched her inhale the silvery stream of smoke simultaneously into her nose and mouth, and then back out. She blew a few smoke rings with the faint remains. The O's trailed off until they faded and finally vanished. I was hypnotized.

"Wow!" I blurted out, not realizing until it was too late how stupid that must have sounded to her. She walked back into the kitchen, turned the corner, took the last hit off her cigarette, and flicked it all the way out into the street as she walked out our front door. She turned around, gave me the peace sign, and then disappeared down the street. She didn't even say good-bye. That, from my Wonder Bread perspective, was the epitome of cool. My mother was definitely going to hate her!

'Perfect!' I thought to myself.

PART TWO

■ *Who I Wanted To Be*

ASSOCIATING WITH VERONICA was like bungee jumping with a telephone cord. Odds were you were quite possibly going to die or, at the very least, someone was going to end up in the hospital. I only hoped it wouldn't be me.

Veronica wasn't really someone I would have called a friend. Mostly because I didn't want anyone to think I was like her. However, not being friends with Veronica wasn't exactly an option. It wasn't up to me: I had been appointed her friend and wasn't about to argue—she scared the crap out of me. Either way, seeing as she rarely went to school, I was spared having to explain, which was a relief because I don't think most of my rah-rah friends would have understood my relationship with that kind of girl. Most of my friends were cheer-leaders, wore Chemin de Fer jeans, and were still virgins. Veronica used the edge of condom wrappers to pick her teeth.

Anyhoo, I think right about the time I burned our new house down was when I started to cross the line. The line between the Veronicas and the cheerleaders. The line that, if I got too close, would sound alarms and trigger my Good Girl programming. Now there was a welcome mat on a conveyor belt with my name on it waiting for me to step on so it could take me right across the border.

I was in seventh grade now, and things started happening that I couldn't explain, nor did I want to—least of all to God, with whom I had recently exercised my "out" clause. I just hoped he wasn't look-ing. I had taken temporary leaves of belief before, but now I was running from the shame that my recent Bad Girl choices had engen-dered. When I got into trouble, I started to exercise the power of four-letter words other than PRAY. "Our Father who art in hea—"? 'Forget this. Why am I praying anyway? I don't even know if you're up there.' (I looked around for a lightning bolt.)

Since I was a very little girl, I had said my prayers before going to bed almost every night that I can remember. And now? It had been weeks, and I had become someone I didn't recognize. No one in my life cared enough to even notice that I was crossing this critical line. I had tried so hard to fit in with my cheerleader friends, dressing the way I thought I should dress, saying what I thought I should say, acting how I thought they wanted me to act. When it was all said and done, I was disposable. I didn't have the support or the self-esteem to handle that, so I gravitated to Veronica and her crowd, to the kids who seemed to be in a similar situation to mine. We were all unhappy for one reason or another and we all had a lot to lose.

They seemed to accept me just the way I was, and I didn't care that they smoked and did drugs and had sex. Acceptance was the glue that held us together. These friends *were* my family. I was so lonely, so lonely, that I believed I had no right to be picky about who I associated with. My criterion was pretty simple: Any attention was better than none. No one else wanted me, and they did. That was good enough for me.

There was no room for God in that equation. And the truth is, it wasn't hard to let him go, because I figured, 'If he really was there, he would have never let my life be so awful.'

But underneath my bravado, I had a flash: What if God *is* there? I clutched my stomach, suddenly wracked with fear, and then guilt that I hadn't talked to God in such a long time. I'd been drinking almost every day, and smoking pot as often as I could get my hands on it. And then the guilt gave way to something else. I felt so sick, that for just a few moments, I was raw and defenseless enough to encounter my own innocence. From that place came the last real prayer I said for years, a prayer that was not a bargain or a demand or a complaint:

"I want you to know I am sooo sorry for how I have been acting lately—you know, drinking and stuff. Like when I threw up all over Jackie's room and told her mom we ate bad pickles. And the time Marcie and I drank a whole bottle of her dad's Red Label Scotch and I don't remember how I got home. You get the picture. And I'm sorry I haven't prayed in a while. Hopefully you're not too mad. God bless Shelley and Marcie and Mickie and Dana and Lorna and Rocky and my family and all my friends on earth and all my relatives in heaven and all the animals on earth and . . ."

That prayer would be my last pass. Waking up in my own barf on a school day would become more familiar to me than God. Being a Good Girl was rapidly becoming a thing of the past. I didn't know how to hang on to that place where God could get in because it became buried so far underneath the wreckage of my childhood, past and present. So I concluded that having virtue in the land of Oz was as useless as knowing how to drive when you're legally blind. I didn't even know what was driving me. And really, what difference did it make, anyway?

He Loves Me, She Loves Me Not

"WHERE DID VERONICA GO?" I nervously asked Leif, Veronica's latest boyfriend. Most boys couldn't get the time of day from me. Not because I thought I was so great; I didn't. Because they were like my brothers. People I threw things at, like footballs and knives. But sometime after second grade, get me anywhere near a boy I found attractive and that was it—speaking English became a chore.

"Uhh, she went to buy some smokes," he said, as he searched the pockets of his flannel shirt.

"Oh," I said. I sat on my bedroom floor and leaned against my waterbed, stiff with self-consciousness. I searched my mind for anything to say. Indifferent to my presence, he pulled a little white package out of the pocket of his brown corduroys. It looked like a miniature envelope, but the paper was thicker and kind of glossy.

"You snort?" he asked, suddenly including me in his reality.

"Snort?"

"Yeah, cocaine! Do you snort?" I knew he thought I was an idiot.

"Uhhmm, no thanks," I graciously replied. I wasn't sure what snorting was, but something about it scared me.

"Come on, here. It's good shit. Peruvian flake!" he sang. "It's almost pure. It's cut with baby laxative though." He thought that was funny. He laughed and nodded his head in that "you know what that means" kind of way. But I didn't know what the hell he was talking about.

"Yeah, but . . . No thanks, I uhmm . . ." I shook my head.

He interrupted me. "Here, look. A nice fatty for ya." I watched him scoop out some of the white powder from the mini envelope with the end of a razor blade and dump it on the top shelf of my black lacquered headboard. Then he chopped the powder up in little tiny motions.

'Who is he, Benihana?' I thought. After that, he sectioned the powder into two piles, took the razor, and drew each part into a line with a checkmark for a tail. He looked over at me, grinned, and handed me what looked like a small straw, but was really a rolled-up dollar bill with the edge tucked tightly underneath a corner of itself.

"Go ahead," he said. "You first."

Me first what? I didn't want any. What should I do? So I just sat there holding the tightly scrolled bill in my hand.

"Whatsa matter?" he asked, staring at me impatiently. I imagined "no" wasn't the answer he was looking for, so I punted.

"You know, my brothers are going to be home in a little while and, uuhh, it's probably not a good idea if . . ."

"That's cool," he said, as he snatched the rolled-up bill from my hand, hovered over the powder, and sniffed up both lines. "More for me!" he laughed, coughed a little bit, and then shook his head back and forth like a dog shaking the water off his fur. Then he lay back on my bed.

"Come here," he said, in a provocative tone.

Come here? Me? Come where?

"Come here," he repeated, motioning me toward him. I shyly

looked down at the floor and then innocently at him. When he could see that I wasn't going to "come here," he leaned up and gently but firmly grabbed my arm and pulled me toward him.

"Come here!" Then he reached up and held my face in his hands. He looked directly into my eyes and then kissed me. Then he pushed my face away from his so he could look at me, then pressed his full lips against mine again. But this time he slipped his tongue inside my mouth. I had never kissed a boy before, so I freaked. I wasn't sure what I was supposed to do. I could feel his tongue making perfect clockwise, circular motions around my own. So I followed his lead. Awkwardly at first, but then I just melted into his mouth.

My heart was pounding, my mind went blank, and I was in heaven. 'Oh-my-God!' I thought. I wanted to say it out loud—"Oh my God!" But I didn't. I had never been so excited and so—excited—at the same time. We must have kissed for ten whole minutes. He rolled me over onto my back and started to press and grind himself against my body. I wrapped my legs up and around his as we slowly, rhythmically lulled the water bed back and forth, back and forth.

He took my hand and placed it on the enormous bulge in his pants, while he rubbed and squeezed my breasts. Then he slid his hand under my shirt, feeling underneath my bra. I froze. My body became rigid, including my tongue. My breathing became shallow. He kept kissing me like he didn't notice. He began unzipping his pants and I started to panic.

"Come on, baby." He clutched his boxers at the bottom of his undone zipper, revealing his stiff, swollen penis. It all looked so . . . big and . . . hairy. Now I was petrified. I truly did not know what to do.

"Come on, baby, suck me," he said, climbing up my body. I squeezed my eyes shut; now I was holding my breath. Tears began to well in my eyes and run down my temples. "Here," he said, hovering over me. He grabbed the back of my neck and pulled my face toward his giant, erect penis. I stretched my arms out in front of me to try to push him off me and stop him from stuffing himself into my mouth. The more I resisted, the harder he pulled.

"Come on, baby, the coke makes me so horny. Look at how hard I am; it hurts me. Just suck me for a little while, please," he pleaded. Finally I was able to mutter something.

"I can't . . . it's just that . . . I don't . . ." I kept shaking my head. But I couldn't say the words. I was screaming them inside: 'No! No, no, no! Please, somebody, help me—please!' I knew no one was home. And what would I say if they were? And the truth is, I wanted him to want me. But not necessarily like this. I wanted to kiss him and grind together with him and have him hold my face in his hands. I wanted all of that to happen. I was letting that happen. So it was my fault that I'd gotten into this mess, and no one was going to rescue me. The other thought that kept me paralyzed was that he was on drugs, which for all I knew, might make him crazy. What if he hurt me? He told me I was hurting him. Why couldn't I just do what he wanted and get it over with?

"Hang on," he said, and stood up.

'Oh God, thank you,' I exhaled, prematurely, figuring that God, after a year-long absence since my last prayer, had taken pity on me. Or that Leif had come to his senses. Either way I was off the hook. He was busy whiffing up the rest of the cocaine, so I took my opening and pulled my shirt back down and flung my legs over the side of the bed. Next thing I knew, he was standing right in front of me. And instead of pulling up his pants, he dropped them to the floor.

He grabbed my hair and pulled my face to his crotch and said, "Lick me." This time it was a command. I didn't dare look at him. I knew I had no choice—something I had learned a long time ago.

Tears streamed down my cheeks. After several minutes of gagging, dry heaving, and gasping for air as he plunged his erection in and out of the hole I made with my mouth, I heard him say, "Do you swallow?" But before I could answer, my mouth was flooded with a warm, slimy, salty liquid. It spilled out the sides of my mouth and ran down my chin. I was choking and sputtering, trying not to swallow any more of it. By then he had let go of my hair and was laughing at me.

Horrified and embarrassed, I ran to the bathroom to spit up whatever was left of what he had ejaculated into my mouth. I couldn't rinse my mouth out enough. I brushed and brushed my teeth, scraped my tongue, but still couldn't get the taste out of my mouth. It felt like it was stuck in the back of my throat. As I rinsed my mouth out for the last time, I thought to myself, 'Was I supposed to like that? And why was he laughing at me? Did I do something wrong?'

And then I wondered if he liked me. I looked up at myself in the mirror. I didn't think so. It's funny, too, because when I went back into the room, the subject never came up. He could have anyone he wanted. Why me? Compared to Veronica, I was a dog. Actually, when it came right down to it, compared to anybody, I thought I was a dog. I was sick to my stomach and wanted my mother.

When I came back into my room he was sitting on the edge of my bed, rubbing his gums with the rest of the powder left on my headboard. He stood up and asked, "Smoke a doob?"

"No, thanks. My mom's probably on her way home. She should be here any minute."

"Cool." He got up from the bed, grabbed his leather jacket, and said, "Tell Veronica I'll be at the loft." He ducked his lanky six-foot, five-inch body under my bedroom doorway. "Later," was the last thing I heard him say. He didn't even look at me.

For days, all I could hear were his words, "Suck me, baby, come on, suck me," over and over in my head. I never did tell anyone, not even my mother. I knew it wouldn't have made a difference. So—true to form—I swallowed it.

Okay, how did I not see that coming? Why didn't I pay attention to the billboards telling me to get away from this person? Me, alone in my house, in my room with some guy I just met. A guy who just happens to walk around with hard drugs in his pocket and who associates with a girl that, by all appearances, is destined to become either a prostitute or a felon. Maybe it was the convincing lies I told myself that somehow cut off the circulation to my brain. Or at least the part of it responsible for logic and reason, causing distorted emissions to dance about my mind—like he would never do anything to me because he's too cute. Or he's Veronica's boyfriend, so he must be okay, right? Or that I was making it out to be worse than it really was, I was overreacting, that it wasn't really a big deal—I was just being a baby. That it was all my fault.

I didn't know what I felt, so how could I know what I needed? This confusion was compounded by a growing, burning need to be held, to be loved. And the twisted version of that is choking down some guy's sperm because I didn't know how to ask for what I needed. I didn't even feel worthy of a towel, never mind a good-bye.

So why didn't I run out the door when I had the chance? This guy was on probation and had ditched his parole officer and would be going to Folsom Prison as soon as they caught him. Plus the fact that Veronica and her girlfriend had already had sex with this boy on numerous occasions—that in itself should have been a clue.

Bottom line: I would have done almost anything to feel wanted, including disrespect myself—and so I did. When you mix a need to be held, low self-esteem, and strong hormones, you end up saying yes when you mean no.

Burnin' Down the House

SO, RIGHT. THE HOUSE. Well, that was not my fault. It was an accident. Really. My brother asked me to go to the mall with him, which happened, well, never. So I was overcome with jubilation and forgot to turn off the deep fryer. My girlfriend and I were making french fries. And then—*poof!* Bye-bye house. Anyway, we got to stay at a wonderful hotel for three months that had an indoor pool and 24/7 room service. The good news is, the insurance covered everything. The fire department said it was an electrical problem, a faulty wire or something. It's not like anybody died. Whatever. . . This was the least of my problems. Let's just say that in light of everything, it was a nice distraction.

I wasn't exactly proud of this, but it was a worthy entry at the back of my Good Girl Handbook. I mean, how many people can say they burned down their own house and lived to talk about it?

Shelley, Shelley, Shelley

SHELLEY WAS ONE OF THE FEW FRIENDS of mine who had my mother's approval. What her criteria were, I never knew. My mother was never very specific. I think you got points if you curtsied and called her Mrs. DelRiccio rather than Caroline. Oh, and if you had a nickname for me, forget it. My name was Maryaaaaane, not Maryannie, or M, or anything else. She would say, "It's Maryaaaaane." And enunciate it for you like you were hearing-impaired.

Shelley and I were like Frick and Frack. We did everything together. For two years we were inseparable. We got drunk together, threw up together. She even taught me how to use a tampon. Well, she explained it to me anyway. Somehow, having her as a best friend made my life seem less like the way it really was. Shelley was an in-between person like me. She was a cheerleader, but had friends who smoked. She knew how to kiss, but had never gone all the way. She said "screw" instead of "f—," and knew how to play the piano. She had her own set of problems, and from time to time we cried together.

The difference between us was that Shelley was tougher than I was. She didn't take crap from anyone. I, on the other hand, could have opened a fertilizer shop.

Shelley was my lifeline. She was the place that stood between me and doom. She was everything I wasn't. She was strong and brave; she was her own person. I was whomever you wanted me to be. My father said she was trash.

"Go sit on his lap," she whispered.

"No way. I'm sure," I replied.

"Come on. You know he wants you to," she teased me. Shelley's older brother, Tye, and two of his friends sat in the living room watching Sunday football while she and I conspired around the corner in her kitchen.

"He's so adorable. I'm totally in love with him," I squealed, trying to keep quiet so he wouldn't hear me.

"Go out there. Go. He totally likes you, I can totally tell." I waited a few seconds and then wandered out into the living room and sat down. The guys were glued to the set until one of them asked for a beer. Reese was his name, the one I liked.

"Is there any more beer in there?" Reese asked.

"Uhhhh . . . I dunno," said Tye, not even looking up from the set.

"I'll get it." I jumped up. I sashayed into the kitchen, hoping he was watching me. I had on pink satin Dolphin shorts and a tank top. "Does anybody else want one?" I shouted from the kitchen.

"Yeah, I'll take one," I heard. I grabbed two Miller Genuine Drafts, flipped the tops off, and headed back into the living room. I handed one to Tye, who already had his hand up to grab it.

"Cool. Thanks," he said, and winked at me. I walked toward Reese in anticipation, holding his beer in my hands.

"Here," I said.

He watched me look at him, took a swig off the beer, and then said, "Sip?" I took it carefully out of his hand, put it to my lips, and guzzled down enough to quench my thirst.

"Thanks," I said, and handed it back to him.

"Who do you want, Dallas or the Niners?"

"Uhhmm, I don't know—who's winning?"

He laughed. I turned red; I could feel it. I was embarrassed, but I didn't know why.

"Here, sit here," he said, pointing to the arm of the La-Z-Boy. I turned around and slid back up on the arm of his chair.

"Yeah, that's right, baby! Go go *go*—yes!" Tye jumped off the couch and started doing some kind of victory dance. "Woo-hooo!" he shouted. He turned and looked at Reese. "Did you see that? Did you see that guy? Unbelievable. Fifty-two yards!" he bellowed. "Watch, they're gonna show it again." He turned back toward the TV. "Watch, watch. There he goes . . . oh yeah, that's right! Touchdown!"

I didn't want to move. Reese was leaning against me, his arm was touching my leg. Energy was pulsing through my whole body. I wondered if he knew he was touching me. I wondered if he was doing it on purpose. My whole body was filled with longing. I wanted him to move closer to me.

"Another sip?" he asked, handing me his beer. We were sharing his beer; now it was *our* beer. I drank some more and handed it back. He leaned in closer to me. I could feel my breath get heavier. I could hear his too. We were breathing in the same rhythm. I wasn't sure if it was my imagination or not until he put his arm around my waist and pulled me onto his lap. He held his half-empty beer in front of me and fed me another sip.

Maybe it was because I thought he was absolutely gorgeous—he looked like a blonde-haired, green-eyed god. Maybe it was because he was nineteen and I was thirteen, or maybe it was that I knew he had a girlfriend who had just graduated from high school, and I was only about to start ninth grade. Maybe the whole thing seemed forbidden. I didn't care. All that mattered was right now, and that nothing stop this moment. I was in absolute bliss.

Shelley finally came out of her room; she had been on the phone the whole time. "Your dad just called. He said he'll come pick you up after the game."

"'Kay," I replied, unaffected. The fourth quarter was just starting. I knew I had about another half hour before my father showed up and this nirvana came to an end. I didn't even want to think about it. Right now all that existed was Reese and me.

I don't remember hearing my father come through the door. But I did hear him say, "Get the f— off his lap, girl." I jumped off and he started toward Reese. "What's your name, son?" he asked. Everyone in the room froze, like in musical chairs. "I said, 'What's your name, son?'" my father demanded.

"Look, she was just sitting on my lap; she didn't do anything wrong," Reese tried to say. I was astonished that anyone had the nerve to talk back to my father; no one ever did that.

My father pointed to me and then to the door. "You get in the car." As I walked away, I could hear him threaten Reese, "Listen, you little puke. You touch my daughter again and you'll be sitting down permanently." I was mortified. I was humiliated *and* mortified. And I was in trouble. But I was still glowing from the fact that I had triumphed. I got what I wanted despite all the odds. So whatever was coming to me really didn't matter. I had won the prize. Reese wanted me. Me! Besides, I only had to stay with my father for the rest of that day. How bad could that be? I didn't think about it much until I got home that night and my mother informed me that I would be going to live with my father—permanently.

I knew something was wrong when my father didn't hit me or anything that day. He didn't make a peep. He didn't need to. He had something better in store for me. Living with him was going to be like going to jail—and he knew it.

My mother told my brother Tony and me that she didn't want to separate us, so he had to come with me to live with my father. This made no sense to me, seeing as we also had an older brother. The decision only illustrated her preference for Johnny and her disdain for me. In fact, she confessed that she couldn't handle me anymore. She cried and swore she didn't know what else to do. But her flood of emotion didn't fool me; I could tell she was relieved. And I would have been furious had it dawned on me that I had just been thrown to the lions by my own mother. Evolution, my ass. This way she could blame him when he spit out the bones.

Wake Up, Little Susie

ASIDE FROM MY UNDERSTANDABLE FEAR of coliseum games, what was my reluctance about living with my father? Let me put it this way—it would be like asking your cat if he wants to go for a swim. No matter how nice you make it sound, he doesn't want to go. Trust me. He doesn't even know why, he just knows he doesn't. It's instinctual. The same way I don't want to stand in front of a freight train coming down the track, jump in front of a bus, or throw myself into a snake pit. Sure, I loved my father. I mean, who didn't love their father? Though "love" is such a tricky word, isn't it? It's so vague, yet so committal, so effectual, so . . . Hallmark. Besides, what's love got to do with anything here? Let's face it: my father was an animal. And it's not like my mother didn't know this . . . although this fact conveniently escaped her now. He was the devil; she told me so herself. Suddenly, however, it would be okay to live with him because, well, "He's your father." Yeah, sure, I get it. He's a really "conscious" evil man. Hitler had friends, didn't he? I mean, at least until they pissed him off, right?

The bottom line was that I was out. My father was going to "handle" me now. And the truth is, my mother was the lesser of two evils, as far as I was concerned. At least she left me alone. All right, so I lifted her credit card a few times. Well, actually I let a friend use it. But how was I supposed to know he and his buddies were going to rent a hotel room and trash it? He told me he needed it to fix his car. It's not like he spent a million dollars. And when I cut school all those times, I was . . . well, I—I hated school. All those classes and the homework. I figured as long as I passed all my tests and stuff—you know, like for college—everything would be fine. And I swear I didn't know anything about those other kids who showed up at our house one night when she was out of town. I only told a couple of people about the party. Whoever called the cops was totally overreacting.

Johnny had parties all the time, and he cut school. I know that for a fact, and he had a D average in his senior year. How come he got to stay? Why not me? She just didn't want to take care of us anymore—not that she ever made me feel like she did.

You ever ride your big wheel down the corridor of a deserted ski lodge when all of a sudden two dead twin girls start chasing you, and no matter how fast you ride you can't get away? No? Well, that's what it was like living with Bruno—on a good day!

Until now, my relationship with my father had consisted mainly of random weekend visits that were more like acid trips. (I never needed to take any to know what a bad trip was.) And it was always the same, with only an occasional variation. But for the record, what he started to do once I moved in with him should illustrate, without a doubt, my lack of enthusiasm for going to live with him.

R-o-o-o-xannne . . .

"WAKE UP, SWEETHEART. Honey, wake up. Your father wants to talk to you," she would say.

"What? Huh? Uugghhh. I'm sleeping! Can't you tell him I'm sleeping?"

"I know, sweetie. He asked for you. Come on," said the second wife. They would all have to do it at some point—except my mother, of course. She must have been a heavy sleeper.

I knew where he was; wife number two didn't have to tell me. He was always in the same place, doing the same thing: sitting in his favorite chair in front of the fireplace with a glass of wine in his hand and a beer nearby. My chair was waiting for me, right in front of him, always just a few feet away.

"Sit down, I want to talk to you," he'd say. I could tell he was drunk because he had that stupid smarmy smile on his face. It was creepy. "Come on and talk to your old man . . ." The thing was, there would be no conversation. There would only be him talking and me sitting frozen, hugging my knees to my chest, watching the clock, waiting until I was released so I could go back to bed, like everyone else.

"You know, girl?" he'd say, like he was going to tell me something deep. Like he was going to tell me something new. "All men want to do is f— you. That's it, that's all they want. So what you have to do is hold out for the highest bidder." At eight years old I'd had no idea what that meant and I still wasn't sure at thirteen. "Look, I'm not going to send you to college because I think you're smart. No, it's because I want you to find a man who is going somewhere. That's right, a doctor or a lawyer." Then he'd wait, squint his eyes like he was trying to pluck just the right words out to postulate my fate, drink some more of his wine, and continue. Sometimes he'd add how much I reminded him of my mother, obviously forgetting all the other times he'd remind me what a no-good whore she was.

But his closing sentiments were the most disturbing. "Have you had sex yet? With a boy? It's okay. You can tell me." Which I knew was a lie. I didn't even want to think of what he'd do to me if I told him I'd even kissed a boy. Still, who tells their father about their sex life? Whose father asks? Gross. Especially the crude way that he did. I mean, I could see if he were actually concerned and said something like, "So, honey, are you seeing anyone at school? Any crushes?" You know, corny things like that. Like a dad is supposed to say. And why did he want to know anyway? That was the weirdest part of all.

I would cringe and wonder if it was me, or was he as demented as I thought he was? But what was I going to do? I knew better than to say a word. My father didn't make threats. Your only warning was about as long as the distance between where you were and the time it took him to get there.

Like I said, what I had to say didn't matter, so I didn't bother anymore. If I did speak, he'd only say the same thing: "Maryanne, you are so full of shit, you don't even know you're full of shit. You can't bullshit a bullshitter." Or he'd smack me. I don't know which was worse. To have your feelings invalidated and not even know what you feel or to be pounded on. It all feels the same after a while.

Bruno was God, and if you asked him, it was his way or the highway. As for the highest-bidder guy? Well, supposedly, someday I would know what my father was talking about, and hence reap the value of such Mafia machismo.

And when my father had finished tormenting me, he would make my stepmother bring her daughter into bed with them while they had sex, which would explain his second wife's outrageous behavior. Inevitably, at some point during one of these "sessions," she would come out of the bedroom, grab his glass of wine, smash it up against the wall, and scream and swear at him while pulling his hair. He would just laugh and tell her to calm down. She would storm off back into the bedroom. And sometimes she'd take all five of us kids to their office and we'd sleep in sleeping bags on the floor. And he—well, he would simply continue wherever he left off, while the wine still trickled down the wall. It was all so . . . lovely.

So why did I believe him? Why didn't I just tell myself he was crazy and that he was just making all that crap up to entertain himself? Why didn't I tell myself that he was an alcoholic and a sick man who had no boundaries and was simply projecting onto me his own incredibly grim views of the way things were? Why couldn't I be like some other kids I saw in the movies who had the guts to stand up to their old man and tell him where to get off? And why didn't I just let it roll off my back when he repeatedly reduced me to a worthless human being, good for nothing but to be f—d by a man?

The truth is, I was terrified of him. He literally put the fear of God in me and I believed him when he told me at every turn that the only sound I would hear is my body dropping to the ground or him pulling his foot out of my ass. At that age my mind wasn't strong enough to ward off the influence of his venomous abuse of power. So I took it on. All of it. I believed every word of it, only I didn't realize it. I didn't understand the universal law of attraction. I didn't know that whatever I believed about myself would become a self-fulfilling prophecy. I didn't know that this simple cosmic law would cause me so much pain. I didn't know how to not be victimized. I didn't even know what being a victim really meant.

All I knew was that he made every woman in his life feel like a victim, like she was weak and stupid and trapped. I didn't know I had a choice yet. I didn't know how to nurture myself, to feed my mind with only good thoughts. Because I didn't yet understand the other equally powerful law of physics—that no two things can occupy the same space at the same time. And I didn't know that if I honored my feelings and found an enlightened witness who could be present for me to consciously express my feelings out loud—all the way—that I would stand a better chance of realizing yet another law of physics— that a system reorganizes itself to the highest truth available. My father's word was the loudest truth I knew. So loud that my own was continually drowned out by his.

I spent years dreading spending even one moment alone with him. I never knew what maniacal, absolutely inappropriate, gruesome thing was coming. My relationship with this man set up a fierce dynamic of how I would be in the world. Simply put, my father taught me that I had to constantly be on my guard, never a moment's rest. He represented the world's chaos theory to a T, and if I were going to survive, I could never not be ready for whatever was coming down the pike.

Breathing deeply was a luxury most people took for granted. I didn't even know it was possible until I was thirty-three years old. Listening to my body, feeling my feelings, putting only good things in my mind—yeah, right. I had no context or concept. I have grieved much over the loss of what it might have been like for me to know.

Woke Up This Morning, Got Myself a Gun

BOOM, BOOM, BOOM (my father's version of knocking). "Pick up the phone," I heard him say. It was about seven thirty in the morning. I was in my room getting ready for school. I wondered who was calling me so early.

"Hello?" I answered. There was a long pause at the other end. "Helllooo," I repeated.

"Maryanne?" the girl's voice said. I muffled the phone and shouted, "You can hang up the phone now, I got it!"

"This is Maryanne, who's this?"

"It's me, Veronica." Her voice was so low I could barely hear her.

"Veronica? Hi, what's up? Why are you calling so early?" Again a long pause.

"It's about Yvonne, Maryanne. They were in an accident. Didn't you see the news? She's—they're all dead," she whimpered.

"What? Wait, what are you talking about? Who's all dead? Veronica? Veronica, who's dead?" My mouth went dry and my heart started to beat faster.

"Yvonne and Lorna and Shelley and—" she began to say.

"Shelley? Shelley Fletcher? *My* Shelley?" I demanded.

"Yeah, all of them."

"Wait. What happened? What are you saying?" I asked, totally freaked out.

"Lorna took her mom's car out. Well, actually, it was supposed to be a surprise for her birthday. And—"

"What surprise?"

"The car was. Lorna's mom bought her a car for her birthday. It was supposed to be a surprise, but Lorna found out and took the car out the day before. They were up on 280, racing some guys on motorcycles, and they smacked into a tree. They all died on impact." She was crying now.

I couldn't believe what I was hearing. I think I was in shock.

"The funeral is this Thursday. You're going, aren't you?" she asked.

"Yes, of course. I mean, where is it?" I asked. "Call me later. I gotta go. Someone's at the door. Call me."

"Later," she said, and hung up. I looked up and saw my father standing in the doorway.

"I don't care who died! You're grounded. You're not going anywhere." And he walked out. I wondered how he knew anybody died. Had he been listening on the other end of the phone?

If he were anybody else, I would have tried to reason with him. But he was Bruno and I knew it was useless. I could have slit my wrists before his eyes and he would have told me I was an amazing actress, thrown me a towel, and told me to clean up the mess when I was done. He was a heartless prick and proud of it. My only hope now was my stepmother. She was more likely to be sympathetic to my plight.

I had been living with my father for only three weeks and had missed Shelley every day. Had I not moved, I would have been with her right now. Dead. I think this occurred to my stepmother, and whatever she said to Bruno made him let me go.

The day of the funeral, he came into my room and made it clear I wasn't allowed to wear makeup or anything that would make me look like a whore. He told me I wasn't going to get any pleasure out of going and that as soon at it was over, "you'd better get your ass home."

The strange thing was that I was looking forward to going to the funeral. But not for the reasons he thought. It wasn't because I was sad and needed to grieve the loss of my friends. I hated funerals; I had been to enough already. And anyway, I wasn't particularly upset, which to be honest, disturbed me more than anything. My best friend in the whole world had just died and I hadn't shed a tear. The truth was, I wanted to get away from him, away from that house.

I stood and watched four of my friends being put in the ground and felt nothing but the familiar thickness in the air when something terrible has happened. I looked around me and saw people weeping and sobbing. I saw my girlfriends' parents dressed in black, some of them so grief-stricken that they were barely able to stand. Other family and friends hugged in an attempt to comfort one another after the tragic loss. And I knew I should be feeling something. But I can only remember feeling relieved that I was out of jail. There was something perverse about the sensationalism of such a tragedy, but in an odd way I was used to it. And I didn't want to force myself to cry. Such a display seemed fake. However, I worried that appearing detached was inappropriate.

The dark cloud I couldn't avoid was the guilty pleasure I could savor—only in secret—that I had used my best friend's funeral to temporarily escape my father's grip. I wondered what kind of person that made me. I put a rose on Shelley's coffin and said my good-byes like everybody else, but when I stood in front of the gaping hole, I felt jealous instead of sad. Jealous that she was getting all the attention, that she had been so loved and admired. I knew I was evil to think such thoughts, which confirmed my feelings that I was no better than the dirt they were covering her with.

Give Me a W
Give Me an H
Give Me an O
Give Me an R
Give Me an E

A MONTH OR SO HAD PASSED and the event of Shelley's death was "over." I just shoved it down into the depths of my unconscious, as usual. According to my Good Girl Handbook, sadness, grief, depression, and negativity in general were unacceptable. A line was drawn through each of these "unnatural" emotions, and superimposed over them in red letters was "Get Over It." So, if you had a delayed reaction to things of this nature, which I seemed to invariably have, you simply felt like you were probably going mad.

The best way I can describe the cumulative lunacy is: you know how, when somebody tells you a joke and you don't get it right away, and then hours or maybe days later you get it and laugh your ass off, slap yourself upside the head—like, duh—and feel stupid? Well, it's like that, except imagine the laughing hysterically part without the joke. There is no connection. In my case, I was actually full of grief, but it had been a whole month—for cryin' out loud—since her death. So what was I so sad about? I should have been over it by now. But because I couldn't make the connection between my feelings and my suppression programming, I figured something must be wrong with me—instead of being able to accept the plain truth that I had lost my best friend and needed to grieve.

I signed up for cheerleading, track, and anything else that would keep me away from my father's house during my freshman year. Shelley was dead and I managed to place her where I believed she belonged—in the deepest part of my subconscious. Which is where whoever I really was resided. Like I said, there was no me. Except with my brother Tony. I could totally be myself with him.

I soon became focused on a boy I was falling in love with. Antonio was his name, and I would have done almost anything to be able to spend time with him. So, one Friday after school I asked my father if I could spend the night at a friend's and I convinced her to do the same. It seemed like a flawless plan. My father approved of Lorraine. She was a straight-A student and pretty square, so it didn't give him cause to be suspicious, though he didn't generally need a reason. I told him we had a football game and then a party afterward. We would be home early. I knew the party was a reach, but figured that my dad would respect that I was telling him the truth and not make a fuss. Antonio would be at Eliza's party after the game.

Eliza had become my new best friend. Remember Pippi on steroids in the fourth grade? That was her. Now she wasn't so scary, just cool. She liked Antonio too—in fact she liked him first—but he and I were in love. Who could argue with that? I told her she shouldn't try. She didn't; lucky for my face—she would have punched it in.

After the party a group of us went to spend the night at a friend of Antonio's. It was late by then, and Lorraine was getting tired and nervous. She started complaining of a stomach ache and, before we knew it, she was throwing up all over the street. Everything would have been fine had Lorraine not wanted to go home. But she did. She swore she wouldn't tell on me, but she did that too.

Sometime around five o'clock in the morning we heard someone come through the front door. We were all crashed in sleeping bags in front of the TV. Antonio and I happened to be sharing one.

"What the—?" Antonio yelped, waking us all up. I looked up to see my stepmother, Isabella, punching and scratching at him. "How could you do such a thing?" she yelled. "You bastard!"

"We didn't do anything. Honest, I didn't touch her." I remember thinking that Isabella shouldn't be getting so upset; she was nine months pregnant. The things you think about when you're about to get the crap beat out of you . . .

I froze when I saw my father's hulking figure standing over me. "You f—ing whore." *Smack!* "Did you f— him, you stupid"— *smack!*—"whore?" He grabbed me by the collar of my cheerleading outfit and pulled me out of the sleeping bag.

The next thing I knew, I was flying head first down a flight of stairs. I can remember looking up when I landed and seeing all the kids huddled together, helpless, crying, and looking down at me. Next thing I knew, Bruno grabbed me off the floor, dragged me out the door, threw me in the back of the car, and then proceeded to beat the hell out of me.

At first I didn't realize it was my car we were in. Not until he slammed the driver's side door of my classic 1965 Cougar, shattering all the glass. I watched my cowboy hat fly out the busted window as we sped away. To this day I can remember the stench of his bad breath and his spitting as he swore at me.

"You're a goddamned embarrassment to this family, you dirty whore." *Smack!* "What did I tell you, you stupid . . ." *Smack!*

His backhand had the force of a wrecking ball. Did I mention that my father was a competitive body builder?

Only a couple of blows after my trip down the stairs—maybe it was a dozen; at that point, who was counting?—and it was lights out. However, I do remember him—sometime after I stumbled into my room when we got back home—waving his enormous finger and pointing it in my face, saying, "You're nothing but a no-good whore, girl, just like your mother, and you have brought shame to this family."

I didn't wake up for two days. When I did, my mother was sitting beside me on my bed. I was happy to see her, but I couldn't ignore the fact that she had left me there to live with this creature. Whatever lies my mother told herself about my situation must have done the trick, because after she made sure I wasn't dead or permanently injured, she left me there with my father again and went back to her own reality.

Come Monday morning, I was dressed in black and blue, even though they apparently were not my colors. Most everyone at school steered clear of the likes of me that day, but they didn't miss an opportunity to stare and whisper as I hobbled past. A few of the braver souls took pity on me and bothered to ask if I was okay. The truth is, I didn't know if I was okay. I was in pain, I was embarrassed, I was angry, and I didn't know what I was supposed to do or how I was supposed to be acting. My ribs hurt so bad, I could barely take in a full breath. I could understand no one wanting to come near me, given my father's reputation.

I was desperately alone. I was trapped. I could not leave, but I could not stay. My life until now, in a nutshell—no wait, in a bullet shell—was . . .

Speaking of Bullets . . .

"BURLINGAME POLICE DEPARTMENT. How may I direct your call?"

"Hello, is this the police department?" I asked, my voice shaking with fury.

"Yes, this is the Burlingame Police Department. Can I help you?"

"Can I ask you something?" I inquired.

"Is this an emergency?"

"Mmmm, kind of. I mean, not anymore."

"Go ahead," she said. I could hear a clicking sound in the receiver. I wondered if the call was being recorded.

"If somebody hits you—me—you know, beats me up . . . like one of my parents . . . do I have to stay there—here—with them, I mean?" I forced back my tears. I did not want to cry.

"How old are you?"

"I just turned fifteen."

There was a pause, like the line had gone dead, and then she came back on and said, "If what you're asking is whether you have to stay in a home when a parent is physically abusing you, the answer is no. No, you do not."

Tears spilled out of my eyes. In that instant I felt like she had given me a get-out-of-jail-free card. Someone had finally heard my plea for help and had given me back my power.

"Thank you. Thank you so much. That's all I needed to know," I said, and hung up. I walked out the door of my father's house that afternoon with my shoulders back, swearing that he would never touch me again. I didn't know where I was going, but anywhere, I thought, was better than here.

"If You Wanna Get High and You Wanna Take a Ride— Cocaine!"

I DIDN'T HAVE SEX WITH ANTONIO that fated night but, no matter how you slice it, I got screwed. And even though I managed to temporarily escape the bondage of my father's demonic clutches, evil would introduce himself as another.

My first night on the road, I celebrated my newfound emancipation with my friend Justin Chang and a six-pack of Mickey's Big

Mouth. So it seems fitting for metaphor's sake that I slept that night in his car. A stock green GTO with leather interior and dual exhausts. I told myself that when my forefathers set out for new frontiers, they slept on dirt under the stars, night after night, without food or water, heaters, or blow-dryers. That made my immediate arrangement more . . . bearable. Being inebriated definitely helped. To my good fortune I was able to upgrade to his closet the next evening and maintained impermanent residency therein for the next fortnight.

Justin and his brother occupied the bottom half of the family house on their enormous estate smack in the middle of old Hillsborough, which put me approximately a half mile from harm's way. Keeping a minor—never mind one that was on the lam and holed up in one's closet—a secret was no easy feat. Especially with my appetite, not to mention culinary preferences. Justin's family was Asian—Chinese, to be more specific; off the boat, to be more to the point. So Justin's sudden need for Lucky Charms, mac and cheese, and a fork definitely raised some eyebrows.

When I wasn't busy plotting my next meal or waiting impatiently for the gate to clang shut—signaling my freedom to roam the premises—I was trying to avoid the heaviness that welled up in my chest. I still could not escape the impending doom I felt even though I was "free."

I had seen cocaine a few times before, but had always considered it a "hard" drug. I associated it with scumbag, rocker people—burner types. But when Justin offered it to me, that all changed. Justin was a senior, was smart, and liked the same bands I did: Wild Cherry, The Gap, and Jimi Hendrix. He knew how to dance and was very popular. Most important, he adored me. The latest addition to my Good Girl Handbook: The only requirement for discipleship—adoration.

Justin taught me everything I ever wanted to know about cocaine, including how to never pay for it. I watched him dry it, cut it, weigh it, package it, sell it, snort it, and smoke it. I even learned how to make those little white envelopes he called bindles. It was all so glamorous, so '80s, so gold chains and polyester, so—Scarface. And then there was how it made me feel.

"Here, hold this end in your nose," he said. "No, like this. Here let me do it," he interrupted, correcting me and then demonstrating the technique. He stuffed an end of a rolled-up hundred dollar bill in his left nostril, closing his right nostril with his index finger, held the other end of the straw at the beginning of the powdery line, and slowly sniffed it up little by little until half the line was gone.

"Aaahh, like that," he nodded, holding his nose shut and then sniffing up the rest of whatever was left in the cavity. "Here," he said, offering me the straw.

"Like I'm stupid?" I said, and snatched the straw. I was nervous and excited. I mean, I had seen it done before, but it was always someone else's nose, so until now the danger had only been peripheral.

Justin was no drug addict and most certainly not a loser, I reminded myself. He was cool and one of the most responsible people I knew. With that, I shoved the straw in my nose like an old pro. He reached over and pushed it in a little farther.

"You have to get it way up in there or it will spill out all over," he said.

"Okay, okay. Stop," I said, playfully slapping his hand away, knocking my elbow against the mirror tray.

"Hey, watch it," he said. He grabbed the razor blade and straightened out the delicate lines that I had just deconstructed. "Go ahead," he said, impatiently.

"All right, all right," I snapped back. I leaned over the mirror and carefully placed the end of the straw at the base of "my line" and sniffed the whole thing up in one go.

My eyes watered lightly and my nose stung a little. A distinct, bitter taste dripped down the back of my throat. I handed Justin the rolled-up bill, mildly triumphant, half expecting some kind of accolade, then waited for something to happen. I wasn't sure what.

But nothing did. At least I thought so. It was subtle, like a cool breeze when you're warm, but you don't realize you were warm until the breeze comes over you. So the only thing I noticed was that I felt good when there was nothing in particular to feel good about. That was it.

What was not so subtle was my increasing urge to do more. The powder was like magic, and the more I did, the more I wanted. But that was nothing new for me. As usual, anything that felt good, I was a glutton for. But until now, the things I was drawn to were merely forbidden; now they were illegal.

Eventually, Justin's parents found out that I was camping out downstairs. I think it was the day I was having myself a frosty mug of beer, watching *All My Children* in the family room when Justin's mother walked in unexpectedly. And I, in a sincere gesture of appreciation, held up my beer and asked, "Can I get you anything?" It was time for me to go. Where, was the question.

Before I secured a less temporary address, I slept in a car, three closets, a tent, and the guest room of some guy I called Salad (because that's all he had for me to eat). In the meantime, Justin knew of a friend who said I could stay with her for as long as I needed to. Her name was Lisa.

Lisa was twenty years old. She was tall and slender, and had long, wavy, chestnut-colored hair. She wore a small gold cross around her neck and thick glasses. Her mother had recently died, leaving Lisa the only living kin. Lisa was kind and generous and only asked two things of me: to clean up after myself (that was easy, I was a neat freak) and to contribute when I could (which meant I needed a job). So I got one.

I started working part-time as a babysitter for a health club near our apartment. But not for long, as it seriously interfered with my social schedule. You see, Eliza and I had made an agreement that we were going to get drunk every day for as long as possible or until the end of summer, whichever came first, because . . . we could. Never mind the rest of my calendar events: snorting cocaine as often as possible, and hosting *Breakfast at Tiffany's* parties. The whole job thing was just so—jobbish. The clincher was when they fired me. They said one of the club members smelled alcohol on my breath at one in the afternoon. I was so pissed. I mean, how could they fire me? What did I do? I'd only had three beers. Besides, I was chewing gum. No one could smell anything. They just didn't like me. Which was all beside the point. I needed this job. What was I going to do now?

I pleaded with the manager to give me another chance. I even apologized and admitted I was wrong. My theatrics were ineffective. She wouldn't budge. And I, unable to rid myself of the shame she had shed upon me, resented and then hated her. In that order and proportionate to the amount of alcohol I drank the rest of that day. I got drunk enough to convince myself it wasn't really my fault, but not drunk enough to drown the disgrace and humiliation I felt.

The thing is, I really felt like a victim in this situation, despite the fact that nobody poured the alcohol down my throat. I felt that she had fired me because she simply didn't like me. I couldn't see my part in it at all, nor did I have any comprehension of the concept of taking responsibility for my actions. Nope, the filter I saw through, the lie I told myself, was that life was doing me wrong—again.

That next morning the phone woke me up; I was lying face down in the walk-in closet that separated the kitchen from the bedroom. I could hear Eliza pick up the phone—she had moved in with us several weeks before. "It's your mom," she yelped as she handed me the receiver. She was calling to remind me to show up for the family portrait she had arranged for the following day. After I hung up the phone, I sat up and looked at myself in the long, skinny mirror that hung on the back of the closet door. My head was throbbing and my eyes were still a bit fuzzy. And I wasn't sure, but I could swear it was me I saw with a big, fat shiner in the reflection. I moved closer to the mirror to get a better look, and sure enough, I had a black eye.

"Are you okay? How do you feel?" Eliza called from the bedroom. I slowly got up off the floor and stomped into the bedroom.

"What's this?" I asked indignantly, pointing to my eye.

"Oh my God," she said, trying not to laugh.

"How did this happen?"

"You don't remember?"

"If I remembered, why would I be asking you?" I glared at her.

"Don't you remember that last night you kept telling me you could kick my ass? You were trying to get me to box with you." I shook my head. "Well," she continued, "I was only trying to stop you from hurting yourself, but the more I tried, the . . . Anyway, you started punching and slapping—you were out of control—so I got pissed and punched you in the face." She lit up a cigarette.

"So you punched me in the face?" I responded in disbelief.

"Yeah! What was I supposed to do?" She nonchalantly took another drag off her cigarette.

"Great! That's just great. I have a family portrait tomorrow! What am I going to tell my mother, Eliza?"

She examined the cuticle of her thumb, bit a part off of it and blew it onto the carpet, and when she realized I was actually waiting for an answer, she looked over at me and said, "I don't know. Tell her you got jumped." Like throwing spaghetti at the wall.

"Jumped? Jumped? By who?" I demanded.

"I don't know. Some guy," she said, flicking her ash into an empty beer bottle.

"Some guy," I repeated blandly. "Oh sure. 'Hello, Mother. My eye? Oh this? It's nothing, I was just jumped by *some guy!*'" I stormed into the bathroom, slammed the door behind me, and walked up to the sink. I leaned into the mirror to reexamine the damage. 'Jesus H. Christ,' I thought. 'What the hell? Where am I? What am I doing here?'

I knew I didn't belong there. And certainly not with a black eye; this wasn't me. I didn't belong in any of the places I had been recently. 'Who wakes up face down—in a closet—with a black eye, Maryanne?' I thought to myself. Not me! I was enveloped with a kind of homesickness. 'There's no place like home,' I thought, and was immediately comforted by my own sentimentality. But the home I longed for was no place I had ever known.

Heeeeere's Johnny!

I'LL ADMIT MY HOMECOMING was a bit dramatic. Being escorted by the police this time was probably not the most strategic move in terms of winning my mother over. But it wasn't my fault. How was I supposed to know that you couldn't be drunk in public, especially if you're a minor and technically a runaway? I wouldn't have said anything had the police officer not asked me where my parents were. Okay, so the black-eye thing probably wasn't very swift, but that wasn't my fault either, I mean theoretically. I didn't know what the big deal was. You'd have thought I robbed a bank or pierced my clitoris. I was fifteen. How bad can a person be at fifteen?

Apparently bad enough to have to qualify my existence because, as far as my mother was concerned, it was definitely negotiable.

Shortly after my mother asked the police to "be so kind as to *not* sound your sirens" when they left, she herself left town, but not before she suggested I not be there when she returned. Needless to say, my mother canceled the portrait.

My brother Johnny was home from college, visiting for the weekend. He shared my mother's sentiments.

"Who do you think you are?" asked Johnny, as I leaned against the kitchen sink, wolfing down a sandwich.

"What? I'm hungry. I haven't eaten anything." He talked right over me and started toward me. I began to tremble, but held perfectly still.

"You make me sick! You know she can't even stand to be in the same house with you," he said, with disgust. I looked directly at him, my fear instantly transformed into anger, my blood boiling at each utterance.

"You're a huge disappointment to Mother." He looked me up and down like the lowest of life forms. "You don't go to school, you don't have a job, you don't do anything," he said. By now I was pulsing with rage. But I didn't say a word, I just stood there holding my sandwich, holding my tongue.

"You're such a loser. You're no good to anybody, so why don't you do us all a favor and get out of here," he said finally, and then pushed me backward into the counter.

Whatever self-respect I had left leaked out all over the kitchen floor. I had just been drained of any life that was inside of me, and I stood there, immobilized by the cruelty and heartlessness of his words. In that moment, I had come face to face with what I feared was true about me. I was ugly, dirty, lazy, and no one wanted me. The feeling was worse than being fat, pasty, and poor. There were remedies for those. But nothing could erase the shame I felt. There was nowhere to go; I had been cornered.

I told myself that what he was saying must be true. After all, he was the epitome of Mr. Perfect: he won best-looking every year in school, all the girls wanted him, and most painful of all, my mother loved him more than she loved me. So who would know better than he that I was a loser?

After my brother walked away, all the clever things I ought to have said in my own defense occurred to me, like, "Who do you think you are, you arrogant bastard, you spoiled brat, you . . . you . . . ? The truth is, I had no defense. He had hit me where I was most vulnerable. I had no self-respect—none to speak of, anyway—so it was pretty easy to take me out. I also knew, as the clock ticked while I waited for my mother to come home, that my only hope was to fabricate enough sincere humility or remorse for being an awful excuse for a human being. So that—God willing—she would take pity on me and let me stay.

I had no place to go—I had outworn my welcome with my friends, I couldn't go back to my father's, and my mother was hostile. I didn't even know if I was going to have a place to sleep that night.

The irony is that as helpless as I felt, I had a lot of pride. There was no way I was going to go to my straight friends or distant relatives, where I would have to uncover this whole ugly mess that was my life and earn their pity. I'd rather grovel and figure out some way to convince my mother to let me stay.

With the help of God—if he was willing to pay a visit and distribute a blessing—I'd be home free.

So once again, I reached into my prayer arsenal, which had been in arrears for at least four years, since my last brush with innocence.

"God, please help me. I can't do this anymore. Please help me. Whatever you want from me, please help me." And I really meant it. I would have done almost anything.

Two days passed and then I heard the electric garage door open. She was home. I figured my brother must have left; I didn't see him again after he had sliced me to bits in the kitchen. To keep myself sane I had cleaned the house from top to bottom—something that usually made my mother happy. As she walked past the washer and dryer into the kitchen, I mustered the most sincere look of prudence I could manage. She was surprised to see me, but said nothing. As a matter of fact, she didn't talk to me for three days. She didn't even acknowledge that I'd cleaned the house. Finally, I couldn't stand it anymore. "Are you ever going to talk to me?" I asked. Silence. I followed her around the house. She abruptly stopped in the hall when she could tell I wasn't going to relent.

"What do you want me to say, Maryanne? You know how I feel."

"No, I don't. You won't even talk to me," I said. She didn't respond. "Mother?!" I insisted.

"What, Maryanne? What do you want me to say to you?"

"Look, I'm sorry. I know I screwed up, but please tell me what to do. Tell me what you want me to do," I cried. She did her best to resist comforting me, but I could see she was tired. She walked into her bedroom and resumed unpacking her bag.

"Okay, Maryanne," she relented. With that I leapt into her arms and wrapped myself around her neck, jiggling up and down. "But you're going to have to go back to school, Maryanne, and get your diploma, and there are going to be rules around here—and a contract. You're going to have to sign an agreement, do you understand, young lady?"

"Yes, yes, whatever you say, of course—anything," I gushed, still hanging on to her neck. "Thank you, Mommy, thank you. I'll be good, you'll see, I promise!"

'Oh thank you, God,' I thought to myself. A wave of relief flushed my whole body, the same way it does when you're driving while you've been drinking and a cop car puts on its flashing lights and you panic, but then it speeds past you and you can't believe you barely escaped, and you promise yourself you'll never do it again.

"Thank you, God. Thank you!" I kept saying, as though my gratitude could pad my overdrawn account with him. For me, being abandoned seemed a fate worse than death. My life had just been spared.

But how soon we forget . . .

As soon as I had put out that fire, my Bad Girl impulses and desires started becoming stronger than ever. No matter how hard I tried, I couldn't not want what I wanted, so the only way I could stay within the guidelines of my Good Girl Handbook was to make absolutely sure I didn't get caught being bad. My mother put me into a small private school for "difficult" kids like me. She promptly solicited my cocaine-dealer buddy Justin—that's how oblivious she was—to be my personal watchdog, knowing full well that if I listened to anyone, it was him. I couldn't have been more jubilant. Not only was my bodyguard one of my best friends, I also had an unlimited supply of nose candy whenever I wanted it. What could be more fabulous than that?

So was it salvation I was seeking? Clearly not. I had been given another get-out-of-jail card and didn't use it. Why not? Why recidivist and not reformed? My only hope for real redemption at this point was having someone see me, really see me, so that I could tell them the truth, so that I could tell them I spent most of my time not wanting to live. But I didn't know such a person yet—and I didn't know how to ask for anything more than crisis intervention. So my answer for everything was to medicate. I wanted to get high so I wouldn't have to feel.

Not Much and Not This

ONE NIGHT THE WHOLE GANG was over. Justin, Justin's best friend Brian, Eliza, Antonio, my friend Matt, and one of Eliza's friends, Collette, who I didn't really know. My mother took us all to dinner, as she often did those days, and had too much to drink, which she often did, as well.

"Do you love her?" she slurred, sloshing her drink all over Matt's sleeve. We were all sitting around the enormous glass dining room table, playing poker. "Do you love her?" my mother asked again as she slid her hand between Matt's legs, grabbing his crotch.

"Uhh, yeah," said Matt, trying to discreetly pull her hand off his testicles.

"Are you in?" I asked Eliza, barely able to believe what I was seeing and trying to ignore my mother.

"Yeah, I'm in."

Mother started up again. "No, really, do you love her?" she slurred, this time slopping her drink all over herself. You could see the relief in Matt's face when she let go of his crotch in order to attend to the mess she had made.

"I'll call," said Brian.

"You can't call!" shouted Justin. "You're out, man."

"Do you want to kiss me?" Mother asked, leaning over and smothering Matt's face and mouth with hers. Matt lurched backward in his chair.

"Mother!" I shrieked.

"Come on, Caroline, behave. Leave the poor guy alone . . . I think it's time for bed," said Justin, as he stood up. Running interference was something Justin was becoming accustomed to. Unfortunately, everyone else had not. They all sat bewildered, if not stunned, by Mother's flagrant attempt to get it on with Matt. I was mortified—and furious.

"Okay, party's over. Time for Caroline to go to bed." I walked around the table, reached over, and grabbed her arm. She pulled away from me, wriggled onto Matt's lap, and then flipped me off.

"Fff— you." She could barely say the words.

"Okay, Mother, f— me. Right, let's go, come on; time to go to sleep." I motioned to Justin to help me grab her.

She ripped her arm out of my grasp and shouted, "Fff— you, I am nnnot going anywhere." She looked toward Matt and said, "Get me anotha drink." By now Matt was simply trying to hold her up so she didn't hurt herself.

"Come on, Caroline, you don't want another drink. Let's go get in bed," he said, and winked at me in an attempt to let me know it was all somehow okay. Like this was normal.

My mother was grabbing my friend's penis and trying to make out with him. Someone please explain how this is normal.

Eventually Justin and Brian managed to get my mother to bed. They made her a turkey sandwich, tucked her in, and then everybody left. Everyone except Antonio, that is.

Strip Poker, Anyone?

"DO YOU THINK SHE'S ASLEEP?" he asked, pulling his shirt over his head, grabbing it from the back of his neck. Antonio and I had spent the night together before. Not that we'd slept much, but aside from heavy breathing and some heavy petting, I was technically still chaste. It's not exactly that I wanted to be a virgin; it's just that I didn't necessarily want to have sex. I had heard people on TV and other places "do it." There always seemed to be a lot of screaming and moaning. As far as I could tell, it sounded like it hurt. And I had no interest in pain, self-inflicted or otherwise.

"Totally asleep," I said. With that he started kissing me, which I loved. He was such a good kisser. But all he had to do was breathe in my ear and it would drive me wild. Something about that boy made me crazy.

"Stop it," I said, pushing his hands away from my zipper. "I said stop it," laughing because he was now tickling me, trying to distract me. We kissed passionately for hours into the night. My face was raw, my lips were swollen, and somewhere along the line he had slipped my shirt off. By then I was defenseless. I wanted him to take me, I wanted to be his.

"I feel like I can't get close enough to you," he whispered into my ear. "I want to be inside of you," he said. He grabbed onto my hair and kissed me so hard I could taste the blood from my lip where he'd bitten me.

"Okay," I yielded.

He rocked gently back and forth, wriggling free of his pants, his face barely an inch from mine. His breath smelled of corn chips and beer, and his eyes were as bright and tender as the moon. He enclosed my hands in his over my head. Then he kissed my forehead, then my eyes, my nose, my cheeks, my lips, my neck, all the way down to places I had never been kissed before. He licked and sucked my fingers like popsicles and gazed into my eyes like no one ever had.

"Have you ever . . . ?" he inquired sweetly. I shook my head. I could feel a tear roll down my cheek into my hair. I could only lay there motionless, struck silent. I knew something extraordinary was happening to me, but I could barely stay afloat.

"Don't be scared," he said, gently. "It won't hurt at all, I promise."

With that, he wrapped my now bare legs around his own and began to carefully push himself inside of me. I clung on to him like a cat gripping its prey so it won't get away.

"Relax, baby, its okay," he whispered, pushing himself deeper inside.

"Ohhh," I said, reluctantly. The sound forced its way from my mouth each time he thrust deeper. Tears now streamed from my eyes. I didn't want him to push anymore, but I didn't want him to let go of me either. I could feel his breath deepen and his gentle rhythm give way to something more fierce. And just when I could feel him plunge all the way inside me, I looked up into his face. He seemed to be lost in some place I didn't understand but I felt included me. His body shuddered for a few seconds and then he collapsed on top of me. I burst silently into tears.

After a few minutes he brushed my hair away from my face and whispered, "I love you, Maryanne." I drank in his words, insatiable.

"I love you too," I cooed, dreamily.

My tears wouldn't stop, and eventually he fell asleep. I rolled over and lay in a fetal position for most of the night, staring off into nowhere, feeling a familiar emptiness that I couldn't place. Even though he lay touching me the entire night, I felt completely alone.

Oh, if I had known then that no one can get all they need from merely having sex. The tenderness I felt in Antonio was authentic, but no way could it fill my gaping emptiness. It was close to something I knew I needed, so I thought if I could get more of it, then I would be okay.

How come I couldn't see the obvious connection between my parents' behavior and my insatiable need to be loved? What I can tell you is that that need was overwhelming. And no one was around to tell me that wanting to be held was perfectly normal—healthy even. In my world I didn't know any form of touching that wasn't sexual.

My family rarely touched. We gave courtesy kisses and hugs that resembled the real thing. And my distorted relationship with my father only made things worse. I was so accustomed to his continual emotional and physical abuse and the cold wind of indifference and neglect from my mother, that I didn't have a clue about the messages my body was sending me.

The next morning Antonio snuck out of my room before my mother regained consciousness. I had a sliding glass door, so it wasn't difficult to do. He kissed me on the forehead, said he needed to borrow my car and that he'd call me later, and left. I was still a bit groggy, but strangely relieved that he had gone. I climbed up off the floor, where we had spent the night, found my undies, and slipped them back on. I remembered hearing that the first time you have sex you bleed, so I looked at the carpet and sheets to see if there was any blood. There wasn't any.

I climbed into bed, pulled the covers up over me, and wondered if I was different now. If having sex made me more . . . anything. I held my hand to my face and breathed in the smell of him, the smell of us. The emptiness in me evaporated, replaced with fresh desire. I could hardly wait to see him again.

My mother woke up later that morning—probably closer to noon. She asked me the routine questions, like where were her car and her keys, and would I get her some juice. Then she handed me her credit card and told me to go and buy myself whatever thing I had mentioned that I needed. Her way to pacify me, if not rectify any damage from the night before.

I called Eliza to see if she wanted to go to the mall and then picked her up in my mom's car, since Antonio had mine. Before I could tell her all the details of what had happened between Antonio and me, she threw up her arms and legs and shrieked, "Oh my God!

You did it!" Eliza had already had sex, more than a few times, and she had been waiting on me to catch up.

"Isn't that your car?" Eliza asked, as we stood in the mall parking lot and noticed a car that looked suspiciously like mine drive by. "And isn't that Antonio . . . and Gina Razzoli?" I squinted my eyes tighter to see if I could see what she was seeing. Impossible! Antonio? I was just with him. I mean I was just *with him*. He would never borrow my car and pick up another girl in it. He loves me.

I felt like I was going to throw up. Nothing made any sense.

"What a complete asshole," she said, shaking her head. "You knew he was seeing her, right?"

"What?" I said, dazed.

"Oh God, you didn't know? How could you not know?" I shook my head. "Yeah, he's totally sleeping with her—and, Abby too," she said.

"Abby? Abby Lombardi?" I cried.

"Yeah, Antonio's been living at her parents' for the last two months." I shook my head again. "God, I thought you knew all this. Well, his mom kicked him out of the house. You knew *that,* right?"

"Yah, but I thought he moved in with his father. I mean, I stayed there with him."

"Well, I heard his mom is signing him up for the army and that his dad is moving back to Honduras," she reported.

My mother lived only ten minutes from my old neighborhood, which was apparently far enough for certain developments to take place without my immediate knowledge.

"What should I do? I can't believe he would do this to me," I said, wiping my tears away. I was devastated.

"Kick her ass, Maryanne. She knew you were with him. Bitch." That was Eliza's answer for everything. Beating the piss out of it.

"She knew I was with him?" I broke into tears again.

"Yeah, I saw her at the twins' party last week. She was totally talking about him like she was with him. I told her to back off." she said.

"Why didn't you tell me?"

"I *am* telling you."

"You told me she wanted him, but I didn't know they were together or anything like that."

"Look, let's go back to your house and call him and see what he says," she suggested. "Maybe it wasn't him," she said, trying to invoke some optimism.

The Glass . . . Tennis Shoe

"LOOK, I TOLD YOU she's just my friend and she needed a ride," he said, walking toward the front door to leave.

"No . . . please don't go . . . wait." I stood in front of him trying to block his departure. "Then why didn't you tell me that's where you were going? I mean, why didn't you say so?" I screeched.

"Look at yourself." He tried to get around me.

"No, please, I'll stop. I'm sorry, I'm sorry. Don't go, please," I begged. He stopped and stood dead in his tracks, waiting for me to move. I couldn't help myself. I burst out, "Why? Why did you have to do this?"

"Do what?" he said, still trying to get past me without having to touch me.

"Why did you have to be with her?" I pleaded, tears pouring like waterfalls from my eyes.

"I wasn't *with* her. Now let me go." He tried to get past me again. I grabbed on to his legs.

"Let go of me. You're wacked," he said, pushing me aside, climbing out of my grip. I fell back onto the ground but managed to grab his ankle as he opened the front door.

"Please Antonio, don't leave. Please, I beg you. I love you. Don't leave," I screamed, still holding on to his ankle. He shimmied loose from my grip, leaving his tennis shoe behind, and when I reached out to grab him again, he slapped my hands away and sprinted out the door.

"Nooooo, nooooo, please don't leave me, Antonio, pleeeease. I'm sorry, I am soo sorry," I wailed. I collapsed to the floor in a heap, absolutely broken. I lay there on the floor, hysterical, sobbing, holding on to his tennis shoe. I thought about how only hours before we had held each other bound by a love that I believed was so true that nothing could ever destroy it. It didn't occur to me that he would lie or that I should worry he ever might. I thought love was all-supreme, and that it was a safe place to surrender into. I assumed he thought so too.

In any case, I convinced Antonio to forgive me. I apologized incessantly for my behavior until he gave in. But not until I admitted it was somehow my fault that he had cheated on me. So he took me back.

What was I thinking? This boy, who incidentally had just told me he loved me, had taken my car and used it to pick up another girl whom he was cheating on me with—*I* asked him to forgive *me*? How does this make any sense? It didn't. So why did I plead with him desperately to take me back? What kind of person behaves this way?

I loved this boy more than I loved myself. I would have done anything, including humiliate myself, to feel the way I believed he made me feel. He told me he loved me; he told me I was beautiful. Who says those kinds of things if they don't really mean it? I could not afford to believe it wasn't true. Because that would have meant that what I felt was all in my imagination—it would have meant that either I was crazy or unworthy of being loved. I couldn't bear the thought of either. I refused to believe what was right in front of me because I could not handle that magnitude of pain.

When my father left us, I barely recovered. I couldn't handle it again. So I lied to myself. I figured if Antonio would only give me another chance, I could prove to him that I could be what he wanted me to be, and he would stay. Does someone smell a pattern here? How about a filter for reality? This is what we call a clue!

★★★★

Right about then I started hanging around Alishay Farooq, a new girl at school who immediately became very popular, not that it mattered to her or that she even noticed. Everyone called her Allie. Alishay dated Chad, the guy every girl in my school wanted—including Eliza—and who was also Antonio's friend.

Alishay's family was Pakistani, extremely wealthy, and very private. Allie was unusually pretty and very comfortable with herself for a girl our age. But what I liked most about her was that she was a bit on the eccentric side. She was the type of girl who would, if you asked her what her name was, recite a nursery rhyme, kiss you on the mouth, and then tell you what time it was in London. Sort of like the trippy chick in *The Breakfast Club*, except she wasn't ugly and no one thought she was weird. I used to wonder what it would have been like to be her.

Because Alishay was Chad's girlfriend, I had the added bonus of being privy to any and all of Antonio's potential indiscretions. If you were me and paranoid, this was very cool. Except that Allie thought Antonio was a saint—although she thought everyone was a saint, even Chad, who had recently spent the weekend in jail for stealing a car.

Anyway, about a week before her sixteenth birthday, Alishay spent almost every day at my house and at some point she would tell me she had a terrible headache, start crying, and then lock herself in my closet. I would ask her what was wrong and she would cry out the same thing to me every time: "I'm going to die, I know it—before my birthday, Maryanne. I'm going to die. And someday you'll know why I'm telling you."

That was the spooky part. I had heard this kind of thing before. I didn't want to be the person people told things to, who someday would know why they did. Either explain it to me now or tell someone else. What am I? A human Crock-Pot for death, destruction, and other related topics? Anyway, I knew she wasn't going to die, but I did consider the possibility that she may have been on heavy medication.

About a week or so later on the night of Allie's birthday, Eliza had a small party for her at Eliza's parents' house.

"I want to go see Chad," said Allie, bouncing up and down in a faux tantrum. Antonio, Eliza, and I were sitting on Eliza's parents' bed, kickin' it, listening to Led Zeppelin, watching Alishay rock back and forth to some other beat.

"So go," said Eliza, "he's probably home by now."

"I knoooow," she whined. "Someone needs to take me." No one said anything. Then she looked at Antonio. "Antonio, come on, you take me, you give me a ride; you're not that wasted," she kept whining.

"No way, forget it. He's been drinking seven and sevens all night. He's not taking you anywhere," I said, and looked at Antonio for reassurance. As you can imagine, letting Antonio out of my sight for any reason was anxiety-producing.

"Pleeease," she said. "Come on, it's only a mile. I just want to say hi for one minute and then we'll come right back. Pleeease," she pleaded, now on her knees.

"Allie, call him and tell him to come over here," said Eliza. Alishay lit up like a Christmas tree and disappeared around the corner for a minute.

"What time is it anyway?" said Antonio.

"Uuuuhh . . . ," Eliza leaned over to the other side of the bed. "It's one fifteen," she said, then pulled herself back up.

"He won't answer the phone, you guys," Allie said, traipsing back into the room, tucking back a lock of her wavy black hair behind her left ear. "Come on! Give me a ride, Antonio," she begged.

"Come on, Allie, it's late," he said. I could tell he didn't want to go either.

"Allie, forget it. He said he's not taking you," I said. I could see the look of disappointment on her face and it made me feel guilty. After all, it was her birthday. Then I had an idea. "Hey Allie, go ask Eric." Eric was Eliza's older brother. "He knows how to drive a motorcycle; he'll take you." I looked at Antonio for his approval.

"Yeah, whatever, as long as he doesn't"—his words escalated into a yell as Alishay darted out the door—"mess up my bike." A few minutes later she skipped back into the bedroom.

"He's gonna take me!" She jumped up and down and clapped, highlighting her extraordinarily long, slender fingers. "I'm so excited! I get to see my baby, yaaay," she sang.

Eric poked his head in the bedroom and said, "Hey Antonio, is it cool if I give Allie a ride up to Chad's on your bike, man?"

"No problem." Antonio reached in his pocket for the keys and then tossed them to Eric.

"Be back in a few," said Allie, frolicking out the door with her hands on each side of Eric's jacket, like she'd jumped in line to do the bunny hop.

A second later Alishay popped back into the room, looked right at me, and said, "If I'm not back in an hour, *you* know what happened to me." We all chuckled.

"Yeah, right, whatever—'I know what happened,' right." And then there was a wicked silence that sort of hung there in the room. We all noticed it. We were laughing and there was music and people were talking and then, in the middle of it, silence—you could hear a pin drop—and then everybody started talking again, and the music started playing right where it left off. The moment was truly bizarre. But because no one said anything, we carried on, right over it.

Just when we started to wonder where Eric and Allie were, the phone rang. I glanced at the clock; the display said two fifteen. Besides Antonio, Eliza, and me, our friend Wendy was the only one left at the party. She picked up the phone. We could hear her talking to someone. I thought maybe it was Eliza's dad calling to say he would be home late. But it wasn't him.

Wendy walked into the room with a glazed look on her face, which usually meant she was stoned. She held out the phone, offering it to no one in particular and mumbled, "They want to speak to your parents."

"Who wants to speak to my parents?" asked Eliza.

"Who is it, Wendy?" I demanded.

"It's the hospital, and they . . ." she trailed off.

"Give me the phone." I took it from her.

'Dumb shit,' I thought to myself. Wendy was no genius and was a true blonde—so she had that going for her, but when she did drugs she was worthless. She and Allie had split some

Quaaludes earlier, and that, mixed with whiskey, was lethal.

"Hello. Yes, this is Mrs. Moran," I lied. "What's going on?" I asked, expecting to hear anything other than what she was about to say.

"Mrs. Moran, your son has been involved in an accident. I think you should come to the hospital right away," said the woman on the other end of the line, in a sharp but vacant way.

"Is he okay?" I asked.

"Ma'am, I can't give out that information over the phone," she replied blandly.

"Yeah, but is he okay? I mean . . ."

'Oh God,' I thought.

"What about Alishay?" I asked. "The girl he was with, is she okay?" My voice quivered.

"Like I said, ma'am, you need to come to the hospital and speak to the attending physician."

"Thank you," I said, and then hung up the phone.

I looked at the others in the room, huddled in anticipation for the answer to the only question on all our minds: Were they okay or not? I could only repeat what the woman had told me on the phone.

In about thirty seconds the four of us tore out the front door and ran the less than two miles it took to get from Eliza's to the hospital. We exploded through the emergency room entrance sometime after three thirty. The waiting room was completely empty. It smelled sterile, like rubbing alcohol and bandages. There were rows of unfilled metal chairs with blue plastic seats, and the large windows made it seem icy cold. You could feel the expectation of doom all around you.

No one was at the reception desk and, except for the voices over the intercom, you'd have thought they were closed. So I took it upon myself to ferret out someone who could help us. I hurried through the double doors behind the reception area and grabbed the first person in a uniform I could find.

"Excuse me." I stopped a small woman in scrubs in the hall. I could tell by the look on her face that I wasn't supposed to be back there. "I'm sorry," I said, "but we just got a call from someone saying that our friends were here, that they were in an accident. Eric Moran and Alishay Farooq?" I puffed, barely able to catch my breath. "Does anyone know anything?" I asked, anxiously.

The woman studied me carefully and said, "Stay here and let me go see what I can find out."

I walked back out into the waiting room and told the others what was going on. No one even looked at me. We were all in some strange suspended animation, like a collective pause. I paced back and forth.

Then, without warning, the double doors opened at the far end of the room. Eric was being pushed out in a wheelchair. His clothes were stained with blood all over. He was slumped over in the chair with his forehead resting wearily against his limp fist. He didn't look up at us; he just sat there, lifeless. Eliza knelt down next to him and tried to ask him what happened, but he didn't respond. We could see that his eyes were swollen from crying, and dried blood was caked under his fingernails. Even his hair was soaked, like straw, with blood. He started to whimper and then slumped over like a rag doll into Eliza's arms.

I walked over to him, knelt down, and gently put my hand on his back. "Eric," I said, reluctantly, "can you tell us what happened? Where's Allie?" He looked up, dazed and barely able to form a sentence.

"We were coming . . . around the . . . corner on Adeline and . . . I don't know, we hit a telephone pole. Allie flew off the bike . . . behind . . . me, and . . ." —he started to cry—"smacked into the pole and . . ." He was sobbing. "It all happened so fast . . . I . . . she was just laying there. There was so much blood . . . everywhere. It was . . ." He tried to collect himself. "So I picked her up and told her to hang on and . . . Oh God . . ." He lost it and was wailing now. His anguish swelled inside each of us. We all surrounded him with hugs, wiping his tears, choking back our own horror, rocking him back and forth in our arms.

Through the double doors, I saw a nurse walk by. I ran through them, grabbed her hand and asked, "What about Alishay, the girl?" Startled by my outburst, I could see she didn't know who I meant.

"The girl that was with him." I looked over and pointed at Eric. "Is she okay? I mean, is she going to be okay?" I asked again.

"I'm sure the doctor will be out soon," she said perfunctorily, and then hurried off.

"Can't you tell us *anything*?" I called after her.

"She may be in surgery," she offered, looking back at me, and then vanished around the corner.

When I walked back into the waiting room, Wendy asked, "What did she say?" tugging at my sleeve, "Maryanne? Maryanne, did she say something? Hello?" I stood there, spaced out. I realized Wendy was asking me a question.

"She said she thinks that she's in surgery—that's it," I said, in a voice that threatened defeat. And then I went and sat down next to Antonio, who had his face buried in his hands. We all sat in silence waiting for someone to tell us what was going on. I watched the clock *tick, tick, tick*; it was approaching four o'clock in the morning.

Several minutes later another woman in scrubs walked through the double doors; her mask was pulled back on top of her head and her shoes were covered with turquoise paper slippers. She walked over to us and said with tremendous regret, "I'm sorry." My heart sunk. "Your friend didn't make it; she died on impact. It was very quick. I'm so sorry." She looked at each of us and then walked back to where she came from.

I knew it wouldn't be good news, but I couldn't believe that she was dead. It didn't seem possible. They said she was in surgery, but now she's telling us she died before she got here?

"Wait!" I called after the woman. But she had already gone. I looked at Eliza and then Antonio. "Then why did they make us wait so long to tell us? If they knew she was . . . I mean why didn't they tell us?" I protested loudly. No one said a word. What was there left to say?

I walked over to the pay phone to call Chad. No one answered. Eliza called her father and he came to pick us up. When we got back to the house, I talked Antonio into taking me up to Chad's so someone could tell him what happened. I wanted it to come from me.

Tap, tap, tap. "Chad? Chad! Open the window." I was whispering as loud as I could without waking his parents. "Chaaaad!" *Tap, tap.* "Wake up! It's meee, Maryanne. You have to wake up!" His window opened.

"What are you doing?" he asked, rubbing his eyes. He stood there with his arms folded, in his boxers and a Led Zeppelin T-shirt, while I climbed in the window.

"I have to tell you something," I said, and started to cry.

"What is it? What are you doing here? Where are my smokes?" he asked, looking around the room.

"Chad . . . Allie's . . . she died," I said, just like that.

"Is this some kind of joke?" he asked, with the unlit cigarette hanging between his lips.

"I wish to God it was, sweetie, but it's not." We both sat down on the edge of his waterbed. We were both in shock.

"What the f—? It's her birthday, and she was supposed to come up here and . . ." he trailed off. Then he poured his face into his hands and I told him the whole story. What I didn't tell him, what I couldn't tell him, was that it was my idea that Eric take her.

I hugged his rigid body in an attempt to comfort him, but it was like trying to put a Band-Aid on open-heart surgery. We both sat there in the turbulent silence and then Chad looked up at me and asked, "Where's Eric?" I looked at him curiously; his tone was strangely provocative. His pupils were dilated and looked black and cold.

"No, Chad, wait, come on." I reached for his sleeve and stood in front of him, hoping to calm him down. "You're not thinking clearly. Look, Eric didn't . . . It wasn't his fault," I tried to explain.

"I'm gonna kill him!" he roared. He threw on a pair of jeans, slipped his bare feet in his shoes, grabbed his car keys, and bolted out the door. I ran after him. "Chad, you can't . . . No—wait. Chad!" I slapped my hands against his window as he turned on the ignition. "Chad, listen to me. Please . . ." I pleaded. He hit the accelerator and like that, he was gone. And so was Eric.

No one saw Eric again for years. The last we heard, he had flipped out and was living with some guy who sold heroin. As for the rest of us, a morose wave of drama rippled through our world. And after the bell tolled, signaling that the allotted amount of time had passed to display or experience emotion over such a thing (in this case, two weeks), we simultaneously tipped our hats to this chapter of our lives and watched whatever remained swirl down the drain with all the rest of the "very bad things."

Even though people told me it wasn't my fault, that Alishay was relentless when it came to Chad, that Eric didn't have to say yes, and that Antonio would have gone if he'd really wanted to, I believed my selfishness was the hand that took her life. And that was the primary reason I wept at her funeral. I was haunted by her prediction that she would die before her birthday and that I would understand why she had chosen to tell me. But I still didn't know why; I was only an envious, frightened voyeur, who had watched her as she swung from day to day through her life like a playful, carefree chimpanzee. Alishay's death was now the hallmark of the horrible guilt I felt: that there was one less perfect person in the world I would have to compete with.

When they lowered her into the ground, it crossed my mind that I might have traded my whole life to be—for one day—her.

This should have been one of the most emotional points in my life. But it wasn't. By now I was almost numb. Words coming out of people's mouths were like comic strip lines, blood looked like ketchup, and death seemed surreal. I suspected something was very wrong. But I never stood still long enough anymore to feel much.

Things were different after Allie was put to rest. I was watching my life happen as if to someone else, instead of it actually happening to me. Now I was the observer, but it wasn't the kind of observation that made me more conscious; it only split me off further from myelf, and created a constant distortion of reality. That disconnection was how I now survived.

I can remember telling myself I could stop it any time I wanted to; I just didn't want to yet. That someday I would cry and love and feel deeply—but not right now. Ahhh, the lies I told myself.

Let Me Tell Ya a Little Story

"HEY, BABY, HOW WAS YOUR TRIP?" Antonio said on the other end of the line.

"Good," I said, realizing he didn't know that I knew.

"So, what happened? Is she gonna make you go?"

"Nope," I said, flatly.

Mother, Justin, and I had gotten back that afternoon from yet another "special private school" interview—her attempt to keep my nose clean. The funny thing was, most of the kids there were higher than I was. Somehow she concluded that it didn't matter; we would work it out, and everything would be okay. Besides, she was about to hit her own bottom, and she didn't have it in her to deal with me. So she bought a few six-packs and a bottle of vodka. We all got hammered and drove home the next day.

"So what are you gonna do now?"

"I dunno, probably get my GED and start junior college in the spring," I offered, throwing him a bone. "So what did you do this weekend?" I asked, knowing I was setting him up. I sat alert, waiting to pounce.

"Nothin', just hung out with the guys," he said, trying to sound matter-of-fact.

"Really," I said, with a tinge of sarcasm, but not enough to throw him off.

"Yeah, we went over to Matt's to watch the game and then hung out there for a while." He was so good at lying. I could actually see the picture in my mind.

What he didn't know was that I knew he had spent the night with Gina Razzoli and screwed her brains out. And the reason I knew this was that Gina had called to tell me herself.

She and I had decided to join forces one night at a party at my house, not long after the time I caught Antonio and her together in my car. And since it had become obvious that neither one of us was willing to give him up, I decided to fight fire with fire instead of with my fists. (Taking Eliza's advice, I tried to beat up Gina one day at school, but slammed my fist into her locker instead of her face.)

I knew she was into cocaine because she was always trying to kiss up to Justin. Fortunately for me, he thought she was a coke whore and wanted nothing to do with her. Which meant that she would probably do anything to get it, including befriend her enemy.

I strategically fed her coke that night and convinced her that I was really over Antonio, but that I would tell her whenever he and I were together and that she should do the same, so we could really get him back. We came out of the bathroom that night, grinding our teeth, with an unwritten truce to take revenge. "May the best girl win" was the part she so cleverly thought I didn't see. But I was counting on it.

"Sounds like you guys had fun," I said coolly to Antonio. I turned up the radio with my big toe. They were playing "Money" by Pink Floyd. I started singing along to myself, "It's a gas, I'm all dry, Jack, keep your hands offa myyy stash, badam bum bum bum—Moneeehhh."

"Can I see you?" Antonio asked, interrupting my private ballad.

"When?" I responded, trying not to seem too eager, but it was too late.

"I was thinking we could go to that dance thing at the Sheraton this Friday night." He couldn't have said anything more perfect. All my friends were going to be there, as well as all his friends and probably most of the school. Everyone was going to be there.

"Look, I gotta go; my mom needs to use the phone," I lied. Can I call you later?"

"I'll call you later," he said, and then hung up. That was Tuesday, and I didn't hear from him again until Friday.

"Hey baby, it's me. What time should I pick you up tonight?" he asked, cheerily.

"Oh, I should have called you. I'm going to meet you there if that's okay. Eliza's coming over here to get ready and we're driving together," I said, faking regret.

"Why don't I pick you guys up?" he offered. I wasn't expecting that, so I had to come up with something quick.

"No, that's okay. She's kinda bummed out about Chad and stuff so . . . Just go ahead, I'll meet you there," I said, which wasn't a total lie since she was pining for Chad, but knew he wasn't over Allie.

"Okay, then I'll be there around nine thirty. I'm gonna go by Chad's," he said. "Later."

We walked into the lobby of the Sheraton Hotel around eight o'clock that night. I know because I asked the concierge. I wanted to get there in plenty of time before Antonio did; I wanted everything to be just right.

"Wow," said Matt with a seductive grin, looking me over. "What a fox."

"What about me?" asked Eliza.

"Beautiful as always, my lady," retorted Matt. Matt was charming, handsome, and wise beyond his years. I knew some day he'd be sitting behind a big mahogany desk with a cigar poking out of his face, watching the stock market while some woman gave him a blow job.

"And you, aren't you quite the dashing gentleman in your penguin suit," I replied. "Brick House" by the Commodores was playing in the background.

"May I have this dance?" he asked, offering me his arm.

"But of course, Ashley," I said, fluttering my eyelashes like Scarlett O'Hara. Eliza wandered off to find the rest of our group while Matt and I moseyed toward the dance floor.

"So, no Antonio tonight?"

He was reading the lines right off of my script. I replied, "We broke up. I told him I didn't want to see him anymore." I didn't even need to pretend that I was heartbroken. "He told me he was with you Tuesday night, when I knew he was having sex with Gina. I know all about it. She told me," I confessed, perfectly.

"That dude is such an asshole. I told him not to . . . Why would he cheat on you, Maryanne? I don't get it." He shook his head. "The guy's been my best friend since third grade, but he's such a jerk," he said, trying to comfort me over the loud music and keep dancing at the same time.

"I thought he really loved me, Matt." I started to cry, for real. He pulled me into his reach and hugged me.

"Don't worry, it's okay. He's a dick. Here, this will cure what ails you." He pulled a flask out of the inside of his lapel pocket. "One-fifty-one, baby—knock yourself out," he goaded. I pulled, not one, but two enormous mouthfuls off the shiny silver flask filled with Bacardi. I could feel that instant glow fill my hollow chest, make my cheeks rosy, and ease my jilted heart back in the direction of the thickening plot.

"Thanks, Matt. I don't even know what I would have done if you weren't here."

"Stick with me, shweetheart. I'll take care of you," he crooned.

The ballroom didn't take long to fill up, and shortly after that, Matt was holding me close in his arms. And then, by nine fifteen or so, as planned, Matt and I were long gone.

I heard a couple of different versions of what happened that night after we left, but the story I liked best went something like this. Antonio showed up alone about ten o'clock. He tried to find me, but when he couldn't, he asked Gina to dance. But she said no. She knew he came there to be with me, so she told him to—and I quote—"F— off."

A few minutes later, he found Eliza and asked her where I was. She informed him of his recent entry onto her shit list and thanked him very much for telling Chad that she would do whatever it took to get together with him. Well, when Antonio finally caught up with Chad, things got bloody ugly. Supposedly, someone told Chad that Antonio had said Alishay was a nut case and that she was in a better place now, so he punched him in the face and broke his nose. Now I didn't hear any of this until the next morning, of course. I was busy hammering . . . a few more nails.

The next morning, I was talking on the phone with Eliza, eating a strawberry Pop-Tart with white frosting and getting the full low-down about what had happened, when I heard the doorbell ring. It was about ten thirty. For the last hour, Antonio had been trying to make an emergency breakthrough on my line, but I wouldn't accept the call. So I figured it must be him at the door.

I told Eliza I'd call her back, swallowed the rest of what was in my mouth, wiped the crumbs off my face, and checked myself in the mirror. If I was about to destroy someone, I wanted to make sure I looked good.

I opened the door and stood in the middle of the doorway with my hand casually on my hip.

"You're up early," I said.

"Where were you last night?" Antonio demanded. His eyes were wild and swollen. He looked as though he hadn't slept for days.

"None of your business," I said, evenly, exactly as I had rehearsed it.

"Who were you with?" he asked, unable to fight back the tears. I smiled without showing my teeth. "Who were you with last night?" he cried out. I was taken aback by his sudden outburst of emotion. Antonio and I had gone to blows once before. He had called me the C-word and I slapped him so hard it left a handprint on his face for three days. He had wrestled me to the ground, but knew better than to hit me back. He knew my father and my father knew him.

I must say that—for about half a second—I felt a wave of compassion. But then all I had to do was recount the betrayal that burned white-hot in the core of my soul, and remember the lies he whispered in my ear when I gave myself to him completely.

"For the last time," he whimpered, "tell me who you were with. Say it. Say it!"

Now *I* was the one towering over *him,* watching him writhe.

"How do you like it?" I asked.

He looked at me, perplexed. "What?"

"I said, 'How do *you* like it?'" I was relishing my vengeance for his brutal indifference on the night he walked out while I held on to his tennis shoe and begged him not to leave me.

"What are you talking about?" He shook his head back and forth, trying to understand, genuinely confused.

"Go home, Antonio, I don't ever want to see you again." I walked back into the house and firmly closed the door. *Ding-dong, ding-dong, ding-dong. Boom boom boom, bam boom bam.*

"Noooo, Maryanne, please. I'm sorry, please. Open the door, baby. I'm sorry . . . open the door." I leaned back against the door. I could feel his fists pounding it against my back, but other than that, I was unable to feel anything other than triumphant.

After a few more attempts to contact me, and several shipments of red roses, he left me alone and eventually went away. Far away. Argentina, I was told; something about drug charges. But not before I crushed him and not until he knew what it felt like to die while he was still alive.

Around the same time Antonio left the country, my mother casually mentioned one morning after breakfast, while passing me in the hallway, that she was an alcoholic and was now attending AA meetings. I wasn't sure what the Automobile Association had to do with her drinking, but I thought it must have had something to do with the five DUIs she had been charged with. The last one she got, the cops pulled her over a block away from our house. She cleverly turned off her headlights, crouched down in the front seat to hide, and when they came to the window, she thought maybe they couldn't see her. (I know this because I read the report.) I asked her what took so long for her to figure out she was an alcoholic, that all she had to do was ask me. Evidently, she didn't think this was humorous and informed me that my own life was about to change dramatically.

It was barely 1980. I was sixteen and working as a hostess at a popular pie place. I was living part of the time with my new boyfriend, Sean, who was twenty-one and who thought I was eighteen. My mother hadn't really thrown me out. She had simply, for a brief spell, given up trying to control me. Which must have been like trying to stop a nuclear missile with a diaphragm.

I had met Sean at a party one Saturday afternoon. He was a six-foot three-inch, lanky, blonde-haired, blue-eyed, second-generation Irish boy who had legs for days. And he had the most beautiful mouth and lips I had ever seen. His teeth were kind of shnaggly, but he gave me a ride home on his motorcycle and that was it. We were together from that day on.

He had a job as a taxi dispatcher at the airport and worked the night shift. He liked to smoke pot as much as I liked to snort cocaine. However, Justin had recently left for college, so my habit and my stash had dwindled down to the rare occasion when someone offered it. So I drank a lot, and being the good Irish boy he was, so did he.

We both liked to party and mostly did precisely that. Our days consisted of me getting up at five o'clock in the morning and working until three in the afternoon. Then I would pick him up to drive him to work an hour later and go and party with whoever until it was time to go and get him. When we got home, we would get more stoned, drunker, and higher, have sex, and then go to bed. Then do it all over again the next day. Sometimes, to mix it up, we would get drunk with his sister and her husband, who lived close by. The difference being we drank out of glasses instead of the bottle. And then one day his buddy Nate rolled into town.

Nate was slightly shorter than Sean and had light-brown, wavy hair that fell in his eyes every time he leaned forward. His nose looked like it had been broken a few times, apparently because it had been, although he didn't seem to be the kind of guy who would get into a fight. He was actually kind of quiet and less opinionated than Sean, who had something to say about everything. He seemed like the type of guy who would give an old lady his seat on the bus. He and Sean had been friends since the seventh grade; and then he met me.

"So whereabout in Fresno do you live?" I asked, passing Nate the mirror after I finished my line.

"Dinky Creek," he said, wiping at his nose with the back side of his veiny, callused hand. I detected a slight drawl.

"Are you from there?"

"Nope," he said, passing Sean the mirror after he finished snorting the other half of his line.

"Where are you from then?" I pressed.

"The Bay Area." He fired up a cigarette and then blew out the match with the smoke he had just inhaled. I watched him look around the bedroom for someplace to throw the match.

"Here . . ." I handed him an empty Coke can. Sean loved Coca Cola. He drank it like a fiend. Nate popped the match into the can and set it down on the hardwood floor.

Sean's roommate, Dave, had just pulled in from work; he grabbed a beer and sat down with us to join our little soirée. Nate made a few more lines and passed the mirror over to Dave when the doorbell rang.

"I got it," said Sean, climbing over us as he jumped up to answer the door. I could hear a girl's voice. It was his friend Debbie.

"Hey, guys," she said, as she took her coat off and sat on the edge of the bed. Dave passed her the mirror and she sniffed up her line like Miss Piggy. I didn't like her. Something about her bugged me. She and Sean had known each other since they were kids. Supposedly, they were just friends. They acted more like kissing cousins, if you asked me.

Debbie was petite, a little on the chunky side, had shoulder-length, mousy-brown hair, with muddy brown eyes to match. She was a spoiled little rich girl who I suspected had her money and her heart bet on Sean. I told myself there was nothing to worry about, that she was dumpy and had bad skin. This theoretically should have made her less of a threat, but it didn't. She was rich and I was, well . . . I needed another beer.

"So what happened to you guys the other night?" asked Dave, looking at Sean and Debbie.

"What night?" Sean snapped and then tried to change the subject.

"What night?" I said, seconds later. Sean looked at me and then gave Dave the evil eye.

"What night?" I asked again.

Changing the subject, Dave said, "So how was Redding, Maryanne?"

I glared at Sean and then turned back to Dave and said, "Hot!" I wanted everybody to know I was not fooled for a minute. I knew something bad was up, and that it affected me. I had been with my mother at her new real estate development for Easter weekend, along with my girlfriend Wendy. Sean said he had to work and told me to go and have a good time.

"So what did you guys do this weekend?" I asked, looking right at Sean.

"What do you mean? I worked all weekend," he said, angrily, as if I had no right to question him. Which was exactly what I was afraid of. We had only been together about two months. Not long enough for me to drill him without casualties, namely me.

"Here," said Nate, handing me the mirror again and pointing to the fattest line. His gesture was chivalrous, sort of. I could tell he felt sorry for me. I accepted his offer in the manner it was given; in my soft eyes and lingering gaze I offered my appreciation. We had a moment. At least I thought we did; I wasn't sure. Anyway, I snorted half the fatty he'd made for me and then thirty seconds later, the other half. Then I handed the mirror back to him, grateful for the break in the conversation.

Somewhere in that time, Debbie had moved physically closer to Sean. I couldn't help but notice she was touching him with her knee and he didn't seem to mind, which I thought was odd. But I did mind, and became even more threatened by this little chubby chick.

"So, did you guys all hang out here this weekend?" I started up again. Not a peep. Dead silence. Nate was chopping some more coke. Sean was feverishly biting his fingernails, while Debbie was rifling through her purse for her hairbrush—which she was using to groom herself every five minutes—and Dave was rolling a joint. My stomach made an incredibly loud gurgling sound, interrupting our drug summit. I may as well have farted, it was that loud. I was so embarrassed.

"So what did you do?" I said, in a desperate attempt to cover up my gastrointestinal eruption and act like nothing happened.

Then Sean blurted out, "Look, we're not married!"

I must have looked stricken.

"That's harsh, dude," said Nate. "Nobody deserves that."

Sean softened his tone. "I see other people besides you. Okay?" I was shocked by his admission. I thought if you slept in the same bed every night with someone you were having sex with, that made you his girlfriend. I mean, I had told him I loved him, and even though he didn't say he loved me back, I thought it was implied in the fact that we made love every day. I figured he just wasn't very mushy.

Obviously I was wrong. How could this be happening to me again? They all must have thought I was an idiot. Here I was, this nitwit that Sean was boinking. He obviously didn't care about me, and everybody knew it but me. The room seemed suddenly cold. I knew I didn't belong there in the first place, and now I didn't feel welcome. They had all known each other for years. I was the new person.

Dave got up and went into the front room and turned on the TV, clearly annoyed. Debbie followed him.

"Look, I never said I wanted a girlfriend," Sean spat, and then got up and left me sitting there. And Nate, well, he stayed with me in the bedroom and we snorted what was left in his bindle. When he asked me if I wanted to go to the store with him to get some beer, I couldn't get out of there fast enough. When we walked past everyone in the front room, Sean and Debbie were sitting together on the couch, talking to Dave about his new bike. They didn't even bother to look up when we left.

Nate and I drove to the 7-Eleven down the street and bought a six-pack of beer and a pack of Marlboro Light 100s. We drove back to the house and sat in his van, snorting coke, drinking beer, and smoking cigarettes until about three thirty in the morning. It was too late to go home to my mom's and besides, I was way too high. The last time I'd gone home on coke, I'd sat on her bed talking her to death until she told me to hush up and go to bed. She asked me if I was on something. I told her I'd had too much coffee and then went into my room and stared at the wall until the sun came up. My only alternative to sitting in Nate's van with him all night was to go back inside and pretend Sean hadn't blown me off. I may have been naïve, but I wasn't stupid.

I found out that night, while contemplating my housing situation, that Nate worked construction on a batch plant (where they make big rocks into little rocks) in the mountains near Fresno. He said he made about a thousand dollars per week which, for a twenty-year-old in 1980, was great money. But that's not all he did. To support his growing love for Peruvian flake, he had started dealing cocaine. That's why he was visiting, to score a half pound and then bring it back up to the plant to sell. Which meant, minus beer and gas—'cause I knew he wasn't spending anything on his wardrobe—he was making about five G's a week. He told me he was saving up to buy himself a house, one of the many things he mentioned during our teeth-gnawing, jaw-grinding, chain-smoking, empty-beer-bottle-infested marathon chat.

Nate never bothered to say, "Look, Maryanne, Sean's not a bad guy," or to tell me, "You know, my buddy's a jerk and you should forget about him." Uh-uh, he never said any of those things. Instead he put his arm around me and held me next to him. He never tried to kiss me, make a pass, or violate me in any way. He just held me. He made me feel safe, something I had never felt with Sean. I had tried to make Sean love me so I could rest and not have to worry so much about what I said, or how I said it. In the few short hours I spent with Nate, I was starting to understand that I needed someone to give me a bigger down payment on a relationship than a ride on a motorcycle, a full set of lips, and a boner. I needed someone who didn't consider me disposable.

Like two stiff mannequins Nate and I lay down together on a mattress he had in the back of his van, and eventually fell asleep. When we woke up the next morning Sean and his bike were gone, and it looked like I had a new boyfriend. Despite myself, I had clearly traded up.

Nate took me home to my mother's the next morning, gave me an eight ball of cocaine, and said he would be back in two weeks. I made him give me his driver's license to make sure. My mother had left a list of new rules waiting for me on the kitchen counter. One of them was a midnight curfew, which was reasonable, unless you were me. Another was that I remain sober and attend ninety meetings in ninety days, whatever that meant. It sounded okay to me; I liked meetings. As a matter of fact, I didn't mind groups in general. And as far as being "sober" was concerned—sure, I could do that. Alcohol was fattening and made me barf half the time. Besides, nobody said anything about cocaine. At least not yet.

My mother and I walked up the stairs shortly before noon one Monday into some AA club in our neighborhood. At the top of the stairs was a bar lined with steel-colored stools topped with worn, shiny red seat covers. Behind the bar area stood a craggy guy named Joe, who appeared to be a short-order cook, evidenced by half the menu splattered over the front of his apron and the greasy spatula he was waving around. The place looked like a small pool hall and reeked of stale cigarettes. The room was almost filled to capacity and getting fuller by the moment. People were standing in the doorways and leaning up against the walls by the time the meeting started.

No young people were in the room; that is to say, I was, without a doubt—by a good fifteen to twenty years—the youngest person there. Except for the girl sitting at the card table in front of the meeting, who was about to blow my mind.

My mother sat down by a window near the front of the room. At a little past noon, a lady named Nancy introduced herself and told everyone she was an alcoholic. Everyone started clapping. As a matter of fact, every time someone introduced themselves and said they were an alcoholic, people clapped. It didn't make sense to me. First of all, being a loser didn't seem to me like anything you would want to broadcast, and second, what was with all the hoopla? And oh, if you were a new guy and hadn't been sober more than a few days or a week, you practically got a standing ovation.

After everyone quieted down, they read some stuff about God and principles and personalities, which at the time I couldn't have cared less about. I figured if there was a God, my life would have been very different from the way it was. A few minutes later the person who was running the meeting introduced a girl named Denise, who was evidently going to tell us her story.

"My name is Denise and I'm an alcoholic," she said.

"Hi, Denise," the room responded.

I didn't say anything.

She started out by telling us, "I took my first drink when I was about eight years old." That sounded about right; I was probably ten. As a matter of fact, the more she spoke, the eerier it got. Her story and my life had so many parallels, it was starting to freak me out.

Denise was twenty-three years old and looked like Barbara Streisand, but more goyish. She was probably five foot four, and looked like she weighed about as much as my leg. She had on a gray pin striped suit, and had her mink-colored hair in a French twist. She wore black patent leather pumps, sheer crème-colored stockings, and a cargo-style Louis Vuitton bag sat on the floor next to her feet. Her nails were flawlessly manicured, her skin was translucent, and her makeup was impeccable. She was everything that I wanted to be. I thought she was perfect.

Denise finished her story by telling us what had brought her to AA. She said that she and her boyfriend were driving home from a party one night and got into a fight. She couldn't remember why they were fighting, only that they were both drunk. She mentioned that she was having losses of memory more and more often, and referred to them as blackouts. Anyway, supposedly she said something that pissed the boyfriend off. He slammed on the brakes and she flew through the front windshield. She said it was by the grace of God that she was sitting before us that day, and then spent a few minutes telling us all the gifts that God and this program had given her. As if being six feet above ground wasn't enough, she now had a great job, had just bought her first brand-new car, and was engaged to this guy I thought was an absolute babe, who was sitting in the front row to her left. His name was Donald. She closed by saying that if we wanted what she had, to keep coming back.

After the meeting was over, my mother introduced me to Denise. I couldn't tell you what we talked about, but I can tell you that I definitely wanted what she had—her clothes, her jewelry, her boyfriend, even her brother. And her God. I was hoping I could trade mine in. So when she and Donald offered to schlep me around to meetings my first week or so, how could I refuse?

★★★★

I stood in Denise's living room, waiting for her to finish getting ready. It was the Thursday night before Nate was due back in town.

"Make yourself at home," her father said. "Denise should be out in a minute." He had a slight Southern drawl.

"I'll be ready in a second," she yelled from down the hall. Denise lived with her dad, who was also in AA. I nosed around the house a little while I waited, checking out the decor. I noticed a variety of framed pictures scattered on top of their baby grand piano: Denise and her dad . . . Denise at camp . . . Denise in her tutu, Denise and—

"Who's this guy?" I asked, looking closely at one of the pictures. Her father was in the kitchen, making some spaghetti using sauce out of a jar. He stopped what he was doing and came out to see who I was talking about.

"He looks really familiar," I said.

"Oh, that's Denise's little brother, Nate," he said, with his drawl more pronounced.

"Nate?" I echoed back.

"That's right," he said, in a voice straight out of *Hee Haw.*

"Nate Lang?"

"That's the one."

"Your daughter is Denise Lang? I mean, her last name is Lang?" I asked, trying to make sure I wasn't hearing things.

"Yep, that's her all right," he said, in a kind of Gomer Pyle, goofy but polite kind of way.

Just then Denise walked out in the room and said, "Ready?" I gulped. I must have looked like I'd seen a ghost or a flasher. "Are you okay?" she asked.

"Fine. Yeah, I'm good. Let's go," I muttered.

I was stunned. She had told me she had a younger brother who was a good-looking construction worker who lived in the mountains and came home on the weekends. I'd been warned to stay away from him. She'd said that with me being newly sober and all, and seeing as how her brother was really attractive, but drank a lot, it might not be a such a good idea, you know, for me to hang around with someone like him. That was okay. I had no problem staying away from *that* brother. I did have a problem with staying away from the brother who was coming home tomorrow.

What was I supposed to do? How was I supposed to know her brother was my new coke-dealer boyfriend? I mean, what were the odds of that? Okay, I'd promised to stay away from him, but he wasn't "him" when I promised that. And anyway, no one said I had to stop doing coke, right? I mean, no way! Alcohol, okay, sure—that was one thing—but I loved cocaine and I was really starting to like this guy Nate, her brother . . . whatever. 'Forget it,' I thought. 'I'll wait and see what happens when he gets here. Maybe he won't even come.'

Oh, he came all right. In one door and out the other, and me right along with him. I gathered he didn't like his sister or father very well by the tenor of his voice when he told them to go to hell and stay out of his life. You see, I had a stroke of conscience and decided I had better tell Denise the truth about her brother and me. I had learned a few things in the two weeks I hung around those AA meetings. Things about honesty and, well, some other stuff I can't remember. But that honesty thing stuck for some reason. Maybe because I had told so many lies. The point is, I confessed. And it actually made me feel better. Denise, however, did not share my relief. She was pissed.

I didn't understand why she couldn't understand my point of view. Now I was pissed. She said something about incomprehensible demoralization and that I hadn't hit my bottom yet. I said she didn't know what she was talking about. But I was about to find out.

Nate and I left for the mountains that afternoon and rolled up to my new abode sometime shortly after dark. And under the circumstances, it was probably best that I couldn't see where I was. I had been camping, oh, maybe twice in my entire life, and neither time involved actual dirt. That's what cabins are for. My last experience that even slightly resembled camping was when I had slept in Justin's car, which was parked in his parents' four-car garage.

When we woke up the next morning, all I knew was I was going to need a lot of drugs.

You see, Nate lived in a trailer; yes, that is correct—a trailer. And the problem was, now so did I. Not that I was ever going to admit this to anyone, ever, as long as I lived. And it was a very small trailer, and I mean *very* small. It looked like one of those trailers you might see in that movie *Easy Rider*. The kind of place where the woman has three kids from three different guys, one of which was most likely her brother. Now I knew why they called places like this Dinky Creek— no one gave a crap what they called the godforsaken place.

But I had my pride, not to mention a half pound of cocaine, which, from what I understood, was going to be left in my care. Well, this was definitely the bright side, because the rest was absolute shit.

Convincing Nate that if he did not rent us an apartment in town I was going to go completely mad took me approximately two weeks. He must have had an inkling I wasn't kidding when I bashed the television to pieces with a baseball bat one morning because we couldn't get any reception. I'd had to stare at the wall until he came home from work because it was about twelve degrees outside; my other option was to spend the afternoon listening to our neighbor Gladys talk about her husband's cataract surgery for the fifth time while she crocheted another pot holder. We moved into our apartment two days later.

Our new place had a pool and tennis courts and they were usually empty. But that's about the only diversion available for twenty miles. Fresno wasn't exactly a mecca of excitement. It was flat and hot and most of the people there—at least the ones I had been introduced to—managed to speak in terms that I could not decipher. Yes, well, not quite the jet-set crowd I was hoping for that went along with my idea of a glamour life with a foxy coke-dealer boyfriend. I may have read way too many *Cosmo* magazines, but let me tell you, this crowd gave *Spank* magazine a bad name.

For example, one of our frequent guests was a gentleman by the name of Bart Bilkam. They called him Sally, and don't ask me why; I don't think anyone knew. Well, Bart, uh, Sally—Mr. Bilkam—had maybe four teeth, none of which were native to his mouth. He was a very thin man and had a pleasant wife, or at least so I'd heard. He used to stop by, and on the rare occasions I answered the door, he'd come in and sit at the kitchen table—even if I wasn't in the kitchen— and tell the same story about how his dog, Gretel, saved his life one time when he was fourteen years old. Then he would use the bathroom for a really long time and then leave. I didn't even want to wonder what he was doing in there.

Nate was such a kind soul that he never had the heart to say a bad thing about Sally or anybody else. He'd only say, "He's a nice old guy," and then kiss me on the cheek and tell me how beautiful I was. Me? I never said anything about anyone either, but it was because I knew it was either here with Bart and our other distinguished friends, or the sardine can on top of the mountain.

Spring turned into summer, which meant that I definitely needed to go shopping. Which meant I was in trouble. The prospect of finding fashion in Fresno was about as likely as finding the First Lady pole-dancing in a strip club. The equivalent of haute couture here was Frederick's of Hollywood. This was a place where most people had never heard the term "fashion don't," where the average female invested most of her disposable income on white pumps and Aqua Net hairspray. Don't get me wrong, I loved big hair and was definitely a fan of the can. But there was no way I was going to shop at JC Penney for anything.

The buzz of being a kept woman was wearing off, primarily because I was getting lonely and bored. Everyone my age was in school or at work. I had zero interest in either. All I cared about were my soaps— Erica in *All My Children* was my secret role model—and how skinny I could get. I was already on the Hollywood diet of cocaine and pineapple. If I were any skinnier . . . well, that's crap; I knew you could never be too skinny. And my tan—man, when I say bronze, I'm talking Bain de Soleil. I looked Puerto Rican.

Here I was, seventeen years old, and my newfound sobriety was lost in the dust of my chase to be Skinny, Tan & Rich. A mere two weeks' worth of sobriety had collapsed under the pressure of a five-year habit of medicating myself. I was frickin' miserable. The lonelier I got, the more coke I snorted, and the more coke I snorted, the lonelier I got, until finally one morning I woke up spitting up blood all over my white tile vanity.

I was by myself when it happened. Nate had stayed up in the mountains the night before because they needed him to work overtime. I was scared to death. I didn't have any friends to speak of and I couldn't reach Nate even if I wanted to. There were no phones where he was, only two-way radios. I walked outside to get some air. I paced around the grounds, wondering what I should do, and then walked over to check the mail. Strangely enough, there was a letter from my mother in the pile. The postmark was about a week old. Neither of us had checked the mail for a while. I sat down right there at the curb, momentarily distracted from the blood that was still fresh in my mouth, and opened the letter.

My Darling Maryanne,

I hope this letter finds you well. You are greatly missed here at home and I hope you know how much you are loved. Your brother Tony made first string for the football team next year and your brother John made a 4.0 last semester. I thought you would be very proud.

I want you to know, Maryanne, that you are welcome to come home anytime, provided you are willing to get clean and sober. I would ask that you attend ninety meetings in ninety days and that you finish getting your diploma. The world is your oyster, missy. I love you very much and God bless you,

Mother

Tears cascaded down my face as I folded the letter and slid it back into the envelope. I could actually feel how much she loved me. I knew what I had to do. It took me less than five minutes to convince Nate I needed to go back home, but it took me six months to convince him I was never coming back. I couldn't bear the thought of hurting him; he wanted to marry me and had even given me a ring. But I wanted something else—someone else. I wanted more. And I wasn't sure what, but I knew that when I got it, then everything would be okay.

Needing to get clean and sober was the excuse I borrowed to ultimately axe that relationship. I had already tried using the pursuit of fame and fortune as an excuse, explaining that I saw bright lights, the big city, diamonds, and furs. (When I looked into his eyes I saw a station wagon, two kids, a dog, and me being strangled by his white picket fence.) Oh no, not this Chiquita. I was going to be somebody. Somebody big. So about the time Nate finally stopped coming around, I left for Los Angeles. I was going to be a model.

Lucky for me, my mother's cousin was the vice president of well-known swimwear manufacturer. So I went to work straight away.

"I'll have a cheeseburger with french fries, please," I said.

"She'll have a green salad with no dressing," said Albert.

"Excuse me, but I'm hungry."

"Not as hungry as you'll be if you gain even one pound. As it is, you need to lose at least ten," he said, sizing me up.

"What do you mean? Do you think I'm fat?"

"And what's wrong with your face? Do you always look like that?" he said, ignoring my question.

"No. I mean, there's nothing wrong exactly. I thought I needed a tan and I used my roommate's face lamp and I left it on too long and . . ."

"Good, because I can't have you looking like that. Let me put it this way: If you're thin, you're too fat, okay?" he said, sucking down his rum and coke. I wanted to scratch his eyes out. "I'm going to give you one of my cars to use while you're here. You need to be at the studio by eight o'clock in the morning—sharp—on Monday, understood? Your face had better be . . . just make sure it doesn't look like that!" he demanded, making circles with his finger pointing at my face.

"Can I get the check?" he said to the waitress, snapping his fingers. I looked around, salivating at everyone's meal.

"I didn't even get my salad yet," I whined.

"Drink your water," he snapped.

'Nobody told me about this in modeling school. I am in Barbie hell,' I thought.

PART THREE

■ *Who I Thought I Was*

What's Butt Floss?

"DIDN'T ANYBODY TEACH YOU THAT TRICK YET?" asked the girl with the Southern drawl, who was changing next to me.

"What trick?" I asked.

"Throwing up after you eat. We all do it. That way you can eat whatever you want and still look fabulous," she said, showcasing her bony, naked body for me.

"You mean, make myself barf? On purpose?"

"Yeah, silly," she laughed. "You stick your finger down your throat and—voilà."

"Girls, shhh . . . Hurry up and get ready. You're almost on," said Claire, the woman coordinating the models. I couldn't stop thinking about what I'd just heard.

"So how many times do you do it?" I asked her.

"Do what? Throw up?" she asked, putting on another bathing suit top.

"Yeah, I mean, don't you get hungry?" She definitely looked hungry to me.

"Not really," she said, "you get used to it. I don't throw up every time. Like if I eat a salad or a cracker, I won't, but if I eat something bad like ice cream. That comes up pretty easy."

'One cracker? Who eats one cracker?' I thought.

"That's all you eat—one cracker?" I asked, amazed.

"Girls, hush!" said Claire, handing me a copper-colored bikini.

"So that's all you eat," I whispered, "one cracker?"

"Sometimes," she admitted.

Oh my God, I'm going to starve to death. I was already pretty careful about my weight, at least I thought I was. I'd always been pretty lean, which I thought was good enough, but apparently I was too big no matter how thin I believed I was. But no food? Jeez. I didn't think I could handle that.

"So, how long have you been a model?" I asked her.

"Since I was eleven."

"Wow, eleven! Have you been barfing since then too?"

"Pretty much."

"Have you ever, like, choked on it before?" I asked. The girl on the other side of me gave me a dirty look. "What? I was just asking!" There had to be an easier way than this.

✶✶✶✶

I finished off the last of the quart of Haagen-Dazs strawberry ice cream and then headed for the bathroom. I figured I might as well try the barfing thing out, seeing as I hated dieting. This new plan seemed ideal. You eat, you puke, you stay skinny. Cool! I locked the bathroom door behind me, even though my roommate wasn't home, and knelt down in front of the toilet. I leaned my head over the bowl and stuck my finger way down my throat. My eyes started to water and I immediately began to gag, but no ice cream—just a lot of saliva.

'Wow, I must really have to stick it way in here,' I thought. So I did it again. It took me about five minutes of dry heaving and coughing up saliva until I got a good stream going. And then up it all came, in two shots.

"Hello, are you here?" As soon as I heard Sara's voice I reached up and flushed the toilet.

"I'm in here," I hollered, pulling myself up off the floor. I examined myself in the mirror to see if I had any chunks of strawberry on my face. I wiped my mouth off with my sleeve and then shoved some toothpaste in my mouth. I felt kinda lightheaded and my throat hurt.

I wasn't convinced this was the way to go. I mean, when you eat, it's supposed to stay in there. Then it occurred to me that I had wasted a perfectly good pint of ice cream on my little experiment, and I was pissed. I didn't think this was going to work out for me.

"Hey, Sara? What do you call the kind of underwear where you cut the sides off and they go up your butt?" I asked from the other side of the bathroom door.

"What are you talking about?" she replied.

"Some girl at work had on underwear that went up her butt like a string or something," I said, leaning up against the bathroom door while I fussed with my hair.

"Haven't you ever heard of butt floss?" she answered. I opened the door and turned off the light. Sara was a college friend of my brother's and also close with my mother. She lived in L.A., and now I lived with her.

"What are you doing tonight?" she asked.

"Oh, some guy I met on the beach wants to take me to dinner," I said, nonchalantly.

"What guy?"

"Remember that guy who bought me groceries last week?" I reminded her.

"Did you give him our number?"

"Yeah, why? He seemed like a nice guy."

"They all seem like nice guys, Maryanne. Anyway, he was old, like forty," she said, pouring herself a Tab in the kitchen.

"He was not! He was, like, thirty, and he's cute," I shot back, annoyed.

"Cute? How many beers did you have? He looked like the elephant man," she teased.

"He did not. He's got a totally nice body."

"Sure, as long as he doesn't take his clothes off," she laughed. "Where is he taking you?"

"Carlos and something's?" I said, pouting.

"You mean Carlos and Charlie's?" She laughed.

"Well, at least he's buying me dinner."

"He's probably all right. I only want you to be careful. Are you meeting him there?"

"No, he's picking me up."

"You told him where you live?" she shrieked.

"Yes, why?" I said, startled by her reaction.

"Don't tell anyone where we live, Maryanne. You don't know this guy. He could be anybody."

"Yeah, he could be a nice guy or something," I said, and walked out of the room.

"Look, if he turns out to be weird, call me and I'll come get you, 'kay?" she hollered from the kitchen.

"Thanks," I shouted back.

'What-ever,' I thought.

★★★★

"Sara?" I hissed into the pay phone. I was trying to keep my voice low.

"Maryannie?" she replied.

"Yeah, it's me. Sara, can you come get me? He's totally trying to kiss me at the table and he's, like, rubbing my leg and he's all drunk on Long Island Iced Teas. I want to get out of here. Will you come?" I pleaded.

"I told you. What did I tell you?"

"I know, I know—please, hurry, 'kay?"

"I'll be there in ten minutes," she said, and hung up.

"I knew the first time I saw you sitting there on the beach that you were the one," he said, breathing all over me.

"Really?" I said, buying time, trying to stay upwind of his breath.

"No, I mean it, I'm not just saying this either."

"Okay."

"No, really," he insisted, his face inches away from mine.

"I believe you." I looked around for a clock.

"It's like, there you were, an angel that appeared before my eyes—poof!" he said loudly, throwing his hand in the air to illustrate the "poof." People were starting to look over at us. He fell in toward me again.

"I have to tell you a secret," he whispered.

"Okay," I replied. Any conversation was a chore at this point.

He jammed his nose into my ear and whispered, "I want to f— you," and then leaned back and smiled as if he had paid me a compliment. My body recoiled and stiffened. The words "f—" and "you" were still rippling through me like aftershocks. It was like somebody had told me I got a part in a porno movie and then slapped me. I was totally grossed out.

"I have to go to the bathroom," I lied.

"Oh, don't go. Com'mere!" he said, grabbing at me.

"I'll be right back, I promise," I said, barely escaping his grip. I almost ran back to the ladies room, where the phone was, and called home again. No answer.

'Sara, please get here. Please, God . . .'

"Here you are," I heard her say suddenly from behind me.

"Oh my God, I'm so glad you're here," I gasped as I hugged her. "He told me he wanted to f— me and . . . oh God, get me out of here."

"Does he know you're still here?"

"Yeah, I told him I had to go to the bathroom and that I'd be right back."

"Where are you guys sitting?"

"Over by the window, right by the front."

"Okay, walk in front of me. I'm parked right by the side. Don't look at him, and don't say anything; walk right by and then run like hell."

"Okay," I said. I was so nervous, but kind of excited. "Oh God, there he is," I squealed, under my breath.

"Don't look, just go," she said, pushing me faster.

"Maryanne? Maryanne! Hey! Whereya goin'?" he slurred as we rushed past.

"Go go go!"

"I'm trying, I'm going as fast as I can," I said, starting to laugh.

"Maryanne, wait!" he shouted, as we bolted out of the restaurant.

I couldn't help but look back. He stood there in front of the door with his hands on his hips, shaking his head. I actually felt kinda bad for a second.

"I can't believe we just did that," I said, still shaking.

"Yeah, well, next time I might not be there to rescue you," she said.

I saw a bumper sticker in the window of a Mercedes in front of us as we sat in traffic on the Pacific Coast Highway. It read, "Welcome to Los Angeles. Now go home." So I did.

The fact is, I knew I didn't have what it takes to stay in L.A. My self-loathing was bad enough, so being constantly reminded of my inadequacies put even more pressure on me. It was like being in a vise. At least back home I knew how and where to hide and I could be a size 4 and people thought I was skinny.

I apparently preferred the illusion, because moving back in with Beelzebub made L.A. look like Avalon.

Here Today, Gone to Maui

MY MOTHER HAD FILED FOR BANKRUPTCY without consulting me when I was snowdrifting in Fresno. Regardless of our differences, I had been privy to all of her affairs—financial and otherwise—but she had for some reason left me out of this loop. Parting with thirty million dollars and the partner who had embezzled most of it put her in a perpetually bad mood.

But that's not the reason why I moved back home with my father. I had been sober and attending AA meetings going on two years, and I had decided it was a good time to heal my relationship with my father. And besides, being sober *and* poor—I don't think so. So after a very cold war, I decided to wage peace?

Did I say piece?

Things hadn't changed much around the DelRiccio household. Except me. Not that anybody noticed. But I did. Before I got sober I thought something was terribly wrong with me, but now I knew what it was. My family! And thanks to AA and guys like John Bradshaw and Wayne Dyer, now I had names for my neurosis and psychosis: Bruno and Caroline. And if they would just get it and apologize for screwing my life up, I knew everything would be okay.

I moved into my father's house, thinking he and my stepmother should be grateful I was sober. When she informed me that sitting around watching soap operas and eating bon bons wasn't enough, I protested. I saw myself as more—Elizabethan. You know, traveling from one relative's estate to the next, reading poetry, going for long walks on the grounds carrying one's parasol, taking tea in the afternoon, and letting the people who work . . . do that.

I got as far as the "reading poetry" part in my "Life According to Maryanne" diatribe when my father informed me the queen was dead and if I had any questions to take them up at the next revolution. I tried to explain to him that it was all the dirty newsprint and the phone calling, not to mention the annoying interview thing that was taking me so long. He gave me two weeks. I found a job in two days.

On the third day I rose again—no wait, that's another book. That's the day I literally ran home, about five miles from the club where I had landed the job as an aerobics instructor. When I burst through the door to tell him the good news, the first thing out of his mouth was, "How much are they paying you?"

Damn. Took the wind right out of my sails. I thought he would be so proud of me and say, "Oh sweetheart, that's great!" or, "I knew you could do it!" or even, "Atta girl!" But no, all he could think about was the Benjamin; just show me the money. Then he wanted to know if I was stupid. That pissed me off. The truth was, I didn't know how much they were paying me because I forgot to ask. I was just happy they gave me the job. Who was I? Leona Helmsley? Another subtle reminder that there was little difference in my family between money and worth.

I never did ask how much they were paying me per hour. I didn't really want to know how much I was worth; if I asked, I would have to face it. I was just trying not to rock the boat. And keep Bruno out of my hair. So I told my father whatever he wanted to hear. The bonus was that I got to jump around in front of a bunch of fat ladies while I listened to my favorite music and lost weight at the same time. Exercise became my new drug of choice.

And just to show I was a good sport, I would go home every day and display for Bruno whatever new muscle group I was sculpting. My deltoid this, my trapezius that, my gluteus is less maximus, etcetera. He ate it up—there was nothing he liked better than a hard body. Just looking at himself in the mirror gave him a boner, so I was a chip off the old. . . Can I just tell you how proud he was? He was so proud that he started taking me out with him at night instead of his wife. Which really did wonders for my relationship with Isabella.

"Go get ready—and wear something sexy," he barked as I meandered down the hall to my bathroom. "And curl your hair that way I like, and don't put too much crap on your face!" he bellowed from the kitchen table. I shut myself in the bathroom, locked the door, slinked up onto the ledge of the marble vanity, and put my feet in the sink like I always did when I got ready. I reached across to the radio/intercom system, tuned the knob to my favorite station, and cranked up the volume as loud as it would go without distorting the music. My mouth hung wide open the way it does when you're putting on mascara.

I spun my long hair up into a head full of hot rollers and painted my toenails bubble-gum pink while I sang along with a Blondie song. I belted out the lyrics I knew, humming the lines I didn't.

"Call me, on the hmmmm, hmm uh uh uh uh uhuh uh uh, call me, call me, call me any, anytime, call me . . . uhhhh uh."

Boom, boom boom. "Turn that down, I'm trying to do my homework," my brother yelled through his bedroom wall. I waited at least a minute and then turned it down just a hair.

"Okaaayy," I shouted. "It's down." I untwisted my locks from the now-cool rods, shimmied each curler back onto its respective port, then proceeded to flip my hair up and down, loosening and separating the curls with my fingers. When I was convinced that I had achieved the right amount of fluff, I held my head still, careful not to let a hair out of place and then—*pshhhhhhhhh, pshhhhhhhhh, shh, shhh, shh-shh*—applied several coats of hair spray, cementing my Farrah Fawcett do.

"Let's go," my father commanded. I could hear the stylish shuffle of his dress shoes across the marble foyer and I knew that meant I had less than thirty seconds to put on my dress and my shoes and try to find my purse.

"Cuhhhmminnngg," I hollered, flying down the hall and into my room. "Shoes? Okay shoes, where are my . . . Oh here, 'kay. Dress is here, put it on . . . zip it up. There! Purse, purse, okay, where the heck is . . . Good, here . . . Okay!! Here I am," I yelped, as I rushed out the door and up the stairs to the top of our circular driveway.

I was wearing a little white sundress with a slim gold elastic belt that accentuated my twenty-four-inch waist. I had on sand-colored, open-toed, cork-wedge platforms. I looked like an extra on *Charlie's Angels*. My father was sitting in the passenger side of his brand-new black convertible Jag, fussing with the stereo, as I hurriedly approached the car.

He looked up at me over the top of his sunglasses, shot me a nod of approval, and then said, "I said 'half an hour.' Let's go."

"I was just . . . You didn't let . . . What-ever!" I said, as I forced my way into the driver's seat.

Bruno liked me to drive so he could get stoned. And it was always my pleasure to have an opportunity to attempt to break the sound barrier in one of my father's new cars. I'd been driving since I was twelve years old, and had a thing for speed. My father hated to drive and had a thing for volume. I made it from Hillsborough to Marin in about thirty minutes, a trip that normally takes an hour. That cut short the time I had to listen to Rod Stewart and Bruno screeching in tandem, "Do ya think I'm sexy?" over and over again.

It was almost dark when we rolled up to the entrance of the five-acre estate. The wrought-iron gates parted, and we glided through them and along the cascade of manicured hedges that led us to the front of the house.

"Hey-hey, man," Charlie laughed as he opened the car door for my father.

"What it is, Sacramento," said Bruno.

After they were done hugging and slapping each other on the back, Charlie looked over at me and said with his signature booming courtesy laugh, "There she is! Com'ere you and give yo daddy some sugar." He always said the same thing and then he would squeeze me until I thought my eyes were going to pop out of my head. Sacramento Charlie was one of my father's partners in crime. For some reason he liked to come off as a black guy in a B movie. I used to wonder why and then I just decided he was weird. He stood about six feet, was as thick as a side of beef, and looked like Bela Lugosi.

From what I gathered, Charlie had just been released from prison, which apparently was what had given rise to this occasion. My father's "associates" were throwing him a sort of welcome home party.

"*Guarda la bella faccia*," said John, coming down the steps to greet us.

"Oh, you say that to all the girls," I waved him off. I couldn't take a compliment.

"Johnny, hey-hey," said Bruno. They hugged, patted, kissed, etcetera.

"Come here, you," he said, grabbing my cheeks. "Look at you— *che bella*, eh?"

"Hi," I said, smiling, embarrassed by all the fuss.

"Can the girl still dance, Bruno? That's all I wanna know," he said, and started laughing.

"Just like her mother," Bruno replied. My mother minced around like Ann-Margret in *Bye, Bye Birdie*. I was insulted.

Cadillac John was my father's other sidekick. He wasn't as imposing as Charlie, but he was just as loud. He always had his hair slicked back, wore a black turtleneck no matter how hot it was, and was constantly offering to get you some food. "Here, have some salami. Come on, have some calzone. You want I should get you some macaroons?" He was worse than my grandmother, although he had virtue. But there was nothing more embarrassing than being in public with the three of them. It was like being with Larry, Curly, and Moe, except they carried automatic weapons and poked your eyes out for real.

After my father assured Charlie that I would entertain everyone later with a dance number, Charlie scooped me up under his arm and escorted me up the brick staircase that knelt before the house. We stood outside the gigantic double doors ornamented with beveled glass while my father and Charlie smoked a joint.

"You want some?" asked Charlie, passing me the joint.

I furrowed my brow. "Uh, no."

"Don't give her any of that. She's in that AA now," said Bruno.

"Oh, yeah," he said. "That's good. Like Triple-A?"

I rolled my eyes. "It's for people who—" I started to explain, but Bruno cut me off.

"Never mind. All you need to know is she's stayin' out of trouble, got it?"

"Sure, yeah, I got it," he said. Then he looked at me and held the joint out. "You sure you don't want any of this?" Bruno and I looked at each other. My father snatched the joint out of his hand and then smacked him upside the head. "What? Wha'd I say?"

Just then one of the gargantuan doors opened.

"I heard you brought the most beautiful creature in the world with you," said Behrouz, another of my father's associates, and the owner of the house.

Behrouz was an extraordinarily handsome Middle Eastern man with a strong, pointy nose and square jaw. As usual, he was impeccably dressed and had on way too much cologne. Between him and my father it definitely made you want to hurl.

"Halloo, Maryanne. So nice to see you again, my dear," he said in his velvety tenor. He stood by a Ming vase almost as tall as he was, which stood smack in the middle of the shiny black-and-white-swirled marble floor. "Come have something to drink, some food, some wine . . . come, come." He waved his hand and a young man hurried over, took our coats, and asked us our pleasure.

My father turned to me and said, "It's okay. Have a glass of wine, enjoy yourself."

I shook my head. "No, thanks."

"Wine's not fattening. Actually, some red wines are good for you. Bring her a glass of red."

"Thanks, Dad, I don't want any, really," I insisted.

"And bring me a Bud Light," he said, ignoring me. "Keep your eye on her," he told Charlie as he and Behrouz walked around the corner.

I told Charlie I had to go to the bathroom and assured him I could do it by myself. The house was huge. It took me about ten minutes to even find a bathroom. In almost every room I wandered into there was a big old gloomy tapestry on the wall, overlooking a few pieces of musty, ostentatious furniture. The rooms were dark and cold, like the inside of a castle.

I cruised around for a while longer and then heard some music echoing from one of the other rooms—I had counted about seventeen so far. On the far side of the house I found a group of people sitting around a pool table. None of them were playing pool. They were either snorting cocaine or had apparently just done so, judging by the amount of white powder still ringed under their nostrils. Not to mention the incessant chatter and smoking that was going on.

Anyone who knew Bruno knew who I was and, as usual, they were ambitious about getting my attention.

"Oh my God, you're so beautiful . . . Just like your father," squealed some girl whose blouse was on inside out and who had breasts the size of my head.

"Thanks," I said, forcing a smile, and then walking away hoping she wouldn't follow me.

"Oh look, it's Marilyn, Bruno's daughter," said another bimbette.

"It's Maryanne," I said.

I knew better than to get too close to the drugs, and they knew better than to offer. So sooner rather than later I tired of listening to this cluster of Mafia groupies talking about the origins of the clap. It was like listening to Alvin and the Chipmunks discuss the evolution of sentient life. Eventually I found a quiet room to lie down in, downstairs and far away from all the noise. But I was not alone for long.

"Hello, sweetheart," I heard a man's voice say. I had fallen asleep

face down in one of the guest rooms, on a king-sized bed surrounded by a canopy of sheer curtains. He was lying right beside me
and stroking my hair. "Such a beautiful girl," he crooned, like he
would to a baby. His accent was similar to Behrouz's, but I couldn't
tell if it was him. I was too afraid to look. I just froze. He began to
rub my back very sensually and then every second or third long,
languid stroke he would let his hand slip down over my behind
and in between my thighs. It was all happening so fast, and I
wasn't quite awake, so I couldn't register yet what was going on. But
when he peeled back my panties, I was definitely sure. I clamped
my legs together and pulled my arms to my sides like a human
Swiss army knife.

"It's okay, sweetie, I just want to make you feel good." I clenched
even tighter. "Come on, sweetie, let me in there," he said, continuing
to rub my bare legs and bottom with long, rhythmic strokes. His fingers were skinny but smooth, and I could feel the ridge of a ring on
his hand.

He nuzzled his face in my hair, taking long, deep whiffs of my
perfume. I could smell cigarettes and some kind of heavy liquor on
his breath. It made me want to vomit.

"Relax, sweetie. I just want to slide my fingers in and taste your
honey pot," he said, breathing heavily and grinding himself against
my rigid body. I squeezed even tighter, if that was possible. He
reached around underneath me, trying to feel for my breast. I kept
my arms at my sides, unyielding.

"Marn?" I heard my father call my nickname from a distance. The
faceless man jumped off the bed, like a grasshopper, at the sound of
his voice and vanished out of the room. "Maryanne, let's go," my
father called out again. This time the sound of his voice was closer.

I rolled over, still disoriented, pulled myself up to a sitting position, straightened out my dress, and tried to un-muss my hair.

"There you are. Let's go," said my father, annoyed that I hadn't
come the first time he called. But I could tell he was drunk and
stoned so I knew he wouldn't stay mad long. When he was sober he
was a different kind of scary.

I had no time to feel anything. My body was still shaking, and the next thing I knew, my father had handed me the keys and I was supposed to start driving. I had just been stripped of a crucial layer that protected my innocence, left defenseless with no way to comfort myself. And who was I going to ask to do that for me—my father? I was my father's date that night; never mind that I was about to accuse his partner in crime—who I wasn't even certain was the assailant . . . of what? Almost . . . rape?

I can't remember ever being comforted by my father. The few times I had tried—like being scared of the dark at night and crawling into my parents' room trying to feel safe, only to be met with my father's wrath—he would yell, "There's nothing to be afraid of—now get back in your room." Sometimes, when he fell back asleep, I would sneak back into their room and curl up in a ball at the foot of their bed, without any covers. I would try not to move so he wouldn't wake up, and shiver for hours until I finally fell asleep. Part of my terror was that if he woke up, it was going to be way worse than the threat in his voice when he threw me out the first time.

When I finally found some "comfort," it came in the form of drugs and alcohol, which is how I medicated my feelings instead of feeling them. Now I didn't even have that. Now I was trapped, forced not to feel, while the terror and fear were still running through my body. So I curled up inside myself while my body shivered silently, hoping not to awaken the big, bad giant.

And with that came the final disassociation between my mind and my body. It was like being ripped in two: my head was now in total command—the proverbial dictator who would determine the degree to which I was allowed to feel in any given situation. There was no escaping my father; he had just attained full citizenship inside my head and now I took orders from him whether he was around or not.

"You can drive home," he said, handing me the keys—as though driving him home were some kind of honor—and then turned his back on me and walked out of the room. I hopped off the bed and scampered right behind him like a scared little bunny rabbit, knowing on some level that I was in danger around this man without knowing how.

The memories of him smothering my head with a pillow when I was four and five years old, telling me that if I made a sound I wouldn't live to see another day, were exactly where he intended them to stay—in the deep recesses of my subconsious. My father had been a master at twisting reality: at the same time he was molesting me, he was telling me that I was Daddy's little girl and how much he loved me. At the same time that lethal terror was injected into me, I was being imprinted with the conviction that this is what love looks like.

So when Behrouz came onto the scene as understudy, I recognized that familiar, sick feeling whose origins I couldn't place. Since I couldn't remember what happened with my father, the fear and the terror that I'd had no chance to purge were reignited and I had to choke that pill down too—not even realizing why it was now so huge and bitter.

The body tries to warn you when you're in danger, but when you can't afford to listen to it, its signals become more and more urgent. For me, for now, the pain was so bad that I was afraid it would extinguish my life. But not before Bruno put the cherry on the cake of my day . . .

We listened to Rod Stewart screaming all the way back across the Golden Gate Bridge. But I didn't care. Somehow, the absurdity of Mr. Stewart's lyrics was annoying enough to help distract me from the horror I had just escaped. I tried to hold back the sickening feeling that welled up inside of me, as I heard over and over the heavily perfumed words, "Relax, sweetie . . . let me in there" flying about, like bats in the attic dive-bombing into me.

The clock in the car said ten after three when we pulled up to the house and, evidenced by the broom clutched in Isabella's fist, I ventured a guess we were home just in time for the fireworks portion of the evening.

"¡Hijo de puta bastardo, TE ODIO!" she shrieked (which, by the way, means: you son of a bitch, bastard, I hate you), clubbing him over the head and anywhere else she could strike a blow. I took this as my cue and carefully walked around the massacre toward my bedroom.

I had seen this all before. And so had everyone else. So I went to bed. No one even bothered to come out of their room anymore. I only wish my father had stayed in his.

Isabella had given birth to a seven-pound baby girl named Juliana only two weeks before, which may or may not have explained her hysteria. The baby was sleeping in my room until the nursery on the second floor was finished, so I quietly closed my bedroom door, hoping not to wake her. By now all the ruckus had moved into another wing of the house. I slipped off my clothes, pulled on a T-shirt, and slid into bed. I stared at the faint light of the moon through my plantation shutters and wondered what it would be like to be someone else.

Just as I was about to fall asleep my drifting thoughts were interrupted by the sound of footsteps coming upstairs and walking toward the kitchen. Now I was wide awake. A few minutes later I could hear him walk back out and then, instead of tromping down the stairs, there was a pause. My heart stopped and I held perfectly still.

"Maryanne?" he whispered, as he cracked open my door. "Are you awake?" he asked, and then walked into my room. I tried to pretend I was asleep, a trick that felt sickeningly familiar. "Maryaaaane," he whispered louder. I rolled over away from him, but now my eyes were wide open and my breath was quick and shallow. I could feel the bed sink deep as he sat down. I smelled the heavy musk cologne that drenched his terry cloth robe drift past as his sleeve brushed my cheek when he reached for my hand. My mouth went dry and I pulled my arms in more tightly across my chest.

"Maryanne? Maryanne, I just want you to know I love you," I heard him confess. His breath stung my nose with fumes of pot smoke and stale, pungent wine. "Maryanne? I don't know what's happened between us. What's happened between us?" he asked, sounding strange and confused. I was too frightened to consider the question. He leaned down, practically smothering me, and tried to kiss me on the mouth. Disgusted, I abruptly turned my head farther away and buried it into my pillow.

"I love you," he professed. "Don't you love your dad?" he asked, tenuously, and then lay down flush beside me. I completely froze. "I love you, Maryanne, and I want you to love me too," he said, preparing me for his descent and then rolling over on top of me.

He was wearing a royal blue robe, with his initials—B.A.D.— monogrammed near the lapel. The robe was untied and spanned the width of my bed, enveloping me beneath it. He was stark naked underneath. His full weight crushed against me, and the only thing between us was a flimsy fleece blanket, a white Egyptian cotton sheet, and my T-shirt.

"Please, Maryanne. I just want you to love me," he said, abnormally sweet, with what sounded like a tinge of vulnerably. "Just love me," he said, pressing into me, and then he tried to kiss me again.

What was he saying? Love me? Oh my God, help me. Get him off me. My body was an absolute plank. He kept trying to kiss me, holding me like we were lovers, and I kept turning my head from side to side, trying to dodge his open mouth. I could feel the bristle of the hair on his chest against my cheeks and chin and the swipe of his musky terry cloth robe chafing my face.

"Maryanne, hold me," he said, pressing himself against me even harder now.

"Stop it," I managed to say. He didn't. "I mean it," I demanded, now starting to try and push him off me.

"Just tell me you love me, baby, it's okay. I just want to love you," he kept on.

"If you don't stop right now I'm going to scream and wake up the baby," I said, in a loud, seething whisper while pushing up on him, trying desperately to get out from underneath him. He wouldn't stop.

"I mean it!" I said, out loud.

"Okay, okay, sshhhh!" he said, pressing his enormous index finger to my mouth to silence me. He must have believed me because he climbed off me and tiptoed out of the room, closing the door quietly behind himself.

For the moment I was safe, but the truth is there was no safe place for me; there never had been.

The conflict was, I didn't get any attention from my father unless it was twisted. But when he told me he loved me, even though it showed up all wrong, I was still touched by that love I was desperate for. He said he wanted to love me, and part of me needed to believe him. What he should have been doing that night was holding me and comforting me, listening to what had happened with Behrouz and trying to make me feel better. But after so many times of having the thing that should be happening not happen—and the other way around—the normal cycle of need and response got short-circuited. After a while, I started to doubt what was real.

My body knew I was being harmed, but my psyche was being deceived into believing I was being loved. Now, the only way my body knew to cope with this double bind was to send me into panic oblivion.

It took me two days and two sleepless nights to muster up the courage to tell someone what had happened. I chose my stepmother, seeing as how she currently hated my father almost as much as I did, and I hoped she would sympathize or comfort me in some way. Instead, the next day my father informed me that I needed to move out of the house. He used the excuse that Isabella didn't want me there and that there was nothing he could do about it.

Did he think I really believed there was nothing the almighty Bruno couldn't do? That a wife he called "girl" had any significant influence over his ability to make decisions? To ease his conscience, he bought me a charming little cottage downtown, next door to a lovely old couple who thought my Persian cat was a poodle and that Bruno was my boyfriend. I figured somebody up there has a sick sense of humor.

L'Oréal Blonde—and I'm Worth It

LYNETTE WAS NINETEEN, voluptuous, with platinum blonde hair and thick black eyebrows. And she was too tan—the wrong kind of tan to have with such white hair, if you know what I mean. She wore bright pink lipstick and taught aerobics wearing turquoise leg warmers at our club on Mondays, Wednesdays, and Fridays. My best friend, Eliza, had joined the army and most girls hated Lynette, so by default we became friends.

Lynette reminded me a little of Loni Anderson. To men she was attractive in all the right places. She acted the part of the dumb blonde, but she really wasn't. Once you got to know her she was actually pretty bright. Any girl who could wrap a dozen men around her middle finger was my idol. Lynette was the kind of girl who carved notches in her bedpost to glorify her conquests. I was definitely taking notes.

Late one Friday afternoon, I went over to Lynette's and hung out while she got ready for a date. I wanted to see for myself one of these guys she kept talking about that supposedly bought her roses, champagne, and jewelry.

"Hello," she shrilled, picking up her powder pink telephone. "Hi there, handsome . . ." She looked at me and winked. "Uh-huh . . . No, why?" She grabbed her nail file and started lightly sawing at the ends of her bare, inch-long claws. "I won't be ready by then . . . No. I can't!" She looked at me and rolled her eyes like we were in cahoots. "Eight o'clock, that's the best I can do, Boo-Boo . . . Uh-huh, uh so? . . . Well, then you'll just have to wait." She looked at me and winked again. "Never mind what I'm going to wear—you'll love it! . . . Look, I've gotta run sweetie, I've got company . . . What? I don't care. Just . . . whatever . . . Dom Perignon. I have to go now," she said, obviously bothered. "*Ciao.* Kiss, kiss." She rolled her eyes again and then hung up.

Boo-Boo? What is that? Who calls someone that? Who was this guy? I couldn't wait to see what kind of schmoe allows a girl to treat him like that. I wondered if he had a brother.

"The trick is," she said, without my asking, "you never give them what they want."

"What do you mean?" You'd think by now I'd know what she meant. Which just shows you the disparity between my experience and my understanding.

"What they want—you know, what every guy wants." I stared at her blankly with my eyebrows raised, wondering if she was referring to the same thing my father was always saying. "To *have* you, silly," she said, rifling through her drawers.

"To have you?" I asked, wondering if my father's "truths" were in fact universal.

"Yeah, you know—control," she said, matter-of-factly.

'Oh, control . . .' I thought, taking note of the difference in their philosophies.

"Here it is," she said, relieved, holding on to some white, lacy thing with strings all over the place. "It's simple, Maryanne. The more you give a guy, the more he takes, but the more you say no, the more he wants," she said, and walked into her bathroom.

Her room looked like a prostitute's boudoir. It was painted pale rose and had curtains that matched. Her canopy bed was cloaked with a velvet purple spread and strewn with decorative pillows. Instead of art she had mirrors, and instead of posters of famous people she had pictures of herself.

"Could you hand me that bag?" she yelped from the bathroom. I reached for the Louis Vuitton sac by her nightstand. "Not that one, the little green one by the door." Who was I, the bell boy? I grabbed it and brought it over to her. "Thank you," she sang, batting her big, fluffy eyelashes at me.

I could see firsthand, in action, my mother's old adage: "You catch more flies with honey than vinegar." Lynette had it down to a science.

I watched her roll and unroll rows of curlers as big as Coke cans. She painted on a face that Renoir would have been proud of and wore an outfit that would have made Marilyn Monroe blush. Had I put the same outfit on, I would have looked like the Flying Nun in garter belts. She sprayed on enough perfume to make me gag and then proceeded to paint her chiseled fingernails red.

"Brandon owns his own company," she said, fanning her fingers and blowing on her nails. "He's totally rich," she said, trying to move a piece of hair out of her face without it touching her almost dry nails.

"Really?" I said, curiously.

Knock, knock, knock.

"Lynette? Sweetheart, I think your friend is here," said her father from the other side of her door.

"Thanks, Daddy," she cooed.

Her father seemed so nice. My father had told me I couldn't date until I was twenty-five.

"He's here," she squealed. "Look, look and see if that's him," she giggled. I peeked through the curtains down to the front of the house. I could not believe my eyes. A shiny white Lincoln Continental limousine with two sunroofs sat out front, and before I could say anything, a six-foot-something godlike creature with wavy brown hair and an ultra-cool smile stepped out of the limousine. He adjusted his cuffs like a man of substance and then walked gallantly to the door. I thought I was going to faint. I felt slightly embarrassed that I had taken such pleasure in looking at this boy . . . guy—man. Whatever he was.

"Come and meet him," she squealed with delight, clutching her furry white rabbit coat that would be quite the cherry on top of her already *débauchée* ensemble. Compared to Lynette I thought myself painfully plain. I wanted to hide in the closet and disappear.

I followed her down the swirling staircase that would lead us to her date. She reached out for my hand, and with the other, squeezed the banister so she didn't fall down the stairs. It was like right out of *Dynasty,* only I was the homely twin they included in the show because they needed to thicken the plot.

"You look absolutely gorgeous," he delivered seamlessly. Who was he talking to? She looked like a cheap tramp.

"Thank you," she replied. "This is my girlfriend Maryanne." I felt like an old shoe.

"*Enchanté,*" he said.

'Did he just bow?' I thought to myself. I wasn't sure. And I didn't know what "ashantay" meant either, so I raised the corners of my mouth and forced a smile.

"All right then, I'll call you this weekend," she said with a vague look in my direction. Then she took his arm, and they were gone. I went home and headed straight for the hard stuff—three peanut butter and jelly sandwiches, two bowls of oatmeal, a couple of oranges—and then had dinner. I was feeling very unattractive. I wished I looked like Lynette. I thought if I did, everything would be perfect. I would have a rich boyfriend who was wild about me and everything would be okay.

This is a classic example of how I compared my insides to everyone's outsides, and then made life-altering decisions as a result.

It's My Turn

AND THEN ONE MORNING, my phone rang. I dove for it, as usual, thrilled that anybody would be calling.

"Hello," I said, eagerly.

"Maryanne?" said the man's voice on the other end.

"Hey, Michael? What are you doing?"

"Talking to you," he joked. I wondered why guys thought this was funny.

"I know that; I mean, what's going on?"

I knew Michael from AA. He was about forty, very handsome in a biker, leather-chaps kind of way. He looked really young for his age, had captivating blue eyes and a crush on me. I liked Michael, but for me he was more like a mentor. He was the one who had introduced me to the concept of honesty. I remember the time he asked me to try and go a whole day without lying. I agreed, but asked him if he would first define the word "lie" for me.

"Do you remember me talking about my buddy Rob, from high school?"

"Rob," I said, trying to remember. "No, not really, why?"

"He's the one who was having trouble with the pipe, remember?"

"Oh yeah, the cocaine guy, right!"

"Right, Rob. Well, he's not doing too good, and since cocaine was your thing, I thought maybe you would come and talk to him."

"Yeah, sure! When?" I replied. One thing I had learned by being a member of AA was if someone needed help, you always said yes. It was just part of the deal.

"Tomorrow about three o'clock. Is that cool?" he asked.

"Sure," I said. "Where?"

"The Fisherman."

"Okay. I'll see ya there."

"Maryanne? Thanks!" he said, earnestly, and then hung up.

I had done a fair amount of volunteer work at the local hospital with kids who were recovering from substance abuse and had been around the rooms of the program long enough now to know how to deal with a practicing alcoholic. But nothing could have prepared me for what I was about to experience. Nothing except my childhood.

The restaurant was dark and practically empty when I arrived; it was off-hours, so technically the place was closed. I went inside anyway and found Michael and his friend sitting in a corner near the bar in a booth with a spectacular view of the bay.

"Maryanne!" said Michael, excitedly, and got up to give me a giant bear hug.

"Hello, Michael," I said, out of the side of my mouth as he squeezed my face against his musty-smelling flannel shirt. Then he sat back down. I brushed myself off.

"And you must be Rob," I said, extending a handshake to his friend, and then sat down myself. Michael was a little rusty when it came to etiquette. He was busy stuffing as many cocktail peanuts as he could into his mouth while Rob and I exchanged greetings.

"Hi," he said, flatly but pleasantly from somewhere behind his expensive, very dark, gold-framed sunglasses. I was a bit surprised; I had been expecting some low-life scumbag crackhead, not this elegant, sophisticated-looking gentleman.

"I hope you don't mind that I didn't get up," he said in a mild voice. He was sitting between Michael and me, with a beer in one hand and a glass of red wine in front of the other.

"Not at all," I said.

"I haven't slept in several days and I'm afraid I might seem a little crazy right now. I don't know how long I'm going to be able to sit here."

Underneath a week of five o'clock shadows, his square jaw was noticeably tense.

"I totally understand," I said, totally understanding.

"It's crazy, Maryanne," he said, shaking his head. "When I called Michael I was sure I was going to die, and the next thing I know, the pipe is calling me again. I just can't beat this thing."

"I know exactly how you feel," I said. "I loved cocaine. There's probably nothing I wouldn't have done to get it. The doctors even told me my nose was caving in and it was starting to make me paranoid and sick. In the end I just couldn't take it anymore. Then one morning . . ." I tried to finish.

"I'm sick, Maryanne, do you know what I'm saying? I tell myself to stop, but the pipe keeps calling. I don't know what to do." He tried to keep his voice even, but I could hear him hyperventilating. I wondered if, when the pipe called him, the voice he heard sounded like Tattoo's from *Fantasy Island*? 'De pipe, de pipe, Rob, come and get de pipe.'

The day I met Rob was my birthday. I was eighteen going on forty, and he was thirty-nine. The only thing we had in common was our love of cocaine, mine past tense, his in a bullet vial in his pocket. We were a match made in—Colombia. Consequently, the first few months of our relationship consisted of me trying to help him get off the drug. All it took to change that was a trip to Las Vegas, a Rolls-Royce, one full-length, black mink coat, a diamond ring, and an eight-ounce jar of pharmaceutical cocaine. Oh, and partial paralysis.

✸✸✸✸

"PSST . . . MARYANNE . . . MARYAAAAAANE," hissed Molly. I didn't look up. I was crouched down behind the waitress station, stocking the French armoire with napkins. When I wasn't working at the bookstore, I had a part-time job at a health food restaurant. "Maryanne!" she said, again.

"What's the matter?" I said curtly. I thought she was going

to tell me I had seated someone in the wrong section.

"Nothing's the matter," she said, surprised by my tone. "There's some guy up front asking for you."

"Well, did he say who he was?"

"No, but whoever it is, Dale said he drove up in a Rolls-Royce," she said in her best hoity-toity voice. Two seconds later Dale sashayed through the curtain, formally announcing the arrival of the mystery man.

"Look at you, aren't *you* gorgeous today. Good thing too, honey, because there's a *very* handsome gentleman up front looking for you—a sharp dresser too," he said, with his contagious affect.

"Okay, I get there's a man up front, you guys. Did anybody bother to find out who he is?" I asked, frustrated. They both looked at each other, clueless. "Is it my father? Is he tall?" I asked.

"I don't know. Is your father fat?" asked Molly.

"Fat? No, why, is this guy fat or something?"

"No, but he looks kinda old though," she reported, pulling on her chewing gum and then wrapping it around her tongue.

"Old? Like how old? Old-old or just older-old?"

Molly rolled her eyes and said, "I don't know! Do you want me to cut him open and see how many rings he has? He's *old*—old-enough-to-be-your-father old."

"Who cares! Whoever he is, he drives a Rolls-Royce. How bad can he be?" said Dale, interrupting our banter.

"You don't know my father," I said, under my breath.

"Would you just go," he said, pulling me out from behind the waitress station. "Whoever he is, just remember, you are the hostess with the mostest, honey—now scat!"

"Okay, okay, I'm going. Would you stop!" I said, as he herded me toward the front entrance. I managed to catch my balance as he pushed me through the curtain.

"Hello," said Rob, who was leaning against one of the pillars. He was wearing a pair of 501 jeans, a blue cashmere jacket, Gucci loafers, and a pair of very dark Porsche sunglasses.

"Hi," I replied. He walked toward me.

"I hope you don't mind that I came by your work. I tried to reach you first, but—"

"Yeah, I know, my machine's broken," I said. He looked confused by my response. "No, it's okay. I mean, sure, no problem—that you're here, I mean. Are you hungry?" I asked, suddenly embarrassed.

He smiled, amused by my rambling, and said, "Actually I came by to ask if you would like to have dinner with me tonight."

"Tonight? Uuhmm, well, I—I don't really . . ." I started.

"Do you already have plans?" he asked.

"No, it's not that," I replied. He looked concerned. "It's nothing, it's just that . . . I don't really have anything to wear," I confessed. 'Nothing that warrants a ride in a Rolls,' I thought to myself. He smiled and then chuckled.

"What time are you done here?"

"Three."

"I'll be back at three this afternoon and we'll go and get you something to wear. How does that sound?"

'Shopping?' I thought. 'Oh my God, yes!'

"Okay," I said, submissively, trying not to act too excited.

"Great, be back at three o'clock then, okay?"

"Okay." I waved to him as he looked back at me through the window. He is so nice, I thought, and he wants to take me shopping. Something must be wrong. I wondered if he was gay.

✦✦✦✦

Rob insisted I sit in the back seat of his Rolls and told me that he would be my chauffeur. I loved the idea. One of my favorite things in the whole wide world was to be driven around and watch people wonder if I was someone important. He drove us into the city, had the valet park the car when we reached Union Square, and then took my hand and led me directly to the fifth floor of I. Magnin. The sign in the elevator read "Designer Dresswear." I didn't care if Rob *was* gay, I was in heaven and, well, he seemed to like me.

"Hello, how may I be of assistance?" asked a petite woman with a French accent who wore bright red lipstick and a tailored gray suit.

"Whatever she wants," Rob instructed her.

"Of course, monsieur! May we get you a glass of champagne while you wait?" she asked, showing him to the sitting area.

"Thank you," he said, sitting down on a delicate love seat with a red crushed-velvet cushion.

"My name is Rochelle and I will be back in a moment," I heard her say. I was still buzzing from the "whatever she wants." I decided I had better hurry up before he changed his mind, so I took off toward anything black or shiny.

I looked over from one of the racks, holding up a dress I'd found, trying to get his attention, when I saw him reach into his lapel pocket and pull out a small brown-colored glass vial with a black rounded top. He bumped it under the glass table top in front of him a couple of times, pulled a lever, and then blasted it up his nose. I couldn't believe it. What was he doing? He was snorting cocaine right here in I. Magnin. What the . . .

"Albert Nipon! This is fabulous!" she exclaimed, startling me as she took the black silk and satin coat dress from my hand. "I'll put it in your room with the others."

"Thank you," I said, nervously.

"What size is your shoe, dear?" she asked.

"I'm sorry, what?" I responded, half-listening.

"Your shoes, what size do you take?"

"Oh, sorry. Uuhmm, 8-1/2."

"Very good," she said, and then carried my dress off with her. I mean, it's not like I hadn't snorted cocaine every chance I had, but in my opinion, I had been more discreet . . . and besides, that wasn't the point. We weren't talking about my addiction.

'How rude,' I thought. 'How inconsiderate. How am I going to stay away from it if I'm hanging out with him? Just go try on the clothes, Maryanne.'

"Find anything?" he asked from behind his glasses as I attempted to whisk past him into the dressing rooms.

"Uh-huh," I said. "I'll be out and show you in a minute." I wasn't sure why I felt so frightened all of a sudden, or if I should be frightened at all. But for some reason there seemed to be a dank heaviness in the air. I felt strange and unsafe, but this feeling was oddly familiar. There was something compelling about it, something dark and wrong. It was like looking over the side of a bridge and wondering what it would be like to jump off. And then you remember yourself and snap out of it. I wanted to go home, but I didn't say a word. I stayed and leaned farther over the edge to get a better look.

"That's unbelievable," he said, "Turn around."

"Do you like it, really?" I asked, deliriously distracted by the change of focus.

"Do I like it? You're a knockout," he said, swallowing down his second glass of champagne. "What about the blue dress?"

"Yeah. It's a toss-up between the blue one and this one, I think."

"Let's get 'em both," he said, and then jumped up from his seat. He pulled out his wallet and handed Rochelle a credit card.

"Thank you, monsieur. I'll take care of this right away."

"Really?" I squealed, jumping up and hugging him.

"Absolutely. They both look terrific." He peeled my arms gently from around his neck. "I'll be right back. Go ahead and sign the card." And then he walked off.

"All right," I said, suspicious about where he was going.

"Here you are," said the lady, handing me the credit card and the bill to sign. I looked at the card. It was an American Express Platinum. Robert C. Windham was the name on the card. I wondered what the *C* stood for, and then signed the bill.

"Thank you so much," she said, handing me a gold-colored garment bag and a handled bag for the shoes.

"Thank you," I replied. Still no Rob in sight. Where was he? Did he leave me? I was starting to panic.

"How's the most beautiful girl in the whole store?" he asked, coming up from behind me.

"Oh God." I was relieved to hear his voice. "I thought you left me here," I said, like a puppy, my eyes half-full with tears.

"Leave you? Why would you think that?"

"I don't know . . . whatever—here," I said, unable to articulate my panic, and handed him his credit card and the receipt.

"What's this?" he asked. My stomach tightened.

"What's what?" He showed me the receipt.

"Charles Jourdan shoes," he accused.

"Uhhhmm, the shoes . . ." I said, nervously.

"I don't remember saying anything about shoes," he said, sharply. I didn't know what to say. I was confused. I thought he said, "whatever she wants." Didn't he? He did, I heard him. I didn't know that meant no shoes. How was I supposed to know? How am I supposed to wear a new dress without new shoes? Everyone knows that. Why was he being like this? Why was he being so mean? I contracted inside but that had no direct link to any feeling.

And then I said, "Should I take them back?" He shot me a look of disappointment, which further confused me, seeing as I didn't know what I had done wrong in the first place.

"Let's get out of here!" he said. I was so uncomfortable, I didn't even want the stuff anymore. I wanted to throw it in his face and say, "Here, take your stupid clothes and shoes, you bastard—who needs them? I don't want them—and take me home now. You're mean." I wanted to say it so bad. I imagined it over and over as I walked behind him all the way to the car, lugging the packages over my shoulder. But I didn't say anything. I was too afraid. I was trapped, stuck between the desire to stand up for myself and the fear of loss.

Having dinner with Rob that night was about as much fun as watching paint dry with toothpicks holding your eyes open. He spent half the night in the bathroom and the other half vehemently complaining about the service. In between, he guzzled a couple of bottles of Chateau Margaux. He had remained distant since our shoe altercation, and of course we didn't talk about it, so there was this unspoken thing wedged between us, and we filled the space with unbearable vacant chitchat.

Even though he had invited me into the intimacy of his desperation, I still didn't feel like I knew him well enough to discuss what had happened. I found it more effective to be how he wanted in order to ensure homeostasis. I figured that my best bet was to wait and see how he was going to handle it. So I sat attentively, my body assuming the proper apology, with a hint of grateful demeanor and remorse. Had I told him the truth, I would have told him to go f— himself. The widening gap between my mind and body was my silent hell, and headquarters for my survival.

Rob didn't touch his food, and didn't miss a chance to take a blast of cocaine right there at the table between courses.

"How long have you been off the stuff?" he asked.

"Over a year now," I said, for about the hundredth time since I'd met him.

"Man, I think that's great. I wish I could do it. It's gonna kill me, Maryanne. I haven't slept for almost a week." He took another blast. "Really? A year? No kidding. Wow, that's something," he said, repeating himself.

"Rob, if I can do it, so can you," I said, easily able to feel my empathy for this man, even though he'd just treated me like shit. He picked up his glass of wine and drank it down.

"Do you want some dessert?" he asked, gentleman that he was, despite his obvious flaws.

"Dessert? Yes, please," I said. I needed something.

He flagged the waiter.

"Uh, when you have a chance . . ." Rob said, impatiently, as the waiter, apparently busy, walked by.

Finally the waiter reappeared. "Can I bring you something else?"

"I don't know," Rob deliberated. "Maybe we should come back when you're not so busy, hmm? What do you think, Dan? Or is it Dean?" I wanted to crawl underneath the table, I was so embarrassed. Okay, the waiter had been rather aloof, but Rob was being an asshole, and on top of that, he was now drunk besides high on cocaine. I decided to pass on dessert. I had suddenly lost my appetite. It was time to go.

"Do you want to come and see my house?" he asked, barely coherent. I wasn't sure what to say. "No" did cross my mind, but unfortunately it only crossed my mind and stopped there. "Okay," I said. He opened my door for me and I climbed into his Pantera. He'd switched cars before coming to pick me up.

"Are you sure you're all right to drive?" I asked.

"What are you talking about? I'm fine." He slammed my door shut.

'Fine?' I thought. 'You haven't slept for days, you're drunk and high, and this is your definition of fine?' Before I knew it we were headed east toward Oakland on the Bay Bridge. It was raining fairly hard and Rob was having trouble picking a lane. I was scared stiff. And I'd had lots of experience driving with drunks. My mother would sometimes pass out at the wheel and drive up freeway embankments with us in the car. I wasn't about to let that happen again.

"Hey, Rob, why don't you let me drive? Come on, you're tired— really, " I said gingerly but firmly.

"What's wrong? Am I going too fast for you?" he said angrily, and then floored the accelerator, increasing our speed to eighty, all the time weaving in and out of the lanes. I thought I was going to die.

"Rob, please, come on, stop. Seriously, this is crazy," I pleaded.

"So now I'm crazy?" he said, going even faster. By now we were coming off the bridge and I could see a couple of police cars parked at the toll center.

"Rob, you should slow down; there are cops up ahead, see? Look!" I said, pointing toward the center divide. That was all it took. Just like that, he let off the accelerator. Then like Dr. Jekyll, he carefully pulled into a parking lot, got out of the car in the now pouring rain, and instructed me to drive. I climbed over the console to the driver's side while he got out and came around my side, got in, shut the door, and proceeded to pull off his wet socks. I took a deep breath, pushed in the clutch, and sighed, relieved to be in control.

He managed to stay coherent enough to steer us home. Within a few minutes he said, "Pull right up to the gate." He gave me the code to punch in, the gate slowly opened, and he directed me to park the car underneath the striped awning that jutted out from the four-car garage. His three-story English Tudor house sat nestled under a gigantic oak tree that must have been a hundred years old.

"Nice place," I commented, handing him the keys. He didn't respond. I wasn't sure if he was mad at me or if he was just out of it. I followed him into the house.

"Would you like a drink?" he asked, caustically, as we walked through the back entrance. "Oh that's right, you don't drink, do you? You're perfect! Miss Goody Two-Shoes," he said, laughing to himself. I was suddenly frightened again, or maybe I was still frightened but it just got pumped up a notch. In either case, I didn't know what to make of his behavior. I didn't know if he was psycho or if he was just being a jerk.

"Well, here, let me put some music on for you so that you can enjoy yourself while I excuse myself for a few minutes," he said. I trailed quickly behind him through the house, past the breakfast room, through the kitchen, past the dining room, then the library, to the sliding double-paneled wood doors exposing a room that looked like a parlor. He proceeded toward an imposing-looking armoire and opened it up, revealing an impressive stereo system. He shuffled through some albums that were situated on the bottom shelf, selected one and put it on, and then left the room. A few seconds later the parlor filled with the discordant sound of John Coltrane's jazz ensemble. At least that's what the empty album cover said. I'd never heard of him and now I knew why.

I didn't know what I was waiting for or how long I would have to wait, but after about half an hour I started to look for him. The house was pitch dark and smelled like a library or a museum, which wasn't surprising. It was filled to the gills with antiques. Just as I was about to climb the stairs the grandfather clock at the bottom of the staircase struck midnight. It was as loud as a church bell. I had to wait for my knees to stop knocking together before I could move.

I found a pool room at the end of the hall on the second floor. It had a full bar, another elaborate stereo system, some leather couches, and deep red carpet. Dangling from a beam over the center of a pool table was an enormous stained glass light fixture shaped like a hood. The table itself was covered from end to end with papers, unopened mail, and checks. Out of curiosity I picked up a few of them: one was for twenty thousand dollars; another for one hundred thirty thousand; and another was for sixty thousand. And these were only the ones I grabbed. There were others, many others. Uncashed checks, all made payable to him, just lying around like junk mail. Hundreds of thousands of dollars. I wondered who his bookkeeper was.

I continued to creep around in the stillness, looking for what else his house might reveal about him. I was suddenly intrigued. I was determined to find out what he was all about. A loud crashing sound like breaking glass startled me, interrupting my investigation. The sound came from the other end of the hall. I saw a light underneath a door, so I headed toward it. The hall was paneled with dark wood, so I felt along the dimly lit wall for a light switch. I found another door that opened into a bathroom. I flipped on the light, did a quick once-over. There were a couple of *Playboy* magazines on a stand, half a roll of toilet paper hanging off a brass toilet paper fixture, and a lone bottle of Denorex shampoo perched on the top ledge of the glass shower. I switched the light off, then shut the door. I continued feeling with my hand along the wall as I headed toward the sound. About halfway down the hall, I felt a cold metal plate with a protruding button. So I pushed it. A beautiful crystal chandelier lit up over the stairwell. The door at the end of the empty hall was completely visible now.

I could hear some rustling on the other side, so I knocked on the door. *Knock-knock, knock-knock.* It was that friendly knock that everyone knew.

"Rob? Is that you? Are you in there?" No response, so I knocked again. "Rob? Are you there?" I said, nervously.

"Just a minute," he said. I heard some banging around and then the door flew open. "What are you doin'?" he asked quickly, like he had something to hide. He looked strange. His shirt was untucked, his hair was disheveled, and his eyes looked wild.

"Uhhm, looking for you, actually."

"Okay, well, I'll be down in just a minute, so why don't I just see you in a minute, okay?" he said. I looked over his shoulder, trying to see what was in the room behind him. "What?" he asked, noticing my curiosity.

"Nothing," I assured him. "I was just wondering what you were doing in there." I could see a huge bathroom with dense blue plush carpet and a sunken tub.

"Just give me five more minutes," he said. I stood there with my arms folded, unconvinced. "Look, if you're tired, come in here; you can lie down. Seriously—here, look, I'll put the TV on for you." He flipped the television on and handed me the remote control. "Ten minutes, I promise," he said, trying to placate me, and then he shut me in the room.

I woke up the next morning face up, in my clothes, on top of the black satin comforter on his bed. The TV was still on. The alarm clock blinked nine a.m. I slid off the bed and roamed out into the hall. It looked like someone was still in the bathroom. I knocked on the door.

"Rob?" I said, through the door. The door flew open a few seconds later. He was still wearing the same clothes, only the dark circles under his eyes were more pronounced and he didn't seem to be drunk.

"I know, I know. I'm sorry," he said. "I'm coming out right now."

"Do you know what time it is?"

"Uh, yeah, it's after nine," he replied, looking at his watch.

"Yeah, nine in the morning! It's tomorrow Rob, and I need to go. I have to go to work."

"Right, of course, uhh, here," he handed me a set of keys. "Take the Pantera. The gates will open automatically." He kissed me on the forehead and then closed the bathroom door. I stood there with the keys dangling from my hand for a second, trying to decide what I should do. I knew if I didn't leave right then, I was going to be late. So I did.

Somehow the warmth of the sun shining through any car window always made me feel better, even if I wasn't feeling particularly bad.

Which in this case I was—well, actually, confused was more like it. But it didn't matter, at least for the moment. I was coming across the bay into San Francisco on a clear day with the sun paving my way. The compact city looked like a steely picture springing out of a pop-up book. And I had front-row tickets. It was Saturday morning, hardly anyone on the road, and I was cruising along in a flashy sportscar on the upper deck of the Bay Bridge. What could be better than that?

★★★★

"What's a Pantera?" I asked, emptying the bin of dirty dishes into the sink.

"You mean the animal?" asked Jayla.

"Not a panther. A Pan-tera! It's a car, I know, but what kind of car? I mean, is it cool?"

"Oh, a Pantera, yeah. That's a totally cool car. They're like Lamborghinis, but like, sleeker I think. Why?" she asked.

'I thought I knew every cool car there was,' I thought to myself. "'Cause I have one out front," I said.

"Uh-uh!" she said.

"Uh-huh," I said. "Go look."

She peeled off the yellow Rubbermaid gloves and bounced across the café and up the hardwood stairs. She pressed her face against the window.

"Where is it? I don't see it."

"It's there," I said, pointing, "across the street in front of the bath shop."

"The silver one? Yeah, I see it. Cool. Where'd ya get it?" she asked, tramping back down the stairs.

"It's Rob's," I replied, matter-of-factly.

"Rob the old guy? That guy?"

"He's not old."

"Right, he's like as old as my mom, okay?" she laughed.

"Whatever. Yes then, him," I said. Jayla's boyfriend was eighteen and she thought he was old.

When I wasn't working at the Skinny Gourmet I had a part-time job at the Central Park Bookstore with Jayla and another girl I didn't like either, Heather. I'd been fired from the health club where I'd been teaching aerobics with Lynette, because they said I never turned in my paperwork on time. I told them I never knew I had any paperwork. They said that was the point, so I left. When the job disappeared out of my life, so did she.

"Maryanne, phone's for you," said the freckle-faced cashier over the intercom.

"Jayla, will you get that lady some more water?" I asked, pointing to a woman who sat at the end of the counter. She nodded. "Thanks! I'll be back in a flash." I trotted down the level of stairs that divided the café from the bookstore and scurried over to the phone.

"This is Maryanne," I said, cheerfully. No one replied, but I knew someone was there; I could hear someone breathing. "Hellooo."

"Maryanne?" said a strange voice.

"This is Maryanne."

"It's me, Rob. Maryanne, I think I'm dying. I can't breathe and I feel like I'm going to pass out." I had gotten several of these phone calls the week before our first date (his version of courting me), so I knew what to do.

"Rob, you're okay. You're not going to die, I promise. Where are you right now?"

"I'm at the building," he said. He owned a commercial building that spanned almost an entire block in San Francisco's China Basin.

"Is anyone there with you?" I asked, calmly.

"Yes, Fish is here. He came by to give me some more stuff," he said, meekly.

"Okay, Rob, here's what you're going to do. I want you to tell Fish he needs to go and then I want you to lie down on the couch in your office," I instructed.

"Will you come and get me? I don't think I'm going to make it," he whimpered.

"You're going to be fine, Rob, I told you. And yes, as soon as I'm off I'll come and get you, okay? You are fine. I'll be there as soon as I can, okay?"

"Hurry," he said. And I did.

I pulled into the back entrance of his building, which was about as big as a football field, and parked behind a red '65 Corvette convertible. An office door to my left was slightly open, so I walked in. The small office was connected to a large warehouse full of fancy cars. He'd said he liked cars, but thirteen? He was as bad as my dad. Most of the furniture in the office was covered with dust, and his desk was strewn with papers, unopened mail, and empty beer bottles. The place felt like a ghost town.

"You're here," he said, relieved. I turned around, startled by his voice.

"I got here as soon as I could," I said. "How are you doing?"

"Not so great," he said. "If I don't get some sleep soon I don't know what's going to happen. I did what you said. I tried to lie down, but man, the pipe keeps calling to me, Maryanne. You gotta help me," he said, wearily.

"I have an idea, if you want to hear it."

"Tell me, anything."

"Well, there's an AA conference in Hawaii next week. Maybe you should go," I suggested.

"If that's what you think I should do, why don't we go."

'Hawaii?' I thought, 'I've never been to Hawaii.' All of a sudden, the dire predicament of this man evaporated into visions of hula dancing, tropical sunsets, and the aroma of coconut suntan lotion. But I remembered what the point of the exercise was, and put all that aside.

"It doesn't start until Wednesday."

"Fine. We'll go to Vegas and roll some bones until then," he said, and then headed to the phone.

I had no idea what "roll some bones" meant, but I was ready to sign up for whatever this program was.

We checked into the MGM Grand in Las Vegas late the next afternoon. I had on a black cotton sundress that I'd bought at Cost Plus, black sandals, and a silver headband that smoothed my permed locks away from my bare face. The two dresses, the pair of Charles Jourdan pumps he had bought me, and a small overnight bag filled with toiletries were all I brought. I was feelin' lucky.

"Come on, seven, come on, bring Daddy a seven!" said Rob. He blew on the dice, kissed them, and then flung them like loose change for the poor. The rest of the gathered crowd watched anxiously as the cubes tumbled the length of the craps table.

"Five and two. Lucky seven," reported the croupier guy with the name Seymour on his plastic badge.

"Hurrah!" we all cheered. I wasn't exactly sure what I was yelling about; I didn't know the difference between crap or pass, except that I kept doing exactly what Rob told me to do, and Seymour kept stacking columns of black chips next to me and even more next to Rob.

"Let's go shopping," announced Rob, as he scooped up all his chips. Since he didn't grab mine, I did. We extracted ourselves from the hovering crowd and pushed on to the cashier.

"Four thousand: One one hundred, two one hundred, three one hundred. . ." I heard the lady say through the silver mesh cylinder from behind bulletproof glass. I was just taking it all in. Slot machines were going off in the background, people were buzzing around waitresses, wearing very short skirts and bustiers, delivering complimentary drinks—it was electric. However, it wasn't quite what I had expected. On *Dynasty,* all the women in the casinos wore glamorous gowns sparkling with rhinestones and sequins, and were draped with jewels and furs. Everyone was beautiful and rich. This scene must have been taking place in some other part of the building, because what I saw was a whole lot of spandex and leopard prints mixed ambitiously with polyester and plaid. A fashion frightfest. A collective *don't,* which would explain the strange looks I got in my full-length sapphire-colored satin evening gown. Minus the tiara. People looked like they didn't know whether to curtsey or kick me.

★★★★

"How may we help you?" asked a plump woman with poofy, auburn hair and a Russian accent. I didn't say anything. The question for me was rhetorical, and Rob was looking for the men's room. "No, no dear, let me show you. Rub the fur *with* the grain." She took my hand and made the correct motion with it. "That's right, *with* the grain. We don't want to disturb the natural pattern and oils," she said, politely.

"Oh, look at this one!" I oozed.

"Yes, of course. That is a beautiful coat, one of our finest," she said. "Here, try it on; it will look beautiful on you!"

She removed the full-length black fur from the shiny, thick, rounded hanger. She slipped the coat over my shoulders like a royal cloak, and I wrapped my arms around myself. The feeling was truly divine and absolutely decadent. It felt amazing.

Meep . . . mar sounded the musical motion detector that goes off when someone comes through the door.

"Try the white one on," said Rob.

"That one?" I asked, pointing to a full-length, fluffy-looking long-haired coat.

"Uh-hmm," he replied. The lady took the black one from me and handed me the white. I stood in front of the three-way mirror, admiring myself, doing a mini fashion show for Rob and the lady.

"I like the black one better," he said.

"I do too," said the lady. I gave her back the white one and put the black back on.

"Absolutely," he said. I looked at myself as I held up the collar, striking a pose from my left, then my right. I turned around just enough to see the black fur careen down the length of my body, exposing a small drape of blue satin from the very bottom of my dress.

"Excuse me, please," said the lady. She reached inside the jacket and pulled the tag encased in a thick clear plastic pouch out of the coat. I saw the price tag as she she pulled it out of the coat.

"Here we go," she said, and snipped it off with a pair of shears. I looked over at Rob. He was on the phone. I looked at the lady.

"Your gentleman friend just bought you the coat, my dear," she said, assuring me with a nod and smile.

"What?" I asked, stunned. "That's ten thousand dollars!"

"Yes," she said, and started grabbing around inside the coat. "You may have your initials monogrammed here," she said, pointing to part of the satin lining.

"Wait, did you say he just bought me this coat?" She smiled and nodded again. "Are you sure? This ten-thousand-dollar coat I'm wearing. On me. Right now?" I asked.

"Yes dear, and you can pick it up tomorrow." I looked over at Rob again.

Ten thousand dollars? That was like a whole car, ten thousand dollars. Of course, no car I wanted, but still, for some person it was a car.

"Uuuhmm, I think we're leaving tomorrow. It's okay, I'll just take the coat now. Thank you, though," I said, closing the coat around me.

"Here, let me put it in a climate-controlled bag for you."

"Uhhmm, that's okay. I'll just keep it on, if you don't mind," I said, clutching the coat at my breast and collar. I was trembling. I think I was having a hot flash. Either that or I was roasting to death in the coat. I wondered if I would have to give it back.

Rob finally hung up the phone with his credit card company. I could hardly stand the suspense.

"Is it really mine? I mean, did you really buy this for me?" I asked, barely containing myself.

"Yes, it's really yours and I really bought it for you," he mocked me teasingly.

"Oh my God," I said, and threw myself against him and kissed him. "Thank you so much." Tammy Faye tears filled my eyes, except I didn't want to cry. I didn't want to ruin my mascara, "So I don't have to, like, give it back to you after the trip? I mean, it's really mine?"

"It's really yours. You don't have to give it back after the trip, no," he assured me and kissed me on the nose.

I was bursting at the seams. I felt like I was levitating. I couldn't stand it—I had to tell someone—anyone. I wanted to run out in the middle of the casino, throw my arms up in the air, and shout with glee, "Hey, everyone! Oh my God, look at what I just got!" Do a few pirouettes for their viewing pleasure and then just bask in the glow of their delight for me. Now don't get me wrong, I had been given gifts before—cars, clothes, other stuff. But somehow this was different. This gift was sophisticated, more grown up—and legal. There were always strings attached to the stuff I got—one string in particular: that I had to be a Good Girl. The difference was now I was learning how to make those strings into reins. "You have any of your chips left?" asked Rob.

"Yeah, lots, why?" I wondered if he was going to confiscate them.

"Come with me," he said. We walked down the marble corridor lined with shops and boutiques. I could barely keep up with him; my evening dress was fitted down to my ankles as though I were a mermaid, so my steps were *click, click, click clicking* to his every stride, not to mention that now I was totally sweating. It didn't matter; there was no way I was taking that coat off.

"Hello, how are you this evening?" shrilled a small Middle Eastern–looking man standing behind the jewelry case.

"Great," I said, with distracted enthusiasm, as I was now preoccupied with all the sparkling and shiny things in the cases.

"I'll be right back," said Rob and disappeared to the bathroom again. I was getting used to this by now.

"You're looking very beautiful," said the stout little man in the double-breasted, flashy blue suit. I raised my eyebrows and nodded my head, reluctantly accepting the compliment. I thought he looked sleazy.

"Can I see that one, please?" I asked, trying not to look him in the eye. "Oooh . . . and that one too," I said, reclaiming my excitement.

"Of course," he said, waddling over to the case where I stood. "This is very nice. Two and a half carats with one and a half channeled carats down the sides," he said, holding the ring between his thumb and forefinger. I gave him a courtesy smile, not wanting to offend him, yet not enough of a smile to suggest my interest lay anywhere else but with the ring he was holding. I slipped it reflexively onto my wedding ring finger.

It was more than nice—it was spectacular. It sparkled brighter than a disco ball, except it wasn't cheesy. It screamed good taste, style, and sophistication without being pretentious—and all for the low, low price of . . .

"How much is it?" I inquired, innocently, and reluctantly removed it for him.

"Let me see," he said, as he put on a pair of glasses. He squinted his eyes, holding the ring arm's length away from his face so he could read the fine print on the small gold tag attached to the ring. I looked around the store impatiently.

'Jeez, what's the holdup; was he decoding Phoenician script?' I wondered.

"Ah, yes, here," he said.

'Finally,' I thought.

"It is twenty-three thousand." He handed the ring back to me.

"Dollars?" I asked. "Twenty-three thousand dollars?" I repeated, wanting to make sure I understood him correctly.

"Yes, that is correct. Twenty-three thousand dollars," he confirmed. I stared at it for a moment, then put it back on.

"Wow, that's a lot," I said. He gave me a courtesy smile. "How about that one?" I said, pointing to another.

"That is also very nice," he said. "But nowhere near the quality of this one." He reached for my hand. "You see, this one is what is called a black African diamond. It is flawless, much like the young lady," he gushed like a snake charmer. I pulled my hand away, trying to make it seem as though I only wanted to examine the ring more closely.

"Find anything?" asked Rob, as he walked through the door. He looked disheveled and tired.

"Uhhm, I don't know. I was just looking," I said, too embarrassed to show him the ring I had on.

"Let me see," he said, reaching for my hand. I could think of twenty-three thousand reasons why I didn't want to show him. I held my hand out and looked the other way.

"It's beautiful. Let me look at it," he said. I took it off and handed it to him and then didn't move, just like a mannequin, superstitiously thinking that one wrong move, word, or gesture could wreck the whole fantasy deal.

'What am I thinking? Right, like he's going to buy me a twenty-three-thousand-dollar ring. Well, then why is he looking at it?' I argued with myself while he discussed the particulars of the ring with the slimy little salesman.

"I think you should have it," declared Rob, handing me the ring.

"Excuse me?" I said, choking on my own saliva.

"Put it on," he insisted. The man was already handling the transaction.

"Are you joking?" I said, seriously.

"No, I'm not joking. I want you to have it," he said. "Go on, put it on."

'Somebody slap me,' I thought. All of a sudden I wished I had tried on some tennis bracelets too. 'Just be happy with what you have,' I thought. 'What am I saying? If you added me up—my dress, my shoes, my coat, and now my ring—I was worth about . . . let's see, twelve hundred plus four—that's sixteen hundred . . . plus ten thousand—that's eleven-six. Yeah, and then add twenty-three thousand . . . that's thirty-four thousand, six hundred. Wait! I had seven thousand dollars in my pocket—that makes forty-one thousand dollars and change!'

"Here you are, young lady," said the wonderful little cherub, handing me a small, glossy bag with a handle.

Once again I threw my arms around Rob's neck and kissed him. This time he kissed me back—and I liked it. It made me feel tingly and soft all over.

"You hungry?" he asked.

"Starved," I lied. I was sick with overwhelm. But what the heck. I wanted to keep consuming—bring it on, more whatever. I was ready for more anything!

This restaurant scene was not too dissimilar from the last fiasco. Only this time, instead of offending one waiter, we had six.

And instead of leaving without dessert, we left without paying.

"Excuse me! Sir? Sir?" A police officer, stopping us about fifty feet away from the restaurant. Rob turned around, annoyed. One of the waiters was standing between two police officers, waving a bill and saying something in Farsi that none of us could understand.

"Sir, I'm sorry to bother you, but this gentleman here is saying that you refused to pay your bill. Is that correct, sir?" asked one of the officers. Rob rolled his eyes and I stood there and smiled innocently. I wanted to shrivel up and die, I was so embarrassed. The other police officer was eyeing me up and down, like he was on to me. And for some reason, I felt guilty. Only it was guilt by association. I wanted him to see in my eyes that it wasn't me. I didn't do anything wrong. That it wasn't my idea to dine and dash. That was Rob's doing. I was just trying to eat some dinner that I didn't even want.

After a moment or so of trying to reach out to the officer with my gaze, I realized he was just checking me out, because he winked at me. Then I felt embarrassed, like he knew that Rob was too old for me and he felt sorry for me that I was with an old guy. A drunk, obnoxious, old guy to boot. I quickly looked away, hoping that Rob would just pay the stinking bill so we could get out of there and have all these people stop staring at us.

"That's right, officer, I refused to pay my bill. And I still refuse to pay my bill," he said, his voice escalating. Rob was obviously drunk.

"Can you explain why that is, sir, so we can clear this matter up?" continued the first officer.

"Glad to," said Rob, righteously. "We sat down like everyone else and I expect to be treated like everyone else," he aggressively raised his voice toward the waiter.

"Sir!" warned the other police officer, stepping in front of Rob. "Let's try and keep calm here; just tell us what happened." Rob threw up his hands.

"Fine! Fine. So what happened is that as soon as our friend seated a group of towelheads—" The second cop shot him a look of warning. "Sorry—a group of 'gentlemen'—at the table next to us, we suddenly didn't exist. I ordered a three-hundred-dollar bottle of wine. What did you order?" asked Rob, looking at me.

"Chicken Jerusalem," I said without hesitation.

"Right, and she ordered the Chicken Jerusalem," reported Rob.

"Sir, this man said he brought your dinners to the table. I don't understand where the problem is," said the first officer.

"Look, I have money to spend here, and I want to be treated just like everyone else. And between you and me, I'm a little pissed off that these f—ing towelheads come over here flashing their dirty money around like goddamned big shots and . . ."

"Sir, let's just calm down," said the second officer.

Rob put his hand on the first officer's shoulder and leaned into him, lowering his voice almost to a whisper.

"Do you know what I'm saying? These guys comin' over here, raping our economy—and I get treated like a second-class citizen. It just isn't right!" The officer chuckled, shaking his head in agreement.

"I know what you mean," he said.

"Okay, what do you want me to do? Pay this guy?" He looked at officer two, then back at one.

"That would be best, sir."

"Fine, give me the . . ." Rob snatched the check from the impatient waiter, pulled out his wallet, and flipped him four one-hundred-dollar bills. "Thank you *so* much. Dinner was fabulous," he said.

"Thank you, sir. Sorry for the inconvenience," said the first officer. Rob grabbed my hand and we were gone.

So, instead of enjoying our four-course, five-star meal, I emptied the entire contents of the snack bar in our suite into my belly. Rather than Chicken Jerusalem, I had Viva Las Vegas, which consisted of a jumbo Snickers, two cans of mixed nuts, a brand of chips I didn't recognize and some Asian party mix chased down with a mineral water. I felt huge and thought I looked like a pig after that, but I had a mink coat and a big fat diamond ring. I got over it. It seemed like a good time to call my mother.

"Maryanne? Is that you? Where are you, honey?" asked my mother. She seemed so far away.

"I'm in the bathroom. I'm in Las Vegas," I whispered.

"In the what? Why are you whispering? I've been trying to reach you for two days. Where have you been? Do you know you have an outstanding parking ticket?" she rambled.

"Mother? Stop. I told you I was going to Hawaii with Rob," I said, whispering a bit louder so she could hear me.

"They have a Las Vegas in Hawaii too?"

"Mother, would you listen! I'm with Rob, in Las Vegas, and right now I'm in the bathroom talking to you."

"Why are you talking to me in the bathroom? Who's Rob?" she wanted to know.

"The guy I told you about, remember?"

"What guy you told me about? You didn't tell me about this person, Maryannie," she insisted.

"Yes I did; remember, he's the older guy who lives in the Berkeley Hills, the one who's trying to stop drinking and doing cocaine, remember?" I droned as though repeating the same thing for the millionth time.

"Okay, yes, now I remember. Bob."

"No mother, Rob."

"Right. Rob," she repeated. "What are you doing in Las Vegas?"

"We're going to the Hawaii conference," I answered.

"In Las Vegas?"

"No mother, in Hawaii."

"Well, then, what are you doing in Las Vegas?" she demanded. "And why wasn't I invited? That would have been the proper thing for your Rob to do. I mean . . . really! If he had any class at all he would have—" she started.

"Mother!" I interrupted.

"Where does this person come from, and who are his people?" she kept on.

"Mom!" I barked. She stopped. "Mother, it would have been odd to ask you to come with us under the circumstances, don't you think?"

"What circumstances? He isn't one of those Moonies, is he?"

"What are you talking about? Moonies—jeez, Mother, why would I be with a Moonie? Have I ever been with a Moonie, Mother?" I asked, distracted.

"Well, the last fella, he was into all that—what do ya call it—woo-woo, cult, scientonomy stuff," she started.

"Mother, Kevin was a radiologist," I explained.

"Oh," she acquiesced.

"Anyway, Rob isn't a Moonie and as a matter of fact, that's why I'm calling. Mother, listen, he bought me a mink coat. Can you believe that? It's so beautiful," I squealed, trying to keep my voice down.

"That's lovely, honey. What are you going to do with a mink coat in Hawaii?"

"What difference does that make?" I demanded.

"All I'm saying is he's too old for you, missy."

"What are you talking about? How do you know how old he is?" I said, confused.

"You told me he's almost my age, for God's sake, Maryannie," she hissed.

"Mom, two seconds ago you couldn't even remember his name. Anyway, what does that have to do with anything?"

"So where are his people from?" she asked again.

"I don't know, Texas I think, why?"

"Is he German? As long as he's not German!"

"What does that mean? What, he's going to give me a mink coat and then kill me?"

"Oh, Maryannie, you're so naïve." She paused and sighed. I could always expect something major following one of her sighs. "Maryannie?" she said, shifting gears.

"What's the matter?" I asked, annoyed. I had called to talk about me!

"Maryannie, I met someone." Again, another pause and sigh.

"What do you mean, you met someone? What happened to Lipshitz?"

"Don't use that kind of language, Maryanne. It was Linus," she said, correcting me. "Did I tell you he collected trains? He was a strange man."

"Mother, just tell me who you met. Hurry, I can't stay on the phone too much longer."

"What do you mean you can't stay on the phone too much longer? I thought you were in the bathroom."

"Whatever, Mother. Go, tell me."

"We were at Diane's and, oh Maryannie, I walked into the room and there he was, standing there. His eyes were so blue. You know Diane . . . Diane who has the two girls?" she explained.

"I don't know, who cares? What? Go!"

"Our eyes connected. It was like magic," she said, drifting off.

"What is he, a magician? What are you saying? Who is this guy, Mother? Does he have a job? Does he have hair? What's his name?"

"Don't take that tone with me, missy. Yes, he has a job. He's a Superior Court judge. His name is Lawrence."

"Lawrence? What kind of name is that?"

"He's a lovely man. Stop it. Honestly, Maryanne."

"Okay, so what's the deal with the judge? Does he like you? Did you kiss him?"

"Oh, stop it now. We like each other very much, yes."

"I want to meet this guy, Larry the magician, before you do anything."

"What do you mean—before I do anything?"

"Mom, before that Lipshitz guy, you were dating a guy who had cancer, who had amazing blue eyes. Corey something," I reminded her.

"That was . . . I didn't know he was sick until after— "

"Mother, he told you he was sick on your second date."

"Well, I didn't know he was dying."

"Mother, he had terminal cancer," I said. She didn't say anything. "Anyway, have you told the boys yet?"

"Told them what?"

"About Larry the lawyer."

"No, and don't you either," she demanded.

"Mom, I have to go," I interrupted.

"It's just that our eyes locked. It's like we've known each other before . . . do you know what I mean?"

"Yes Mother, it's like all those books I've been reading about: past lives and reincarnation, all that stuff you call woo-woo that's bending my mind. What sign is he? And then I have to go," I said, hurried.

"He's a Pisces, like me."

"Cool, sounds great. I love you. I'll call you when I get to Hawaii, 'kay?"

"Have a safe trip, dear; tell Ron I said hello. Kiss, kiss, love you."

"Bye, Mom," I said, and hung up. I tiptoed out into the bedroom and saw that Rob was still fast asleep. I was grateful. I was worried he was going to want to do it. Not that I didn't like doing it, but I didn't really feel that way about him yet. So I quietly lay down next to him, on top of the covers, with all my clothes on. I pulled my mink coat over me and fell asleep.

✳✳✳✳

"God, look at that," I gasped. "It's even more beautiful than the postcards," I exclaimed as we descended into Waikiki.

"You know why I never liked traveling with my ex? She never appreciated things the way you do. When I brought her here for the first time, I took her on a helicopter ride through the waterfalls and all she did was complain," he said. All I knew was that I had never seen anyplace so beautiful in my life. I didn't get what there was to complain about. And then we got off the plane.

"What a beautiful room. Look at this view—it's awesome," I said, peeling back the curtains.

"Did they give us a key to the wet bar?" he asked, searching his pockets.

"I don't know. You had the keys," I said, trying not to sound annoyed. "I thought you said you weren't going to drink."

"I told you I wouldn't bring any drugs and that I would stop drinking when the conference started," he said, still looking for the bar key.

'Great,' I thought to myself, 'another night with a drunk guy. God, if he would just get sober, everything would be perfect.' I couldn't wait for tomorrow.

"Can we go swimming?" I asked, hoping to shake my mood. After all, I was in Hawaii. Who gets to just go to Hawaii? Oh my God, me! I couldn't believe it. I trembled with pleasure.

"Sure, as soon as I find this . . . Here it is," he said, then slid the key into the lock. He pulled out three little bottles of vodka and then went looking around for the ice chest.

"Did you bring a suit?" he asked.

"Uhh, no."

"Why don't you go buy yourself one and meet me down at the pool. Give me about five minutes," he said. I knew what that meant, but this time I didn't care. The last thing I wanted to do was sit inside a bloody hotel room and watch him get drunk.

"Okay," I said, just happy to get out of there.

I was into about my twentieth lap in my beautiful new bathing suit when I looked up and saw him sitting in a lounge chair at the edge of the pool. We were practically the only people there.

"I could watch you swim all day long," he said. "You look so graceful." I didn't know what to say. So I smiled and started swimming again, only now I was self-conscious and stiff.

"I'm done," I said, climbing out of the pool. Rob walked over to the edge of the pool to meet me. "I would be dead if it weren't for you, Maryanne," he said, with gratitude in his eyes.

"Don't thank me, Rob. It's God. I didn't do anything anyone else in my position wouldn't have."

After more than a year of attending my support meetings and hanging around people who were practicing what they preached, I'd had a change of tide with the Man Upstairs. There was a new God in town, called the Higher Power. This one replaced the punishing, judgmental, unavailable God I had grown up with. Riding this new pink cloud, it seemed like everything was possible.

Rob handed me a towel. I wrapped it around me and stood staring out at the ocean; it was breathtaking. And then I wondered if tonight was the night he was going to want to do it. I tried not to think about that, and he fell asleep that night before I even had time to worry about it.

★★★★

There was nowhere to sit by the time we got to the conference. We stood for an hour against the rear wall of the auditorium while a man named Gary told us his story. Rob was spellbound.

He concluded his talk by saying, "I would've never quit drinkin' if I thought I could never drink again for the rest of my life. That's why this program has worked for me. For eighteen years all I've had to do is just not drink one day at a time. And if you're new here today, keep comin' back. It works. Thank you." The audience thundered with applause. Rob stood there dumbfounded.

"Unbelievable," was all he could say. And then we left. We never went back to the conference, but we stayed in Hawaii for two more days. Rob didn't touch another drop of alcohol for years after that meeting. Cocaine, however, was another story.

★★★★

"We're not going to be able to get a car at this hour," said Rob, angrily talking to himself as we waited for our bags at the carousel. If I didn't know better I'd have thought he was mad at me.

"Sure we will. I'll just say a little prayer."

"What the hell does God have to do with us getting a ride home? That's ridiculous," he said venomously. I shriveled. I felt foolish and deeply offended at the same time. I didn't know how to respond. God was real for me, but was still outside of me, so I wasn't strong enough to stand up for what I had come to believe. Just then our bags came out. Actually, his bag came out. I was holding all my stuff and was still wearing my mink coat.

Rob called for a limousine. He was in a mood.

"Do you need me to take you home or do you want to come back to the house with me?"

"Uhhmm, I'm not sure. I—"

"Look, no one's forcing you to do anything you don't want to do here. I told you that," he snapped.

"I know, I didn't say you—"

"Look, I think you should just go home." My eyes shot full of tears.

"What did I do?" I wanted to know. Tears were now spilling out of my eyes. He was being so mean. I didn't understand it.

"Please tell the driver how to get to your house," he insisted. So I did.

We pulled up in front of my house and I got out and walked to the rear of the car, waiting for the driver to open the trunk so I could get my stuff. I was trying to conceal the waves of emotion coursing through me. I grabbed my bag from the driver and walked past the car straight into my cottage, without saying good-bye. I heard the car pull away; I didn't look back. I ran into my house, threw myself on my bed, and sobbed. I felt like everything I had ever wanted had suddenly disappeared. I was right back where I started. I wasn't sure where that was, but I was sure I didn't want to be there. I didn't even get to find out what I had done to ruin everything. He just took himself away without giving me a chance to defend myself. It seemed so unfair.

I thought I'd never see him again. I imagined he detested me. It felt like I had missed my big chance—to escape from my life, to be happy and have everything I'd ever wanted. To have someone who actually wanted to take care of me in the lifestyle I was accustomed to—give or take a few detours. Overlooking the mammoth obstacles staring me in the face. But I had spent my life running one obstacle course after another; so that didn't stop me from attempting this one, at my peril.

It didn't occur to me to call him. I just knew it was over.

Okay, so you have to be asking yourself: How is it this guy is giving her all this stuff and she hasn't slept with him yet? The answer is: I was eighteen and, underneath his aggressive behavior, he was a gentleman. That's right, a real one, and that's the truth.

He had married his high school sweetheart. They were together for twelve years and after that he was with a woman named Maddie for the next thirteen. I was the anomaly. But being a gentleman didn't make him any less an alcoholic and a drug addict; it just bought me some time. Two more days, to be exact.

"Maryanne? Are you awake? Are you there?" asked the caller.

"What time is it?" I asked, looking for the glow-in-the-dark numbers illuminating my clock radio.

"It's three o'clock in the morning."

"Rob? Are you okay?" I asked, rubbing my eye.

"I am so sorry about what happened. I think there was a big misunderstanding. I have driven by your house a number of times to apologize," he said.

"No, it's okay," I said. "Really."

"It's not okay. I'm not okay. I need you, Maryanne. I can't do this thing without you." I didn't know what to say. I was half asleep. "Can I see you?"

"Of course."

"When? I mean, can I see you later? Let me take you to dinner."

"Sure. I'm going to the noon meeting at the club and then for a run. I'll be back after that." He didn't respond. "Are you sure you're okay?" I asked. There was a long pause. It sounded like he was crying.

"I'm sorry, Maryanne. I shouldn't have called so late."

"Hey, I told you, you could call me anytime, day or night, and I meant it. You're going to be fine, Rob, I promise. You don't ever have to feel this way again if you don't want to."

"I'll pick you up about four—how's that?"

"Fine, four's good. Now listen, if you need to call me again don't worry, I'm right here, okay? I'm here!"

"I'll see you later." The relief in his voice was palpable.

"Good night, Rob."

I never thought I would talk to Rob again. I couldn't believe he called. I was full of hope and excitement. It was like my ship had come in.

Of course, the question I should have been asking myself was, Why would I speak to this man again? Because he needed me, that's why. And that's what I got my self-esteem from—being needed. I had learned from taking care of my alcoholic mother that my value came from being a caretaker. So, like a homing device, I gravitated to what was familiar. What I had learned was how to be what you wanted me to be so I could get my needs met. That generally manifested as, "I take care of you and then you will let me stay."

The promise of clothes, jewelry, and all the other enticements was just a way to spark the empty place in me that should have been filled with self-worth. A simple case of mistaken identity. A long-term confusion, I'm afraid, and another way to medicate.

If I Just Had a Ferrari, Everything Would Be Okay

"I JUST NEED TO MAKE ONE STOP before we head down south," said Rob, loading up the car. I was used to waiting. Sometimes I'd sit for hours, waiting for Rob to transact a business deal, or talk endlessly to one of his friends about cars, which bored me no end. I never said anything about it, either. It didn't occur to me that I had a choice. I felt lucky to be there at all, kinda like a yellow lab who piles into the car, happy that he's being taken anywhere. I was a low-maintenance high-maintenance girl.

One thing I started to do during my long waits was to clean things. I'd always loved to clean. Anything. I would do it for hours. Aside from cooking, it was something I knew how to do really well.

And other than trying to help Rob get clean and sober, it was all I felt I had to contribute. But remember, there was no me, so there was no use in saying what I wanted—not out loud anyway. I was still learning to master the art of not wanting. Wanting wasn't allowed. The only way I could ensure my position was to not rock the boat; to stay frozen, to not take up space, to contribute, to be an asset, not a burden. Otherwise, I knew I'd get thrown out. And then what would I do? Where would I go? Besides, who did I think I was? I should be grateful that'd I gotten promoted from charwoman to lady-in-waiting.

We stopped at the building on our way out of town. He said he had to meet a doctor about this or that, which would only take ten minutes. So I waited.

"Hey, Maryanne," said Nathan, who rented space in part of Rob's building for his big electrical company.

"Hey, Nathan, how's it going?" I responded, waving. They all knew me there by now. I was the one who was "helping him out of this thing." I was the self-appointed property manager as well. Rob had not collected rents in months, among other things. Anyway, after about a half hour staring at the thick red cement floor, I decided it was filthy. So I went down the hall to one of Rob's tenants and borrowed a bucket and some detergent, got on my hands and knees, and started scrubbing the garage floor from end to end. It took me about three hours to finish, and just when I was ready to start on the hallways, Rob came out of his office, high as a kite.

"What are you doing?" he asked.

"Just cleaning up the floors."

"I am so sorry. I just couldn't get out of there and . . ." he started to say.

"It's okay. I got a lot done. It's fine. Let's just go."

"We have to stop at the bank and by Louis's office and then we're done." There was no mention of the red crust which now covered my knees or the shiny, clean floor. Which, if I were the janitor, would seem appropriate. But I wasn't looking for his approval anyway.

He went back to lock up the office, and a slightly balding, stout man in his late forties slinked out of the door, handed Rob a jar, and scurried past me on his way out of the building. I didn't ask.

"Run in and tell Angela to put these into the 66916 account and these others into the retirement account, and get us some cash," he said, handing me a fistful of checks. God, I always got confused about which account was which. My new position as bookkeeper/personal assistant/counselor/girlfriend/janitor was overwhelming.

His accountant routinely yelled at me and complained that Rob never wrote down his checks, was late for quarterly whatever, and had withdrawn too much out of his 401K—or accused me of taking it out. Then there was Fredo, the nice tax man with an office in North Beach who I spoke to periodically. He liked me and used to say, "Maryanne, you're the best thing that ever happened to him. Make sure this gets in the mail by five." And then there was Angela. She was the vice president of the S&L where Rob kept most of his big money.

"Hello, Maryanne, what can I do for you today?" Angela asked. I loved that I never had to wait in line.

"Okay, I think he wants this in here and then these in the retirement thing and, oh yeah, I need to cash these two." Rob had given me power of attorney, for everything.

"Here you go. Six thousand, seven hundred, one, two . . . eight thousand. You're all set, Maryanne," she smiled.

"We're going to Carmel," I offered.

"Have a great time," she said politely and smiled. I always felt like such an idiot around her. I wondered what she thought of me.

"Here," said Rob, handing me a brown glass jar with a black lid when I hopped back in the car. I carefully took it from him and suspended it in front of me.

"What is this?" I asked.

"I need you to keep it for me. I don't trust myself."

"What is it?"

"It's pharmaceutical cocaine."

"What does that mean?"

"That man you saw at the building, he's a physician. He's in trouble and needed some cash so . . ."

"So what? He gave you cocaine?"

"It's the best you can get. It's pure."

"And you want *me* to hold it?"

"I don't trust myself. Just keep it for now," he said, and then we drove off.

By now I was about two years clean and sober and feeling pretty confident about it. I was living with Rob and my world revolved around him. Which meant I had less and less time for AA because he needed me and didn't understand my dependence on the program. And because I couldn't explain it without feeling foolish, I stopped trying. So when he asked me to watch his stuff, I didn't refuse. His inability to understand the benefits of AA was not the bigger problem. The problem was he had just handed a reformed cocaine addict six ounces of pharmaceutical cocaine.

"I think that's it over there on the right," I said, trying to help him navigate.

"You're right, I see it."

Rob pulled into the parking lot of the European car dealership. 'Oh shit, what am I going to do with the coke?' I thought. I stuffed it in the pocket of my mink coat for the moment.

"Can I help you?" asked the plain-looking guy with thin lips, dressed in tight slacks and a sweater.

"I'm the one who called about the 308," Rob said.

"Right, of course. It's right over here." We walked in a clot over to the car.

"She's a beauty," said the salesman, walking and talking. Rob didn't say anything.

"Oh my God," I gasped, the moment I laid my eyes on the fire-engine red convertible. Rob grabbed my arm firmly and whispered in my ear, "Do not act like you like it."

"Okay," I agreed, a bit startled by his grip. I took another step, his hand still grasping my arm.

"Because if you act like you like it, he'll know we want it." He sounded like my father. Actually he sounded like a lot of people I knew. I just wanted to like it because I did like it. But now I couldn't like it.

'Fine, I'll play your silly game,' I thought.

"Get in," said Rob, opening the driver's side.

"Me?"

"Would you like to take her out for a spin?" asked the salesman. His name was Dan. "You drive; it's a girl's car."

"Okay," I said. My heart was racing. Just getting into the car was a thrill. I was worried that the jar of coke would fall out of my pocket, so I flipped the bottom of the coat up into my lap, just in case.

'Oh my God! A Ferrari 308GTS! I'm sitting in one. It's exactly like Magnum P.I.'s. Nothing is cooler than this,' I thought as I cozied down further into the slick black leather seat.

I shut the door, started the car, and when I say it purred, there's no need to exaggerate. It was like a tiger. I could barely drive straight, I was so amped with adrenaline. Rob and I tore up and down the frontage road near the car lot and then hopped onto the freeway. Zero to eighty in a heartbeat. I almost had a heart attack.

"Do you want to drive?" I asked Rob.

"No, it's not going to be my car," he said. I didn't get it.

"Well, then why are we driving it?"

"Do you like it?"

"Are you crazy?" I asked, downshifting into second as we came up to a light. I noticed that people were staring. My whole body was trembling.

After our high-speed cruise Rob and I walked into the small office building at the south end of the lot. He pulled out a blank check and said, "I'll give you seventy-two thousand cash for it right now." This was a defining moment for Dan, whether he knew it or not, because Rob wasn't going to negotiate.

"Well, it's listed at ninety-six four," said Dan the Man. That was it. Rob didn't even flinch. It was just like my father said: "The first man who speaks loses." Dan was dust, and we were gone. It was like having the first six numbers of a quick pick and then—aaahhhh, too bad! I didn't pretend I wasn't disappointed regardless of whose car it was going to be. This pissed Rob off.

"Did you just want me to give him the money?" he asked, causti-cally. "Just burn it? Here," he pulled out a wad of hundred-dollar bills and a lighter. "Let's just burn it."

"Stop it," I said, grabbing at the money. "Don't." He was behaving like a spoiled child.

We barely spoke on the rest of the ride back to the Peninsula. I couldn't stop thinking about the cocaine that was in my pocket and wondered where I could hide it from Rob when we got home.

"I just want to make one more stop," he said, waking me out of a light sleep, and then pulling into a parking lot.

I looked around, trying to figure out where I was. We were about five minutes from home, as it turns out, at a lot that specialized in high-end sports cars. I didn't say a word as he got out, and just sat in the car and waited. For a couple of minutes I watched him talk to an older man with a mustache who looked like he just got off the boat, and then Rob waved me over. I pointed to myself. He nodded his head and then waved again, smiling.

'Oh goody, he's not mad anymore,' I thought, and hopped out of the car. The heaviness I felt disappeared, just like that.

"What do you think?" he asked, pointing to the brand-new white 308GTS with a black interior.

"Wow, it's beautiful. I've never seen a white one."

"That's what I meant," he said, eyeballing me. "Do you like the white one or the red one better?"

"Uhhmmm, I think I kinda like the white better because it's dif-ferent. I mean, probably there are not too many white ones around, and anyway I like the black leather better than the beige."

"Me too," he agreed, as we walked closer to the car. "Hop in," Rob said, handing me the keys. So I did. I started it up. It had the same purr as the one I'd just driven, but for some reason this one seemed nicer. It was cleaner, sharper—it was more expensive.

"You told me over the phone it was ninety-eight out the door," argued Rob. I stood just outside the office, blandly inspecting some of the other sports cars while the guys haggled.

"Look, Mr. Williams, I told you ninety-eight. With tax and license, that's one hundred twelve thousand dollars," said the Juan Valdez look-alike.

'How long is he going to take? Waiting, waiting—God, I'm always waiting,' I thought, impatient, pressing into one of the tires with the heel of my shoe.

"Here's the deal. I'll give you one-hundred-two right now and that's it," I finally heard Rob say.

'Come on, come on, take it, person,' I thought. And then Rob walked out of the office.

"What's the matter?" I asked.

"Nothing's wrong. I left my wallet in the car," he said, winking at me. I jumped up and down, exploding with delight and then stopped. I reached into my pocket and then froze. It was empty, no jar.

'Oh f—,' I thought. 'Oh wait—*phew*—that's right, I put the jar in my bag when Rob went to use the bathroom at the restaurant.' I started jumping up and down again. 'Wait a minute. He didn't say anything yet . . . don't get carried away,' I thought. 'Maybe he was just saying that, like, it's a girl's car, and I could drive it, but it's his car. Just relax, will you?'

"Are you the lucky lady?" asked the salesman, extending his hand to shake mine as he walked out of the office.

"I guess so," I said, not sure if it was acceptable to be excited yet.

"Go ahead," said Rob, returning with his wallet. It was as if he were reading my mind. "It's all yours."

"Really?" I asked, rattling inside. 'OH MY GOD,' I thought.

"Really," he assured me.

"Mine?" I asked once more, just to be certain.

"Yours," he replied. I looked around one last time, sweeping the area as if *Candid Camera* might be hiding somewhere on the lot. I ran up and jumped on him so hard that I almost knocked him down. "Oh my God, I have a Ferrari!" I sprang up and down like a five-year-old. "I can't believe you bought me this car. Oh my God." I kissed him all over his face like a one-hundred-twenty-pound puppy and almost choked him to death hugging him around his neck.

"So get in—let me look at you . . . You look perfect in it." Even though I loved that word and wore it proudly, I blushed. "I'll see you at the house," he said. I'm right behind you." He leaned in the window and kissed me on the forehead and then walked away. I wondered if he had seen where I'd put the jar.

Monday

'Maybe I should hide the jar in one of my shoe boxes. He'll probably never look there. No, that's too obvious. Just keep it in your mink coat . . . that's so obvious he'll never think to look there. But what if he does? He won't. Yeah, but what if he does? I wonder if maybe I should tell someone I have it. I mean, just in case. Oh wait. I know! I should just keep it with me. That way he'll never be able to find it. That's perfect. That's the safest place for it to be.'

Tuesday

'I'll bet he's looking for it. He's been acting weird. Maybe he knows I have it on me. No, how could he? Maybe he's mad because he can't find it. Maybe that's why he's been so mean today. Or maybe he thinks you're doing it. Yeah, what if he thinks you're taking some? That's stupid. Besides, how would he know, there's so much. I mean, like he'd really know. . . I wonder if I should call my sponsor?'

Wednesday

'God, he seems so paranoid; what's his problem? I just know he's been thinking about it. Why does he want to know if I put it in a cool place? Does he think, like, I'm going to put it in the oven? Anyway, it's not like anyone comes to the house . . . I wonder how many grams are in six ounces. Probably a lot. Like fifty maybe. I wonder if you have to cut pharmaceutical coke with anything? Like it's so pure it would be too much. God, I bet just a tiny bit would be like . . . a rocket launcher.'

Thursday 7:00 a.m.

'Maybe I should hide my purse. I mean, what if he wants something in it? He'll totally find it. I wish he would just go to work, he's making me so nervous. Just go, go, *go*. Come on, get your coffee. Okay, now say good-bye.'

"Do you need any money?" he asked.

"Uhhm, I have some, I'm good."

"I'll call you later," he said, kissing me as he walked out the door.

'Finally! What was he doing anyway? I thought he'd never leave.'

Thursday 10:00 a.m.

'I wonder if I should go to a noon meeting? I haven't been to a meeting for a while. No, forget it, it's Thursday. It's dead on Thursdays. Besides, if you see someone, you're going to have to tell them about the coke. Oh my God. I wonder if Rob . . . Oh *whew*— here it is. I thought for a second he found it. I wonder how long it stays fresh.'

Thursday noon

'You know, I bet if I did just a tiny, tiny bit, it wouldn't make a difference. By the time he gets home I'll be off it, and he'll never know I took some anyway. Just a little—like two lines or half a quarter, that's like nothing.'

Thursday 3:00 p.m.

'If I took a gram and just . . . Yeah, just one gram and kept it in my wallet. That way I'll put the bottle back in my coat. I'm totally sure he won't check there. I can just fluff up the jar. He'll never know. I'm sure, like—what is he going to do, weigh it? One gram, that's, like, nothing.'

Friday 7:00 a.m.

'Just go . . . go!'

"Here's your coffee. Call me?" I said, rushing him out the door.

"What are you up to today?" he asked.

'Why is he asking me that?'

"Uhhmm, I have to—I'm going to the Peninsula. With Denise.

What do you want for dinner?" I asked, walking him out the door.

"Whatever you want. Surprise me."

"Steak?"

"Sounds good," he said. I walked back into the house, relieved he was gone, and went up to my dressing room.

'Oh God, steak. Makes me sick just thinking about it. I hadn't eaten meat in years . . . Anyway, it's not like I can snort a whole ounce. I'm just going to take an eighth out here—just to round it out. That's not much compared to this whole jar. See? Look—there—when I fluff it up you can't even tell.'

Friday 2:30 p.m.

'I wish it would stop raining,' I thought, grinding my jaw, as I looked out the window of the pool room. 'Is someone moving in? What is that truck? It's been parked here all morning. What's in all those boxes? I don't see any labels on them. And that guy. He doesn't look like a delivery man. I don't know that name on the truck. What does that say—Sign Systems something? Where is he taking those boxes? They don't look like anything that anyone would order around here. Oh my God, what if they know I have it? That's it. They must. Why else would people be delivering boxes of stuff no one wants—in the rain. And that car, it keeps driving around the block. This is like the fifth time. And it has out-of-state license plates. Oh my God.'

I dialed Rob at work. "Hey, what are you doing?" I asked nervously. I didn't wait for him to answer. "Hey, uhmm, there's this truck parked out front and this guy is delivering boxes of stuff I know no one wants, and this car with an out-of-state license plate keeps driving around and around and . . ." I rattled on.

"Maryanne, what are you talking about?" he interrupted, firmly.

"Rob, no, I'm totally serious. There's some guy out front and he has boxes of stuff with no labels and I know the bank on the corner doesn't need anything that would look like that," I ranted.

"Look, I'm on another line. I'll talk to you later."

Friday 10:00 p.m.

"Maryanne, it's me. I'm at the building. I need you to come get me. Fish came down and I—I'm so sorry, baby. I need you to bring me the stuff." I could barely speak. My jaw was clenched shut and it took all I had to say anything.

"Rob? Where's that Valium?" was all I could get out. I knew if I didn't come down somehow that I was going to have to call an ambulance. I had snorted the whole eighth ounce and was now almost paralyzed. I managed to eat three Valiums and then sat at the edge of the bed, stiff as a board, waiting for them to work.

Sunday 4:00 p.m.

"Rob? Rob! Open the door, I have to talk to you. Now. Open the door, please," I pleaded, banging on the bathroom door.

"Just a sec," he said, and opened the door.

"Rob, there's something I have to tell you about the coke," I started. "I have been doing some of it. And you need to know that if I keep doing it I'm not going to care about you or anything else." He stared at me with a somewhat concerned look, but he was high, so I didn't know what that meant.

"It's okay, Maryanne, there's plenty."

"You don't understand. I mean it. I will not care about anything except getting high. Are you hearing me?"

Sunday 9:00 p.m.

"Maryanne, Maryanne wake up, wake up, what did you do? Maryanne? Can you hear me?" he yelled.

"I don't know," I slurred.

"Maryanne, what did you take? Did you take these?" he asked, as he held up the empty bottle of Valium.

"Uhhhuh," I said, and passed out again.

"Maryanne, wake up. Maryanne, how many did you take?" he asked, holding my face. "Was the bottle full?"

"Uhhhuh," I said, and that was it.

Monday 10:30 a.m.

"Hey there, beautiful. How are you feeling?" asked Rob. "Do you want some juice?"

"Uh-uh."

"You gave us quite a scare last night."

I rolled over on my side. "Why does my throat hurt so bad?"

"They had to pump your stomach," he answered, wiping the tears away from my eyes. "I called your mom."

"My mother, why?"

"She wants you to go and spend a few days with her," he said, looking at me helplessly.

Tuesday 6:30 a.m.

"Maryannie, sweetheart, I spoke to a woman at the treatment center and she said that they deal with alcoholism, not drugs. Well, honey, they have a bed, but unless you've been drinking they can't take you." She was very kind about it.

"Mother, what time is it?"

"Six thirty, why?"

"Nothing, it's—never mind. What did you just say?" I said, barely awake.

"They can't take you, honey, unless you're an alcoholic, sweetheart," she said, again.

"Okay. Fine. Then I'll just get drunk."

★★★★

Twenty-eight days later Rob came to pick me up from the all-women treatment center in my new black Mercedes 450SEL and took me home to his house.

So why, after all this, would I go back? That's easy. I went back because I had never addressed the truth about why I was with him in the first place. Taking away the drugs—that's the easy part. You take drugs away from an addict and your troubles have only just begun.

I'd had the habit of medicating myself—in different forms—since I was twelve. Now I was nineteen, and the stakes were higher. I was closer to what needed healing in me, but I wasn't ready to go there yet. Had I addressed the deeper truth of who I was and what was real, I might have been able to help myself. But my pain was too deep and the grip of unconsciousness was too strong.

The few tools I had learned in treatment pointed me in the right direction, but I didn't have enough discipline or support to apply them and override my fundamental programming—which was that I am worthless . . . broken . . . damaged goods. All I knew was that Rob could take care of my basic survival needs. So going back was all I was capable of. It took me three more years to leave.

★★★★

"You stupid bitch, I told you to put that check into the retirement account. How difficult is that?" he snapped.

"Why are you being so mean? I'm twenty-one years old, not forty. I get confused sometimes. You have so many accounts."

"Look, if you can't do it correctly, just say so. I'll take your name off the accounts. I ask you to do one simple thing and you mess that up. Stupid, stupid bitch!"

"Quit calling me that. I hate when you call me that."

"'Quit calling me that,'" he mocked me, like a twelve-year-old. "Look, when you act stupid I'm gonna call you stupid."

"Stop—would you just stop? God, you're so mean. Why are you so mean to me?" I said, crying now.

"'Why are you so mean to me?'" he mocked me again. "Don't you have any pride? Any self-respect?"

In fact, I was just starting to. In my spare time, which I had a lot of, I had been devouring self-help books. I was learning something about what it means to feel good about yourself. I was also expanding my understanding of what it means to be God's child. Granted, a lot of this was only conceptual, but as my mother always says, "You gotta fake it till you make it."

"Don't talk to me like that. I can't take it anymore. Do you understand me?" I said, pointing my shaking finger in his face. I moved in front of the sacred television screen to block his view. "You can't talk to me that way," I said, angry, but mostly frightened.

"Get out of my way, you dumb cunt," he snarled. I felt like I was going to vomit. I was shaking.

"No, I won't," I said, my voice quivering. "Not until you stop calling me names."

"Get out of my face," he demanded. "I feel like I'm in a frying pan."

"No," I said, defiant.

In one smooth motion he came out of his chair, walked to where I was standing, and slapped me so hard I flew across the room.

I screamed. He came running over to me.

"Oh God, baby, I'm so sorry. Oh God, let me help you . . . Are you okay?" I sat there in a heap, holding my jaw.

"Get away from me," I screamed. He came closer.

"Don't touch me. Please don't hurt me," I whimpered.

"I'm so sorry, baby, I'm not going to hurt you. I just want to . . . Let me see your face," he said, pulling my hand away from my jaw and trying to comfort me. He took me in his arms. I resisted at first, but my head was spinning. I thought about calling my father, but there was no way to know to what lengths he would go to to avenge his daughter—besides I wasn't sure this wasn't all my fault.

"I know I shouldn't say those things to you, but I guess I think you can take it. You seem so strong, so I think it doesn't bother you," he said, rocking me back and forth in his arms.

"It does," I said through my tears.

"I know, I know, I'm sorry, baby," he said, squeezing me tighter. Then I started to cry even harder, tapping into the well of tears I had never cried.

"I know I should have done it right. I'm sorry. I'm trying, really. I am trying so hard to do everything right. I am. But you have to stop talking to me this way. Please. I really can't take it; it hurts me," I wailed.

"Everything is going to be okay, shhhhh. . . It's okay," he said, stroking my hair away from my face. I laid my head in his lap and we both sat in the calm after the storm.

After a while I sat up and leaned back between his legs, exhausted. Some television special about Elvis and Priscilla Presley was on when I looked up. She had just gone to visit him for the first time at Graceland. She was only sixteen.

"That's kinda like us," said Rob, wrapping his arms around me.

"Uh-hmmm," I complied.

I couldn't leave, but I couldn't stay.

If I Were Famous, Everything Would Be Okay

"MARYANNE, I CAN'T TELL YOU how grateful I am to you. Rob looks great. He's like a new man," said Hal. I hugged my knees into my chest and smiled. We both looked out at the view of the bay from Hal's deck. I never knew what to say around Hal. He made me nervous. "Are you guys comin' to Montana for Thanksgiving?" he asked.

"I think so. Is your dad coming?"

"Yep. Dad, Faye, and then you guys."

"What's Rob watching in there?" I asked.

"Some footage from our shoot at the Galapagos Islands. We're doing a special for Disney," he explained.

"Oh."

"Hey, that reminds me, did Audrey call you?"

"About what?"

"We want you to be in one of the scenes with Christine, a swimming pool scene where she's learning how to dive."

"Okay," I said.

"Before you leave, remind me to have you talk to Audrey. We'll be shooting in two weeks, depending on the weather."

"Okay. Who's Christine?"

★★★★

"What do you think, Hal—should we have her put the other one on?" said some lady, turning me around like a lazy Susan.

"Yeah, what else have we got?" he asked from across the pool and from behind the strange-looking underwater camera.

"I brought four other ones: a blue one, a white one—" I ventured.

"How about a blue one?" she shouted across the pool.

"Fine," he shouted back. "Tell her to use the bathroom inside the house." It was like I wasn't there.

"If you go around—" she started.

"I know where it is," I said.

"You need to hurry. He needs you."

I grabbed my bag and slipped into the house through the sliding glass door that opened into the dining room. I flew down the hall and threw open the bathroom door, not expecting anyone to be inside.

"Can I help you?" asked a young woman, untwisting hot rollers from her hair.

"Uhhmm, I'm sorry, I'm supposed to change . . . They told me in here. I . . . they need me . . ." I said, feeling awkward.

"I'm Christine." She held out her hand.

"I'm sorry," I said, shaking her hand. "It's just that they said I had to change in here and that I should hurry," I started to babble again.

"Don't worry. What's your name?"

"Maryanne. I'm Maryanne, sorry."

"Maryanne. Don't worry, Maryanne. They're not going anywhere without me and I'm not ready yet." Then I realized who she was. Hal had told me all about her. And there I was, sitting in the bathroom with her. But she looked so normal. I mean, if I didn't know who she was, I would have thought she was just like me.

"You want some?" she said, offering me a piece of a Butterfinger.

"That's okay," I said, shaking my head. I was too excited to eat. But from what Hal told me, that's all she did. He told me that they'd made her go on a diet because her butt was getting too big. They'd found candy wrappers everywhere on the boat when they were in the Galapagos and had to cut some of the footage because she looked too fat. And they couldn't have a fat Miss Universe on their prime-time Walt Disney special. Now she was sharing her secret with me. I felt like a traitor because I knew.

"I'd better change. I mean, is it okay—to change in here, I mean?"

"Of course," she said, while putting on some lipstick in the mirror. I yanked off my suit and threw on the blue one as fast as I could. Maybe they would wait for her, but I wasn't so sure they would wait for me.

"I'm not going out there with you!" she said, looking me up and down. I felt even more self-conscious, and compared to her, totally ugly. I knew she had to be saying that to make me feel good.

"I am so fat," I said, seriously. "I don't know why they want me to do this."

"Fat? What are you talking about? You're perfect. Look at your stomach—it's so flat," she said, marveling at my waistline.

"Yeah, well, whatever I don't have on my stomach is definitely on my butt. I'd better get out there," I said, and grabbed my stuff. "See you out there. Nice to meet you." I wondered if I should have asked for her autograph.

"How's this one, Hal?" said the same lady, turning me around and around slowly. I wanted to die. I felt huge. And I knew the camera put on at least ten more pounds.

"It's great. Let's do it. Where's Christine?" he barked.

"She's coming," I said, like we were pals or something.

"Maryanne, you come in from the left and lean down real close so we can get a shot of you and Christine," instructed Hal.

"From the left?" I pointed to my left, a little confused.

"No, no. My left. The other way." I felt so stupid.

"Okay, got it, that way," I said, pointing in the other direction. I wasn't exactly nervous. I loved the whole scene—the lights, the cameras, all the attention. I felt right at home. I just wanted to do it right.

"Here she is. Okay, let's get this thing," said Hal.

Thirteen hours later, my feet were burning, my eyes were stinging, and if I had to say, "Hello, I'm Dr. Talbot from the Seaport Institute" one more time . . .

"That's a wrap. See everybody at six in the morning, sharp," said Hal. "Maryanne, come here."

'Oh my God, what did I do?' I thought.

"Is Rob coming up?" he asked.

"He's already here. I saw him talking to Audrey a while ago," I replied, relieved.

"Did you hear what Christine said?" he asked, putting his arm around my shoulder.

"No, what?" I replied, looking up into his face. "She told Margaret that she refused to stand next to you in any of the shots and asked why we had to pick someone so beautiful," he said, proudly.

I must have turned three shades of red. "She said that, really?"

"Yes, she did." He grinned.

"Did she say that I burst in on her in the bathroom? I mean, was she mad?" He wasn't listening. He had said what he had to say. And what Hal said in Hal's world was the final word, and that was that. So when he announced at the wrap party that I had a hotter body than Priscilla Presley, and in the same breath bragged that I looked better in a bathing suit than Miss Universe, I loved the compliment, but I couldn't let it in. All I saw when I looked in the mirror were my flaws.

This was by no means an end to my aspirations to be Skinny, Tan & Rich. It only intensified my need to be seen, which was becoming insatiable and would rear its ugly head again in the not-so-distant future.

It was Christmas season, my favorite time of year. Everything was possible during Christmas. I loved all the lights and the shopping and the hustle and bustle. And I devoured the good cheer, even though most of it was manufactured. As a matter of fact, I started celebrating the holidays around my birthday in October, so Halloween and Thanksgiving were just preludes to the kiss of Saint Nick. I always used to think it would be cool to marry a Jewish, part-Buddhist guy so I could legitimately celebrate all year around. Anyway, what I didn't like was the traffic. And I despised waiting in lines. It could suck the Christmas spirit out of me faster than anything.

"Rob . . . Raaaahb," I screamed, bursting in the front door.

"What? What happened, baby?" he said, lumbering around the corner.

"Oh God, Rob, I just had a heart attack. I mean, I think I did. I was coming across the bridge back from the Peninsula . . ." I said, hyperventilating as I recounted the story.

"Slow down. Okay, just take a deep breath—relax." I hated when people told me to relax. Why was everyone always telling me to relax? Can't he see that just makes me more—unrelaxed?

"I'm trying to tell you something here," I said. "I think I just had a heart attack. I'm serious!"

"Tell me what happened. Are you hurt? Did you wreck the car? What happened?" he stammered.

"I'm fine. Nothing's wrecked. The car is fine!" I insisted. He looked confused.

"What happened, then?"

"I'll tell you what happened if you would just be quiet and let me tell you. God!" I said. "I don't know what happened. I was sitting in traffic at the foot of the bridge. I was crocheting that blanket I've been making, you know?" I said, looking up at him. He nodded.

"Anyway, all of a sudden I started getting really hot and my chest started to get tight, like someone was stepping on it. And I couldn't breathe. I mean, I was starting to freak out. So I rolled down all the windows . . . I even opened the sunroof, trying to get some air, and I thought I was going to die, but I was stuck in traffic and kept thinking, 'Oh my God, what if I pass out right here. Who will help me?' So I don't know . . . somehow I made it to the other side of the bridge and I started to breathe better and . . . I don't know, I was so scared, Rob."

"Maybe we should call the doctor."

"You think?" I said, confused. "What do you think that was?"

"How do you feel now?"

"Okay, I guess; a little shaky, but better."

"Why don't you just lie down for a while and then we'll call the doctor. I'm sure it's nothing," he said, trying to comfort me.

"Nothing! I just had a heart attack and you're telling me it's nothing? I can't believe you."

"Come on, you're getting yourself all worked up again. Let's just wait and see what the doctor says. Now lie down," he directed.

'Nothing!' I thought to myself. 'Right, that was nothing. Well, then that was the biggest nothing that has ever happened to me in my life!' I stared up at the ceiling, trying to relax.

The next morning I drove across the bay to my doctor's, who also happened to be my mother's ex-boyfriend.

"So what do ya think, Doc?" I asked.

"Well, Maryanne, I don't see anything abnormal. Your heart and lungs are fine. We'll get your lab work back in a few days, but I doubt if anything will show up."

"So what are you saying?"

"What I'm saying is you're as healthy as a horse."

"What? That's not possible. I just had a heart attack, okay? So something's wrong!" I insisted.

"Have you been under a lot of stress?"

"Stress?" I repeated. "What do you mean, stress?"

"You know, is everything okay at home, are things going well?"

"Yeah, everything's fine. I don't have any stress. What are you trying to say?"

"I want you to see a friend of mine."

"What kind of friend?"

"He's a psychiatrist. He's got a lot of experience with this kind of thing."

"With what kind of thing? I thought you said nothing's wrong with me."

"Here, this is his phone number. Call him. If you tell him I referred you, he'll see you right away," he replied, ignoring my question and handing me the psychiatrist's name and number on a prescription blank. "Just call him, Maryanne," he said, and then kissed me on the cheek and walked out of the room.

I hopped off the examination table and grabbed my mink coat. 'Why won't anybody listen to me? Fine, I'll call . . . who?' I looked down at the paper. 'Dr. Pierce! Fine, Dr. Pierce . . . whatever. Maybe he'll believe me,' I thought, and walked out in a huff.

★★★★

"Have a seat in here. He'll be with you in just a minute," said the receptionist. I looked around the office. One wall was completely covered with degrees and awards.

'He must be pretty smart,' I thought. Just then the door opened and a pleasant-looking man with a beard rolled into the room in a wheelchair.

"Hello," he said, calmly. The fact that he was in a wheelchair momentarily distracted me, and it shouldn't have made a difference, but it did. From the start I was looking for any excuse to diminish this person's credibility.

"Hi," I said.

"What brings you here today?" he inquired, getting right to the point. I wasn't expecting that.

"Uh, didn't you talk to Stuart?"

"No, I didn't talk to Dr. Osborne, so why don't you tell me what's happening."

"Okay. Well, I think I had a heart attack last week and so I went and saw Stu—Dr. Osborne—and he said I was fine but that I should come and see you," I explained, and then sat back in my chair.

"I see," he said. Then he stayed quiet for a minute. I stared at him, thinking he looked like a dork and probably sat around watching reruns of *Star Trek*. I couldn't take the silence; it made me uncomfortable.

"So I don't know why he told me to come here. I mean, if I had a heart attack why would I need to see a psychiatrist? You know what I mean?"

"No, tell me what you mean," he said, seeming interested.

"I mean, I don't really know why I'm here," I retorted, annoyed.

"Why do you think you're here?" He was starting to bug me.

"I don't *know* why I am here! That is what I am trying to tell you."

"You seem angry," he observed, calmly.

"I seem angry? Well, maybe because I *am* angry."

"Would you like to talk about it?" he asked, evenly.

"Would I like to talk about what?"

"Why you're angry."

Now I was pissed. "I just told you! Look, I just had a heart attack, okay? And I came here because Stu told me to come here and I still don't know why I am here. And now you're asking me if I want to talk about my anger? I don't get it. What are you saying?" I demanded.

"I see . . ."

"You see what?" I asked, now furious.

"How's your relationship with your father?" he asked, with a slight inflection. I studied him for a moment; I couldn't figure out if he was for real.

"Are you kidding me? My father? What the f— does anything have to do with my father?" I yelled, getting up out of my seat.

"It's all right," he said quietly. I sat back down. "It's perfectly understandable," he said, in a reassuring tone I didn't trust. I slid to the edge of my chair, about to get up again.

"What? What's perfectly understandable?"

"It's perfectly normal to have this kind of reaction if and when areas of your past become triggered. For example, when I asked about your father—"

"Look, here's the thing, Doc: My relationship with my father has nothing whatsoever to do with my having a heart attack. And I don't have time to sit around and listen to you tell me a bunch of crap that I already know, okay? So unless you have some new information for me, I'm outta here," I said, and folded my arms.

Then he started, "Exploring your relationship with your parents typically helps one identify—"

"That's it—I can't do this. I'm sorry . . . I have to . . . Thank you. It was . . . nice to meet you but . . . I'm sorry . . ." I said, getting up to leave. And I did.

I just wanted someone to say, "Here is the problem: It's black, the size of a walnut, and we can remove it and—ta da!—it will never come back." Being invited into the depths of my psyche was like asking me to open Pandora's box. I wasn't sure what was in there, but it had to be bad because I had spent an extraordinary amount of effort trying to keep the lid on. I wanted there to be something wrong with me that wasn't my fault, like a heart attack or some disease. I couldn't be with the idea that whatever I suffered from was rooted in my mind. That would have meant that I was sick in the head—that I was crazy. Or emotionally unstable. I couldn't have that. I would not have it.

✦✦✦✦

"You just need to stick with one thing, Maryanne, that's your problem. Last week you wanted to have an aerobics show on HBO, this week you want to—what did you say?—be an alcohol counselor. You want too many things," said Rob.

"I wanted to do the HBO thing because Hal wanted me to do it! It's not my fault I got sick."

"You need to tell Hal that, not me. I'm not the one who had the camera crew from *Entertainment Tonight* waiting for you all afternoon when you never showed up."

"I was sick," I screeched. He walked into the other room. The truth is I'd had another one of those attacks and couldn't drive. I was too embarrassed to tell anyone, and I didn't know what to say anyhow. So I didn't show up.

"I just want to do something big, something important, you know, to help people," I explained.

"So join the Peace Corps," he said, rifling through the mail.

"You're not listening to me." He dropped the mail on his desk.

"You're right. I'm sorry! Here, let's sit down and spend the whole day talking about it. I don't need to do anything. My business will run itself. Don't worry about it! I'll just let it fall to shit until we figure out what poor Maryannie, who has everything anyone could want, wants to do with her life! Okay? Is that what you want me to say?"

"Nooo."

"Then what do you want?" he asked, frustrated.

"I don't know . . . I just . . . I can't explain it."

"Well, while you're trying to figure it all out, I have to go to the building. There's a guy coming in from San Diego who wants to look at some patch panels," he said, walking into the foyer. "Relax! You're so intense! You think too much." He grabbed his jacket off the coat tree. "Everything is fine, Maryanne. You have a good life," he said, more softly, rubbing the intense furrows between my eyebrows. My father used to do that. He told me I was going to get wrinkles.

Why all of a sudden is everybody telling me to relax?

It rained that afternoon, like cats and dogs, as my mother would always say. I sat on the edge of the pool table, watching it come down in sheets. The television was to my back. *All My Children* was on. I was sitting in a three-story Julia Morgan English Tudor house with two thousand cash in my wallet, my Ferrari in the garage, and all I could think about was, 'Is this it? Is this all there is?' Most people spend their entire lives to get here, wherever here is, and I'm here. They say I have everything: I'm skinny, I have my own tanning booth and gym upstairs, I belong to a tennis club and I don't even play tennis, I have more jewelry than Mr. T, I have agreed to marry a man who, even if we both tried, could never spend all his money in this lifetime, and all I can think about is, 'Is this all there is?'

✶✶✶✶

"Maryanne?" I heard from a distance. It was my little brother, Tony. I could tell by the way he cleared his throat and by his imposing gait. Physically speaking, he was a carbon copy of Bruno.

"Hey, you guys," I said, looking up from my book. I was sitting on the floor, leaning up against a bookshelf in the metaphysical section of the bookstore where I used to work when I first met Rob. Tony was with his girlfriend, Kiki.

"What are you doing?" he asked. I held up my book to show him.

"Reading," I replied.

"*Messages from Michael?* What's that, some romance craaap?" he asked, exaggerating for emphasis.

"It's about reincarnation and past-life stuff," I said, getting up from the floor.

"So you're into voodoo now, huh?" he said, waving his hands around.

"Uh-huh, and I'm learning to speak in tongues too. It's great!" I said. Tony had an extraordinary sense of humor, except when he didn't—also like my father.

"Okay, fine, whatever. Who are you here with?" he asked. I looked around for effect.

"Uhh, myself," I said.

"Alone?"

"Yeah, that is correct, just me."

"Maryanne. It's Friday night," he pointed out.

"What? They don't allow people who are alone in bookstores on Friday nights?"

"No really, who are you here with? Some guy?"

"Yeah, I'm here with some six-foot-five-inch, Swahili-speaking guy and I just didn't want you to see us together, so I told him to run to the bathroom." He looked at me for a minute like I was serious. "Fine—if you must know, I'm taking myself on a date. There, I said it."

He stared at me, puzzled, looked at Kiki, and then, pretending he didn't hear that, said, "Do you want to hang out with us?"

"Yeah, we're just gonna have some cappuccino," chimed Kiki.

"You guys! I'm fine. I'm just trying to learn how to love myself, you know, trying to take responsibility for my own happiness." They both had blank looks on their faces.

I continued, "Cleaning up the wreckage of my past . . . ? Oh, never mind." I could tell that they still didn't get it.

"You and Mom, you're so intense. Why do you always have to be so deep about everything?"

"We do not. I—" I realized it was useless to defend myself. "You guys just go. Go into the night and be with each other or whatever you were going to do."

"Did you break up with Rob again?" he asked, unconvinced that I was really all right.

"God! What's your problem? Are you deaf? I told you, I'm just . . . No! I didn't break up with Rob! I'm . . . I just wanted to be by myself. Jeez . . . Bye, you guys. Nice to see you, Kiki. Say hi to your mom," I said, sat back down and picked up the book I'd been reading.

"Hey, did you hear about Dad?" Tony baited.

I took it, not looking up. "What?"

"He's boinking some girl at the office."

"Who told you that?" I asked, unable to resist.

"I was there and she's, like, only seventeen."

"What do you mean you were there?"

"Check this out—Dad made me drive them around in the new limo."

"What new limo?" I said, my curiosity piqued.

"Yah, he and Sacramento Charlie bought a new limo company."

"What are you talking about?"

"What do you mean, what am I talking about? You sound like Mom. Jeez," he said, rolling his eyes. "They bought a new li-mo com-pan-ee, okay? Would you just let me finish the story?"

"God, you look just like Bruno when you flap your hands around like that," I said, interrupting him again.

"Are you going to let me talk?"

Kiki wasn't going to get between us and walked off to another section.

"Fine. Go. Say it!" I waved my hands for him to hurry up.

"Anyway, he and Charlie were in the back of one of the limos having sex with the girl while I drove them around the city," he said, looking around to see where Kiki had walked off to.

"No way; are you serious?"

"Totally."

"That's disgusting!"

"I know, it kinda freaked me out too."

"And then what happened?"

"That's it."

"That's it?"

"Maryanne, they had the privacy thing—the window thing—open so I could see 'em and everything. It was gross."

"He is gross, what do you expect? Does Isabella know?"

"I don't know, maybe. Dad said she rammed the Mercedes into his Corvette two nights ago in the parking lot by the office because he didn't come home or something. Maybe it was that," he reported.

"That's great!" I had suddenly had enough of the conversation. "Tony, why do you stay there?" I asked, and then let out a huge sigh.

"School starts in two months."

"You know you're never gonna see a dime from him," I said, cutting him off. He curled his lips up into a toothless smile, which was his way of saying that he understood my rage, while reminding me without rubbing it in my face that his reality was slightly different than mine.

"Have fun on your 'date'!" he said, making quote marks with his fingers. He started to walk away.

"Okay, then, now that I've had my little family update, I think I'll go and . . . hang myself," I said. He looked back at me, unamused.

"Just kidding. I'm just kidding! See ya. Tell Mom I'll call her if you talk to her."

Keeping up on Bruno was like watching a perpetual train wreck. You couldn't help but look, but you always wished you hadn't. And seeing my brother was usually bittersweet. We were war buddies chewing the fat, but when we started talking body count it was time to *hasta la bye-bye.*

★★★★

I stayed tucked away in the metaphysical book section until I finished reading my book. Lately I had been spending hours devouring one compilation of hope after another in search of the answer to life's mysteries. Which for me amounted to a perennial hunt for immunity from pain. Astrology, numerology, psychology, paleontology, mythology, archaeology, physiology, phrenology—I read it all. My little brain was like a psychic sieve panning for nirvana. Or the keys to the kingdom, whichever came first.

It was a toss-up between Stephen Covey and Shakti Gawain. Where, oh where, were all the rich spiritual people? That's what I wanted to know!

I read somewhere that we pick our parents before we come into each lifetime. And although I couldn't imagine ever agreeing to such a thing, it did make more sense than the whole Adam and Eve deal— life emerging from a metaphor seemed too Walt Disney. And since I had never seen anybody in my neighborhood foraging through a park, snatching up a small rodent and biting its little head off, then sitting back on their haunches enjoying their afternoon snack . . . Darwin's theory? It was all a little too quantum leap for me. I decided that what I needed to cure my ills was a little Pacific Rim shot, some East-meets-jest. And then the funniest thing happened—I got a job. But more about that later.

★★★★

"Are you here?" Denise asked, covering the mouthpiece on the phone with her hand.

"Tell him . . . tell him I'm asleep . . . uh, I'm in the shower . . ." I said, motioning frantically so she'd say anything but that I was there. She held her hand up, signaling me to chill, and then put the phone back to her mouth.

"Rob? Hi. She's in . . . she went to the cleaners." I could hear his muffled voice through the phone and it made my stomach twist in knots. "Do you want me to have her call you when she gets back? Uh-huh. Okay, I'll tell her," she said, and then hung up.

"At the cleaners?" She walked over to the kitchen table, grabbed the pair of Nikes that were on top of her gym bag, and sat down.

"Well, what did he say? Does he want me to call him?" I was dying of curiosity.

"Maryanne, why don't you just tell him you're not coming back?" she asked, putting on her running shoes.

"I don't know. I'm not like you. I'm not good at the whole guy thing; I can't just tell him like that." I was sprawled on my back, lying on the couch, clutching one of the decorative pillows like a security blanket.

"What are you so afraid of?" she asked pointedly, as she took the coated rubber band she was holding between her teeth and pulled her hair back into a ponytail. "You don't have to be honest to tell the truth, you know, Maryanne," she said, pulling her sweatshirt over her head.

"What is that supposed to mean?" I asked, totally lost.

"Just tell him that you need some time. You know, that you're trying to figure yourself out right now."

"Yeah, but what if he meets someone else, or doesn't want me back?"

"Maryanne, he asked you to marry him. He told me to tell you that he and your stupid cat miss you and want you to come home."

"He said that?" I asked, now feeling incredibly homesick.

"Get your shoes. Let's go," she commanded, looking for her car keys.

"It's not that I'm afraid. I just don't know. I don't want him to . . ." I said, hoisting myself up from the couch.

"You don't want him to what?" she asked, perching her sunglasses on top of her head.

"I don't know. I mean, part of me wants to be with him, but the other part, I just want to see what else is out there. He doesn't like to do the same stuff I do. And I'm twenty-two. I haven't done an thing."

"So why don't you two just date?" she asked, poking at the elevator call button. I folded my arms tightly across my chest.

"Uhhmm, can we . . ." I started to say.

"Oh, right. You don't like elevators," she remembered, and let the door close.

"I can't date him! You heard him. He wants me to come home.

What is that anyway—date him?" I said, tromping down the stairs behind her.

"You know, just go out and have fun. Why do you have to be so serious?"

"I want to go dancing," I said, delirious at the thought. "He hates dancing."

"Hey, did I tell you that Joe guy called me?" She was good at abruptly changing the subject.

"The guy you met at your conference thing?"

"Yeah, and he—God, I totally forgot to tell you. He has this friend, Dale, who lives in Sacramento or someplace and they are taking us to dinner this Thursday," she said, unclipping the convertible top to her car.

"Really? Is he cute?" I asked, suddenly interested.

"Who cares? They're taking us out to dinner," she said, as we loaded into the car and blasted out of the tiny garage. This was Denise's bottom line when it came to men. If you had a penis, you paid. Period. I loved her.

★★★★

"Maryanne!" Denise hissed, elbowing me. I was busy looking at all the sailboats on the bay. "Check out this guy in the Porsche next to us," she said, with that look I knew all too well.

"What? What's he doing?" I asked, practically climbing over her to see him.

"See his license plate?"

"Uuuhh, yeah, I see it. It says 'ICEMAN'." I twisted back around in my seat.

"Iceman, what is that?" she replied, obviously repulsed. "Watch this!" At the next stop sign Denise leaned slightly out her window and smiled. "Hey," she called out, in full flirt.

The guy in the Porsche smiled back. "How's it going?" he replied.

Denise shot him an even bigger smile. "Great!" We took off.

At the next stop sign he caught up to us. Denise leaned out again and said, "Hey, ICE Man . . ." He pulled his glasses off and looked over eagerly. "Uh, were they all out of 'ASSHOLE' at DMV?" Then she gave him a flick of her hand and a "ta-ta" and cruised off.

I couldn't believe it. I slid down in my seat as far as I could, absolutely mortified. She, on the other hand, thought this was hilarious. Denise was another of those girls who ate glass and you bled. And the guy, well, he turned left. I felt so sorry for him; that is, until she explained the way it is.

"Maryanne, why do you think he bought that Porsche?" she asked me.

"Uhhh, because it's a cool car?" I ventured, sure this was the wrong answer.

"No, he did not buy the car because it was cool. He bought the car because he wants to screw beautiful girls like me. And that is all," she declared with finality.

'She sounds just like Bruno.' I thought.

"How do you know? Huh? Maybe he's a nice guy and he likes nice cars," I said, defending him.

"ICEMAN?" she said, caustically.

"Maybe he sells freezers."

"You just keep telling yourself that, honey."

"God, what is with you? Not all guys are dicks, you know."

"No, but all guys think with their dicks, and the sooner you realize that, the better." I hated that. I hated the thought of it. I refused to believe she was right.

"I know guys who aren't like that," I countered.

"Like who?"

"Like, uuhmm, like, Mike Finney."

"Mike Finney? Mike Finney's a priest, Maryanne. Nice try." She chuckled.

"So?"

"Maryanne, forget it. You're not gonna win that one."

"Okay, well. What about Dennis Greenly then?" I said, excited that I'd managed to dredge someone up.

"Dennis Greenly? Please, Maryanne. He tried to get me to have sex with him when I was only three weeks sober."

"But he's married!" I exclaimed.

"So?"

I couldn't believe it. Dennis Greenly. He was like the nicest normal man I knew. It was so gross that he wanted to have sex with her. He was like the man on the Wendy's commercial. Like a chubba bubba.

She chimed on, interrupting my inner postmortem. "The married ones are the worst," she explained, pulling into a parking spot.

I thought Bruno was the only dog within a fifty-mile radius. Compared to him, everyone else seemed like a holy man.

"Wake up, Maryanne. Think about it. You can go to the grocery store and get a weekly chronicle of who left who for their secretary. she said. I'm just telling you the way things are. Besides, you don't have anything to worry about," she said, and winked. "I'll always love you."

That's what I was afraid of.

Despite the windfalls of my life, there was one thing I consciously knew—that there had to be a better way to live, that I was missing something big. Now she was forcing me to confront the Second Essential Truth: that men are essentially all pigs—despite my childhood fantasy that there existed, in fact, a knight who had shining armor with my name on it.

But what I didn't know was that this hallucination was killing me. And what I couldn't seem to figure out was how to stay awake long enough to pull all the clues together. As soon as my adrenaline stopped pumping, I fell back to sleep and—*zap!*—like thought in a fly zapper, any progress I seemed to make was snuffed out of my brain, and it felt like I had to start from scratch again.

I knew that I had a propensity for attracting alcoholics into my life. I also knew that I had a tendency to be slightly codependent. By now I didn't know anyone who wasn't—codependent, that is. I'd had a few experiences of freedom from suffering, but I couldn't remember which combination of incantations, affirmations, and bumper-sticker sayings I had concocted to counteract the effects of whatever drama I found myself in. So each time I needed an antidote to suffering I had to go back to the drawing board. But as soon as I figured out one end of a pattern, the other end would come up and smack me in the ass, knocking my feet out from under me.

So what kept me going? Aside from terror, there was a curiosity to know the truth, and a fire inside of me I can't define. They just kept burning, and I wasn't going to give up. But it was going to get worse in some ways before it got better. Like they say, it's always darkest before the dawn.

"When are you coming back up here? I miss you," I said.

"I don't know. Alan has to go back to Kentucky for a week and he wants me to go with him. He's breeding one of his studs back there," said Deborah on the other end of the phone.

"That's cool. Are you all into it now? Do you like to wear the whole gear, with the crop and everything?" I asked, laughing at the visual. Deborah was about six-feet-three-inches in heels, and nothing about her was petite.

"I definitely have the riding boots, but I'm still getting used to the smell," she admitted.

"Hang on a sec," I said, covering the phone. "What's up, Craig?"

"Where is everyone?"

"They're all outside with Tommy, playing volleyball. They should be back in a little while."

"Is anyone else here?" he pressed.

"Nope, just you and me. You should finish up your program packet before they come back. I'll help you in a few minutes . . . Are you there?" I asked, into the phone.

"I'm here."

"Sorry. That's one of the new kids. We just admitted him this morning. He's still in detox." Deborah understood the sobriety lingo; she'd been sober for several years herself.

"How's that going, your job and everything?"

"I love it. It's great. Everyone here at the Adolescent

Recovery Center is wonderful. I feel so lucky."

"I thought about getting into recovery work, but I just don't have the time anymore."

"You don't ever have to work again in your life; what are you talking about?"

"I still think it would be fun."

"Do you know how many people applied for my position?"

"Thirty?" she guessed.

"Two hundred and fifteen," I said.

"Jesus!"

"I know, can you believe that? I'm the only one at the ARC without a degree," I said, mystified. "You know it had to be Spirit—hang on a sec. Craig? What are you doing?" I raised my voice, looking over the nurse's station out into the kitchen area.

"I'm gonna—someone," I heard him mumble, looking in my direction.

"I gotta go. Let me call you back," I said, and hung up the phone. Craig was twirling a knife on its point into the kitchen counter, repeating something, like a song, over and over. I couldn't quite hear what he was saying.

"What did you say?" I asked, listening closely so I could hear him.

"I'm gonna—someone," he said again.

"I can't understand you," I said, standing up. He spun the knife around and around and then said it again, only this time I heard him loud and clear.

"I'm gonna kill someone," he growled, and this time he was looking right at me. I swallowed hard, looked around the room to see if anyone else might be in the unit. Everyone was gone. Tommy, who was on shift with me, had taken the kids out to play. It was just me and the psycho kid.

"Okay, Craig, put the knife down and walk back into your room," I said, trying not to sound terrified.

"I'm gonna kill someone," he repeated in the same eerie monotone, still twirling the knife.

"I said, 'Put the knife down,'" hoping to God this time he would. I thought my stomach was going to come up out of my throat.

"I'm gonna kill someone—and I'm talking to *you*," he said, grabbing the knife and pointing it at me. I had two choices as far as my body was concerned—fight or flight. I figured he was smaller and faster than me, and I really wasn't in the mood to take a knife in the back, so I thought I'd try to intimidate him. I'd had some experience with little boys and knives . . .

"Look, Craig, don't be stupid. You don't want to hurt anybody. Put the knife down," I said. I slowly—and I mean slowly—walked toward him.

Again he repeated, almost hypnotically, "I'm gonna kill someone." Only now he was holding the knife in a ready-to-stab position.

"Look, Craig, you don't scare me. I'm twice your size; what do you think you're going to do?" I asked, using to my advantage the adrenaline that was pumping through me. He didn't take his eyes off me.

Just in case, I flung up a plea to the Divine Master of the Universe: 'Please help me. This kid is crazy. What should I do? Please, please, oh God. . . Think. Think, Maryanne.'

"Put the knife down before someone gets hurt, Craig," I said with firm command. I hated being scared and this kid was pissing me off. He didn't flinch. Now I was mad. Who did he think he was, coming in here and scaring the life out of me like that? "All right, that's it. Game's over," I said, walking toward him. He was going to have to stab me, the little puke, because I was done messing around. "You better put that knife down, punk, or you're gonna be sorry," I said, about two feet away from him.

"Maryanne? Is everything okay?" I heard from behind me. It was Bridget, the head nurse. Craig dropped the knife and ran toward his room.

"Get him!" I screamed, flailing my arms around. "He was going to stab me," I gasped, running back toward the nurse's station.

"Calm down," she said, waving at me to stop. "I'm calling the psych unit. Shhhh . . . Yeah, who's this, John? Yeah, hi, it's Bridget

Medlin over in the ARC. We've got a fifty-one-fifty going down. Uh-hmm. One of the kids got a hold of a knife. Yep, we need someone over here stat. Thanks," she said, and hung up the phone.

"Where did he get the knife from?" she asked, turning to me.

"I don't know. One of the parents must have left it from Thanksgiving," I said, my heart still pounding.

"Don't worry. He's not going to do anything with both of us here. The guys will be over in two minutes," she said, giving me a squeeze. "When did Tommy take the kids out?"

"About forty minutes ago or so," I said, still trembling. "What's going to happen to Criag?"

"Oh, they'll bring him up to the psych unit and give him some meds to calm him down. He was a borderline anyway. We admitted him as a secondary psych, so he's better off up there. As soon as the guys get here you can go."

"Home?"

"Don't worry, Tommy and I are fine and Demetri's on at one. Besides, you worked a double yesterday."

"F—," I gasped. The full impact of what had just happened hit me. "He could have stabbed me. I mean, if you hadn't walked in exactly when you did, I could be dead right now."

"If anything like that ever happens again, all you need to do is call unit two. Don't even try to talk to them."

'Sure, now she tells me,' I thought.

★★★★

Okay, I had just broken up with Rob, moved in with Denise, and had, only hours before, been confronted by a homicidal maniac. So ending up in the emergency room that afternoon was merely the grand finale in the medley of my day. Or so I thought.

"Marn, I'm in a meeting; can I call you right back? Where are you?" asked Bruno.

"I'm at home, at Denise's," I said, barely able to speak.

"I'll call you right back," he said. It was so good to hear my father's voice. I hadn't talked to him in months. I don't know what possessed me to call him; we only spoke on occasion. I would call when I had accomplished something, like when I first got this job as a rehab counselor. But now I needed something. Comfort, assurance, perhaps to be rescued. What was I thinking? My father had never even given me a birthday card.

I lay face down on the carpet with the phone tucked under my arm, waiting anxiously for it to ring. My body was immobilized, my breathing so shallow that it felt as though the next inhale would bring the last air I might ever breathe. I was starting to lose sensation in my legs. My thoughts were frantic, out of control.

The terror I would experience during episodes like these . . . the best way I can describe it is like being woken up out of a dead sleep to find myself pinned down by a terrorist, who, before he blew my brains out with a sawed-off shotgun, was going to dismember me. And there's no way out.

I didn't know how much longer I could suffer through this particular episode. I couldn't believe I'd made it over the bridge and all the way home. In my panic, I'd had to pull over twice, freaking out, certain I was having another heart attack. I just knew I was going to die. Someone needed to help me. And then the phone rang.

"Maryanne?" Bruno said, his tone serious. He knew that if I was calling, it's a big deal.

"Dad?"

"Whatsa matter?"

"I was driving across the bridge from work and I started . . . I couldn't breathe and . . . I had to pull over, and then I got here and now . . . I can't move."

"What's going on?"

"I'm lying on the floor and I can't move. I feel like I'm having a heart attack," I said, gasping for breath after each syllable. "I think I should probably call an ambulance." I tried so hard to sound normal, but I was even more afraid that he would think I was a nut case. "Do you think I'm going to be all right?" I asked, hinging every hope on his answer.

"I think you're going to be fine. You're my daughter, you're tough like me."

"Well, I don't feel so tough right now."

"Where's your roommate?"

"I think I'll call her. Maybe she can come home and get me. What do you think is wrong with me, Dad?"

"You're okay," he said. "Call me back if you need to. I'll be here."

"Thanks, Dad."

"Good-bye," he said, just the way he always did.

I didn't want him to hang up. I was terrified to be alone. I wanted him to come and get me. I wanted to scream into the phone, "Please, help me, something's wrong with me!" But I didn't. I thanked him for nothing and hung up.

I didn't know what I was going to do. I knew it was a matter of moments before I passed out or my heart exploded, but I couldn't tell him what was really happening because I was so afraid of what he would think.

"Denise, it's me, Maryanne. Could you come get me? I think I need to go to the hospital. I think I'm having a heart attack," I said, now wrenched up in a fetal position. My hands were having spasms and I was seeing little electric strobes before my eyes.

"I'll be right there," she said, and hung up. The thought of her racing home to get me brought immediate relief, and by the time she got there I was more exhausted than scared. She practically broke down the front door, came screaming into the bedroom, and helped me up off the ground. I burst into tears, partially due to embarrassment, but also because I was horrified that something was terribly wrong with me.

✶✶✶✶

"Are you a diabetic?" asked the nurse.

"No—I mean, I don't think so. Why, do I look like I am?"

"Are you allergic to any medication?" she asked, not answering me.

"Uhhh, penicillin, I think. Why, do I need some?"

"Are you an epileptic?" she asked, again ignoring my question.

"No, for sure, no on that one. Why, though? Does it seem like I have that?"

"Do you have any heart disease in your family?"

"Uhhh, I don't think so. My grandmother had a stroke, but mostly everybody's just an alcoholic. Why? Do you think I had a heart attack?"

"Are you on any medication?"

"No, I'm a recovering addict. I don't even take aspirin," I said, indignantly, lying on the freezing-cold gurney, wearing nothing but a short hospital gown no thicker than a paper towel. She wasn't interested in my story. She took my pulse again.

She laid my hand on my chest and said, "The doctor will be with you in a minute," and then closed the curtain.

"Maryanne?" I could hear Denise looking for me.

"I'm over here," I said. She slipped inside the curtain.

"What did they say?" she asked.

"I don't know. I haven't talked to the doctor yet."

"You're fine. I'll bet you had food poisoning," she offered. "Yeah, one time when I was traveling in Arizona, I ate some . . . I don't know . . . breaded steak thing, and man, I thought I was going to die. I *wanted* to die, actually. I was lying on the bathroom floor. I couldn't even get my face up to the toilet, so I was lying in my own vomit and—"

"Denise?" I said, cutting her off.

"Yeah, babe?"

"Could you see if they have any water somewhere?"

"Sure, sweetie! I'll be right back," she said, and stroked my forehead. If she didn't shut up, I was going to freak out all over again.

"Hello, Maryanne. I'm Dr. Goldwyn," said the young resident, pulling back the curtain. I started to sit up so I could shake his hand. "No, no, don't get up, just relax. I'm just going to ask you a few questions, examine you and talk about your test results. Is that okay with you?"

"Okay," I said. He seemed so nice. I wondered why he was being so nice. Maybe that's what they do when they have something bad to tell you.

"How have things been for you lately, Maryanne?"

"Fine, I guess. Well, except for this—whatever you call it—heart attack thing."

"Have you been experiencing any stress lately?"

"God, why does everyone keep asking me that? I don't have stress. Something is wrong with me, okay?" I said, completely frustrated.

"I'm just going to press on your abdomen, if you can try and relax for me. How's that feel?"

"Fine, I mean I don't like it, but . . ."

"Does it hurt?" he asked, gently.

"No, it's fine."

"How about here?" he asked, pressing further down my abdomen. I started to laugh uncontrollably.

"No," I said, pushing his hand away. "That tickles, sorry."

"That's all right," he said.

Then he had me breathe in and out, stuck some probe thing in my ear, made me say "ahhhh," and then finally he asked, "Have you had any coffee today?"

"Mmmm, yeah, three café lattes, why?"

"You might want to consider cutting back on the coffee."

"Is that bad? Coffee, I mean? For me?" I shot up off the gurney.

"Coffee is a stimulant and can create feelings of anxiety if you drink enough of it," he explained.

"Anxiety? What do you mean? Am I allergic to coffee? That's what's wrong with me? I'm allergic to coffee? That's why I had a heart attack?" I shouted.

"First of all, you didn't have a heart attack. All your tests came back negative. And I didn't say you were allergic to coffee; I said that you might consider cutting back. Caffeine is a stimulant, and if you ingest too much, sometimes your body has a strong reaction and can set off nervousness and, in the extreme, acute anxiety."

"So I'm not going to die?"

He smiled. "You're fine. You can get dressed and go home now. Just take it easy for the rest of the day," he said, and closed the curtain behind himself.

"Thank you so much," I called after him, hoping he heard me as he walked away.

"Are you gonna live?" asked Denise, dramatically ripping back the curtains.

"Would you shut that—I'm totally naked here," I said, hopping around trying to get my leg into my pants. I was still a little shaky.

"Here's five bucks for a cab. I have to get to a meeting, so if you're okay I'm going to take off," she said, hugging me.

"I'm totally fine. He just said I should stop drinking coffee and that I should probably take a few days off and relax," I said—my own version of the truth.

"Good," she said, walking away, not listening to anything I was saying. "Just don't forget about tonight."

"What's tonight?" She was almost out of earshot.

"The ballet? And that Dale guy, remember? Dinner? Is it coming back now?" she said, and then was gone.

I frantically grabbed my purse; I needed to make sure she hadn't left me without the keys to get in the apartment. And of course she had. "Great, I can't even go home, dammit." I was jumpy and exhausted at the same time. I plopped down on a chair in the waiting room, rummaging through my purse for the tenth time, hoping the keys would magically materialize. I was so pissed. For a moment there I had felt like everything was going to be okay. All I had to do was never drink coffee again and everything would be okay. Finally, I could breathe.

I remembered I had an extra car key in my wallet, so I could at least pick up my car at the apartment and go somewhere until she got home. 'Oh thank you, God,' I said reflexively. I meant it; I was starting to feel more intimate with whoever or whatever I thought God was at that point. Thanking the Divine was something I was doing more frequently, but I still didn't know why sometimes that connection worked and sometimes it didn't.

A wave of something resembling relief washed over me. I slung my purse over my shoulder, took a deliberate, deep breath, and walked outside to catch a cab. No sooner had I held my hand up to hail a taxi, than one pulled up. 'Now that's more like it,' I thought. I opened the door, collapsed inside, and said, "One-four-three-two Jackson Street, please." I felt like I could relax a bit, that I had just glimpsed a light at the end of the tunnel. Then it struck me: that was no light—it was a train. My lattes were all decaf!

★★★★

'Oh, you f—. You took my spot,' I said silently, and then I shouted, "Thanks a lot, buddy! Yeah, thanks! I'm talking to you, ya jerk." I drove past the blue Honda, looking right at the guy who had snagged my place as I was about to circle the block for the fiftieth time. I slammed my hands against the steering wheel and bellowed, "I can't stand this! I have been driving around and around for almost half an hour trying to find a place to park. Fine, screw it!" I threw my car into Park, flung open the door, and slammed it behind me. "I don't care. Whatever. They can tow it, steal it, I can't . . ." I grumbled, knocking on the door in the hope that Denise was home to let me in. I still didn't have my own key.

"What's wrong?" said Denise, as she opened the door. She looked like she had just come out of the bathroom, wearing only a bra and undies.

"It's taking me an hour to find a parking place down there! That's ridiculous. Who has time to drive around and around aaaand around?" I was starting to yell again.

"Where'd you park?"

"I didn't," I said. "I left it out front and I don't give a shit—they can have the thing. Take it."

"Where are your keys?"

"This is insane," I said, handing her my car key. "How do people live like this?" I shouted. I noticed I sounded exactly like my mother. And then I noticed what Denise was wearing. "Is that my bra?" I asked, following her into the bedroom. "I thought we said we weren't going to wear each other's clothes."

"I said as a rule we shouldn't wear each other's clothes. What's the big deal? It's only a bra," she said, walking into the bathroom to finish dressing. I followed her. She tossed my key onto the vanity.

"The big deal is, you said we weren't going to wear each other's clothes, Denise. That's my favorite bra and, as a matter of fact, I was planning on wearing it tonight," I said, fuming.

"Look, it's just a bra. Get over it," she said, pressing her five-foot two-inch self up into my five-foot-eight-inch face.

"You don't want to do that," I warned.

"F— you, you ungrateful little bitch," she said, poking me in the chest. "Here's your f—ing bra," she said, whipping it off and throwing it at me.

"You need to stop," I said.

"Or what?" she mocked in her smart-ass, cocky little way, walking past me.

"Just don't." I followed her into the bathroom.

"Don't tell me what to do. I'll do and say whatever I want, whenever I want, in my house. Got it?" she said, poking me in the chest one last time.

"You know what? I'm sick of you," I said. "Why don't you shut up. You think you're so tough. You're just an obnoxious, loud-mouthed bitch," I said, getting closer.

And that was it. She took her best shot. She threw a punch at me. Luckily I grabbed her hand mid flight and then shielded my face from the subsequent flurry of slapping and flailing that followed. After a few seconds of that, I pushed her off me long enough to catch my balance and then I lost all control. She took off running for the bathroom, but before she could completely shut the door, I forced my way in. I grabbed her by the throat and smashed her up against the wall. Her feet came up off the ground a good three inches.

"If you ever touch me again, ever, I swear to God the last sound you will hear, you little bitch, is your body dropping to the ground. You got it?" I said quietly, through my clenched teeth. She nodded her head as much as she could and I released her from my grip. She grabbed her throat with both hands, gasping and coughing, and slid down the bathroom wall. Adrenaline was still pumping through my body. I felt like I was on fire. I knew if I didn't get out of there, things were going to get even uglier.

I snatched the car key, stuffed all my belongings in my gym bag (I had learned to travel light), and walked out the door. I passed her date in the hall on my way out. He was wearing a full-length, black cashmere overcoat and was carrying not one, but two dozen red roses in his arms, completely unsuspecting.

"Good luck," I said.

"Thanks," he replied, looking back at me over his shoulder with a quizzical expression.

"'Cause you're gonna need it, buddy."

I never spoke to Denise again after that night. There was really nothing to say. However, I did have one regret—I never did get my bra back.

So, how could I turn off my feelings like that? Denise had been good to me. But in the war I was fighting, allies could turn to enemies at the drop of a bra. All's fair in love and war—at least that's what my mother always said. But it went deeper than that. By now I had enough emotional scar tissue to make my heart almost impenetrable. Any access to a sense of loyalty was almost completely shut down. And I didn't have the time or the capacity to stop and think about it either; I was in hot pursuit of the next place where I knew everything was going to be okay. So, naturally the casualties would start to pile up.

I couldn't avoid the fact that I had wanted to hurt Denise, and that scared me. And frankly, I didn't want to know if there was more of that rage inside me. So what I told myself was that she was crazy—which got me off the hook. Shutting off my feelings and walking away felt like the only choice I had. Otherwise, I'd have to look into the void that was growing inside me, and I was still not prepared to do that. I couldn't afford to be that vulnerable. My need to survive was making it necessary to show people less and less of what was real about me, and to live more and more on the surface, which made intimacy almost impossible.

But I had just walked away from the only person who knew how broken I was and loved me anyway. So now, besides having to carry my mammoth inner torment and hide it from the next person who might offer me a safe haven, I would also have to shove down my grief over losing Denise, which was crying out to be felt.

But I was in flight, hunted by this nameless thing that wasn't going to leave me alone, and I wasn't about to stop.

PART FOUR

▪ *Who I Am Certain I Was Not*

I KNEW I WAS BEING PUNISHED for something. Otherwise, why would God be letting this horrible thing happen to me?

Wasn't it enough that I'd had a shitty childhood? That my father was the spawn of hell and my mother didn't care about anyone but herself? And that I was a recovering cocaine addict? By now I couldn't even drive my car without freaking out. I couldn't sit in group at work without making some excuse for leaving. I was panicking more and more often, and I didn't know why. I couldn't sleep through one night without waking up in a feverish sweat, gasping for air, sure I was going to die. I couldn't sit in a restaurant without running out into the street, certain I would suffocate . . . or go to a movie, or get in an elevator, or ride on an airplane without it being a traumatic event.

I was becoming frightened of virtually everything, but I forged on, refusing to cave. As I heard my mother often say, you are as sick as your secrets. This was my secret. And I couldn't tell a soul. I knew if I did they would lock me up and I would never get out. I just needed to make this thing go away—and then for sure everything would be okay.

I didn't have a name for what was wrong with me, so I didn't know how to ask for help. The only question I could ask myself was: What is this horrendous affliction that has been cast upon me? This darkness that came unannounced out of nowhere devoured me like a monster, and spat me out without regard?

It had to be God that did this to me—or at the very least, allowed it to happen. (Okay, I wanted to give him the benefit of the doubt.)

All I had to do was look at my Good Girl Handbook to prove it. By now I had violated every Good Girl "don't" there was. What other explanation could there be?

My childish relationship with the I'll-put-the-fear-of-God-into-you kind of deity had surfaced again. Even if that one were willing to help me, any recent favorable dealings with him were swept away and engulfed by the terror.

"Hi, sweetie, what are you doing here?" asked Stan, looking up from his desk. He was one of my closest friends from AA. Stan was the president of a large paper company, looked like Larry King, and drove a brand-new Riviera.

"Just walk with me, okay?" I said, as I barged unannounced into his office early one morning.

"Okay," he said, looking at me curiously. "How's it going? I haven't talked to you for a while. I heard you got a new job. Isn't that a bit much with going to school?" I had been attending junior college off and on for a couple of years. Mostly off lately, because of the constant anxiety attacks.

"Please, just talk to me while we walk. I can't really breathe right now," I said, annoyed by having to speak, my heart still pounding. He nodded.

"So, I saw Denise last week." He knew we were on the skids and loved to stir it up. "She's pissed at me too," he continued. "She thinks I need to go to see a shrink. She said my food issues are too much for her to deal with. We both know she's the one who's nuts, right?" he asked, laughing. I wouldn't have argued if I could have. He stopped at the end of the parking lot like he was going to go back inside to his office.

"Just a little longer?" I said, still totally wound up.

"Sure," he said, and continued walking. "Yeah, I tell ya, she's something else, that one. Did you hear what happened?" He was clearly at no loss for gossip.

"No, what?" I forced out, still having some trouble breathing normally. My chest felt like a truck was on top of it and I was disoriented.

"Well, she was driving and apparently some poor bastard on a motorcycle was tailing her too close, so she slammed on her brakes and the guy crashed into the back of her new Saab and flew over the top of the car. I guess he was hurt pretty bad," he said, his tone now more serious.

"Wow," I said, taking my first full breath since I'd arrived. He gave me his toothy smile and a squeeze.

"You're terrific, kiddo, you know that? I'm really proud of you," he said.

"Thank you so much, Stan," I said, grabbing on to him, suddenly flooded with emotion. Stan saw things in me that I couldn't even begin to appreciate in myelf, like being one of the few young people who were in AA at that time.

I wanted him to hold me and tell me everything was going to be okay. But he didn't. And I couldn't ask.

"How's it going with that new guy you're seeing—Timmy?" he said, still unaware of how panicked I was. I had met Timmy in the program a few months earlier. He was handsome, tall, and strong, just like my father . . . but *he* was sober and he seemed safe.

"Good," I said. "He asked me to marry him."

"That's great," he said. We turned around and headed back. "Have you talked to Rob lately?"

"No, have you?" I could tell I was starting to come down. And that's all I wanted. I just wanted to be normal.

"Yeah, he called me last week. I'm thinking about buying his Rolls," he said.

I glanced down at his chunky Rolex watch. "Oh God, I have to go, I'm totally late," I said, and grabbed his face and kissed him on the cheek. "Thank you so much. You'll never know how much this meant to me." And almost like nothing had happened, I raced back to my car. My legs felt kind of rubbery and I noticed I was a bit spacey, but compared to the attack I had just had, this was nothing. Without exaggeration, I felt like I had come back from the dead. I was exhausted—and I was late.

Everything Comes in Threes

LIKE I SAID, I HAD BEEN READING voraciously, particularly books slanted toward Eastern spirituality. After much arduous postulation, I had a few hypotheses that attempted to make some sense of the chaos I called my life. First, that we pick our own family before we are born. And for the record, the reasons I didn't choose well were twofold: (a) Apparently my eternal soul was severely neurotic, had low self-esteem, and was slated for a lifetime chock-full of lessons, and (b) Karmically speaking, evidently I had abused my power in my last lifetime. Which, based on the family I chose, had to mean that I must have axed them all to death . . . and now we were even. Another idea I was toying with was that we have agreements to bring other souls into this world.

★★★★

"I'm late! I'm f—ing late!" I shouted. Silence on the other end of the phone. "Did you not hear me? I said, 'I am late.'"

"I heard you. I heard you. . ." he trailed off.

"So? Is that all you have to say? You heard me? What are you, a parrot?" I screeched.

"No. I'm thinking."

"Thinking? About what? What is there to think about?" I shrieked.

"I want us to have it," he said, tentatively.

"Are you crazy? I'm not having this baby! I go away for a weekend with my girlfriend and come home to find blood splattered all over my walls, and you have the audacity to say you want me to have your baby? Are you retarded?" I screamed.

"I didn't know where you were," he said, weakly.

"You didn't know where I was? Of cooourse you didn't know where I was! That's because I broke up with you, which means that it was none of your business where I was."

"Would you stop yelling at me!"

"I wasn't yelling. That is not yelling. I feel sorry for you if you think that is yelling because *this* is f—ing yelling!" I screamed.

"Please stop! I can't talk to you if you're screaming at me," he pleaded.

"What makes you think I even *want* to talk to you? And don't change the subject; that's not the point here."

"What do you want me to say?"

"That's the point. I don't want to have to tell you what to say or what the point is. I'm pregnant, you idiot!" I shouted.

"I love you, Maryanne. Why won't you—" but I cut him off.

"You know, I'm sick of hearing your lies and your promises. I just want you to stay away from me, you f—ing psycho. I don't ever want to come home again and find my windows bashed in because some maniac I'm not even seeing anymore has freaked out because he didn't know where I was. I don't ever want to walk into my house and find it looking like a damned bloodbath and wonder if you killed my cat. So that's why I won't . . . whatever you were going to say. Just stay away from me. I don't know why I even told you. It doesn't matter what you say anymore, Tim, I'm not having this baby," I said, and slammed down the phone.

I had quit my job at the ARC at Marin General because I couldn't make it across the bridge without having a panic attack. I now had a job as a chemical dependency counselor with my own caseload at a hospital within walking distance from where I lived. My shift that day was about to start. 'F—, now I'm really late,' I said to myself, and rushed out the door.

★★★★

"What's wrong?" I asked, shoving my purse in a cubby behind the nursing station. Coming into that vibe was like walking into a spider's web.

"Sara came in this morning. They found her at her dealer's house. She snorted some bad shit," said Jeffrey, the head nurse on duty.

"Well, where is she? Is she okay?"

"She's in the ICU," he said, looking at me with a penetrating gaze.

"Can I go down there and see her; I mean, can she have visitors? What happened, Jeff? Did they tell you anything?"

"I don't really know anything other than that she took off from here, went straight to her dealer's house, and I guess the guy gave her some bogus stuff."

"Son of a bitch, I'm gonna f—ing . . . Can I go down there?"

"She's pretty bad, Maryanne. They don't think she's going to make it."

"I don't care. I'm going down," I said, and started for the stairs. I still couldn't get in an elevator.

"Her parents are in there with her now," he said. I froze for a second.

'Oh God!' I thought. 'What was I going to say to them? It was my fault Sara left. But I made her promise me she wasn't going to run away before I left my shift. I even told her to call me at home if she needed to, and that I would come and be with her. All she had to do was call . . . I knew I should have stayed after my shift. It was my fault. And her parents—they had been totally counting on me. I'd told them she was doing well; I thought she was. When I last saw her, I was sure she was okay.' I started to cry. I didn't know if I could face them.

"She's in 3-A," said the nurse on the intensive care unit.

I pressed against the heavy swinging door and crept into the sterile-smelling, dimly lit room. The fluorescent light above the hospital bed flickered as Sara's parents hovered over her emaciated body. The steely monitor blipped wearily as they watched their daughter slip further and further away. I took a spot at the end of the bed and clung to the footboard, my body turned slightly away from all of them. I could feel the clip on Sara's chart gnash into my leg, but I didn't dare move. I wanted to face her; at the very least, she deserved that. But I couldn't bear to look directly at her. The sight was too horrific.

Her eyes bulged from their sockets as though they were being forced out from her head. Her pallid skin draped across her adolescent skeleton like stretched-out pizza dough, tubes and wires feeding into every orifice. It was like nothing I had ever seen. My body was giving me signals that it wanted to collapse, yet I stood perfectly erect. The silence warranted decorum. I was afraid to even breathe.

"Mr. and Mrs. Nettle, I am so . . . I just want you to know . . ." I couldn't even finish the sentence. I broke down. Sara's mother came over to comfort me. I knew it was they who needed comforting, not me, and I couldn't believe she was being so nice. Why didn't she hate me? It was my fault her daughter was lying there, dying.

I tried to gather myself. I wiped my tears and took a few deep breaths, attempting to compose myself. Mrs. Nettle walked back over to her daughter's side and then one of the nurses came through the door to check Sara's vitals. There was absolutely nothing I could say and I knew it. So I just stood with them silently in the last few moments they had left with their daughter. My eyes poured out all the compassion and grief that I couldn't actually feel, and I offered a halfhearted smile. They smiled back with a love and kindness that I knew I didn't deserve. I looked over my shoulder as I held open the door on my way out, wanting desperately to express some feeling. But my gaze was unmet. With my head still turned toward them, I let the door swing closed behind me. I never saw the Nettles again.

The ICU nurse at the station told me that Sara had run away the Friday night after I'd gone home, even though she promised— crossed her heart and hoped to die—she wouldn't go. And I'd wanted to believe her. The nurse told me the paramedics had found her lying on the bathroom floor at her dealer's house, bleeding from her nose and mouth. Sara had overdosed on synthetic cocaine. She was barely fifteen years old.

A kaleidoscope of Sara's bulbous eyes and her parents' tear-streaked faces and strained smiles haunted me as I continued down the corridor. I wanted to keep going—down the hall, down the stairs, out the lobby, out the front door. Instead, I walked back up the three flights of stairs to the unit where I worked, where Sara had been my patient. My desolation was interrupted periodically by barfing my guts up in the ladies room every few hours. And so went the rest of my day on into the night. The only thing that varied was the reason I was vomiting.

✦✦✦✦

"Are you still up there?" asked Sharon, the night security person, who had just rang up the unit.

"Yeah. Cameron went home sick, so I told him I would stay over. There's only seven kids up here right now."

"Well, there's some guy down here looking for you, but I told him you already left."

"Who is it? I mean, what's he look like?"

"Big, real tall, dark hair—looks kind of like Richard Gere."

'Except he has fuller lips,' I thought.

"He's moping around like somebody done died."

"I'll come down. Don't let him up here, okay?"

"Don't worry. He ain't goin' nowhere as long as I'm standin' here."

"Cheryl? I'm gonna take a mini break and run down to the lobby for a few minutes, okay?" Cheryl was reading a novel with her feet propped up on a file cabinet.

"Of course, sweetie. How are you feeling? Any better?"

"I'm fine. I just need to move around a bit. Be back in ten, 'kay?"

I pushed against the steel bar on the exit door and walked past the elevators into the empty lobby.

"What are you doing here?" I asked, and folded my arms.

"I had to see you, Maryanne. I think you're making a mistake."

"You had to come to my work and jeopardize my job at two in the morning? You couldn't wait and tell me this tomorrow?"

"I couldn't wait, Maryanne. I love you. I want to be with you. Don't you understand?" He started to cry.

"Well, you know, it's too late for me. I don't love you anymore, Tim. You scare me. I don't trust you anymore, and . . . I can't think of the other things right now, but there's other stuff, but we've already been through all that, so just go. I don't want this anymore." I started to walk away.

"Maryanne, no please, just talk to me. You're angry and you have a lot of hormones right now. You're probably not thinking clearly," he said, walking toward me.

"Look, you're starting to scare me. I have to go back upstairs."

"I'm not going to let you do this, Maryannie. I love you, and you have my baby inside you."

"What are you going to do, kidnap me?" I asked, only half joking. "You know . . . whatever. I have nothing to say to you and I'm going back upstairs."

"No, you're not," he said, starting to grab me by the throat. He was six feet five inches and easily weighed two hundred fifty pounds. I jumped back, somehow managing to escape his grasp, and yelled for help.

"Maryanne," I heard from around the corner, "are you okay?" asked Sharon. Tim took off for the door.

"He . . . was trying . . . was going to choke me," I gasped.

"Come over here and sit down, girl. I'll get you some water." She brought me back a Dixie cup with water and I drank it down in one gulp. "Do you want me to call the police, honey?" she asked.

"No. Please, don't. It'll just make it worse," I said, still trembling. I fell over into my lap, held my face in my hands, and started to cry. But no tears came out. Just a strange sound. Like a moaning. It was beyond tears. Beyond exhaustion. Beyond, beyond. "He won't stop. He won't leave me alone. Not unless I disappear," I said into my hands.

"Are you sure you don't want me to call the police? Because they'll come right over."

"No. I'm just gonna go back upstairs and crash. Thanks anyway."

"Well, if he comes back, I'm gonna call them."

"Fine, whatever you want. Whatever you want . . ." I slowly walked away.

What is beyond stress? How can I describe for you that place? There are almost no words that adequately relay the point where nothing makes any sense anymore, yet you must make sense of it all right now. I felt like I had been running and fighting for so long and that I just couldn't take another step. But I knew if I didn't, I was going to cease to exist. I feared I would collapse and never recover. Then some people who didn't even know me, in some hospital somewhere, would have control of my life and I would surely never be free.

So I had to think of something quick. I needed a plan. I feared that if the feelings that were buried in me were unleashed, they would never stop, and then I could not function at all. No, there was no time to stop. There had to be another way out.

★★★★

"Good morning, Maryanne. I'm sorry, I'm meaning to say good after . . . how you call it? Good after noon?"

"God, I'm so glad it's you, Giancarlo. I thought it was. . . Never mind," I said.

"What, who you thought I was? Some boy? Eh?" he asked in his broken English.

"Forget it. No one. I just plugged my phone back in and . . . Anyway, what's up?" I asked. "Is everything okay?"

"Oh yes, everything is okay. You said should I call you and say what I put in my journal."

"Right, right. I'm sorry." I didn't know how to say no. My patients and their families would call me at home whenever they felt like it. And I always picked up the phone. I wouldn't have known what a boundary was if it had come up and slapped me right across my face.

"Tell me how you feel. I'm listening," I said.

Giancarlo was one of my patients. He and his mother had just moved here from Italy. He was absolutely *GQ* beautiful, and barely of legal age. Had his birthday been just a few days earlier, he would have been admitted to the adult unit.

"So, go. Shoot, talk," I said, impatiently.

"How I am feeling today? How I'm-a feeling today is . . . that I am in love for you."

"What?"

"Wait, there is more," he said. I could hear the pages of his journal rustling. He read: *"I am in love for Maryanne and cannot wait to be with her. I want so much to kiss her and hold her hand. She is all I'm-a dreaming about."*

"Giancarlo. Uhhh, you can't put that in there. I mean, you can't write that in your journal."

"Why not?" he demanded. "Who will try and stop me?"

"Did you show anybody that?"

"Yes, of course. I am not afraid."

"I don't care if you're afraid, you fool. I'm going to get in big . . . We're both going to get thrown out of here."

"So what? I do not care. I'm wanting only to be with Your Loveliness," he said, defiantly.

"Well, I do care. This is my job, and I like my job."

"Why you like this job anyway? You should come to Italy with me. My family is very rich and we don't have to live like animals."

"What are you talking about?"

"Come with me, Maryanne. Come away from this stupid place. They don't like you here anyway. I hear they talking about you."

"Who's talking about me?"

"Claire and Jason—and Jeff," he replied.

"Jeff?" I asked, surprised.

"So, who cares about these stupids anyway? Come with me and we will live like kings."

I couldn't believe it. Jeff was talking about me. "What did Jeff say?"

"Nothing. He is stupid."

"Tell me," I commanded.

"Okay, okay. He said you were trying to change things too much and they wanted you to go out from this place."

"He said that?" I was shocked and immediately became paranoid. I wondered what else they said. I wondered if they knew Timmy had been there the other night. Maybe Sharon had said something. "Did anyone else say anything?" I asked.

"Forget it. Don't worry, you are with me."

God. Did everyone hate me? When did that happen? I thought everybody liked me—well, almost everybody. There was one girl who said I might want to rethink my wardrobe. But I thought she was a drip.

As it was, I had called in sick the past three days. I'd gone and had an abortion. How could I bring a baby into this world with a two-hundred-fifty-pound head case for a father? I didn't see it happening. But now I didn't know if I even had a job to go back to.

'Live like kings,' huh? Well, at least somebody was with my program.

★★★★

"Hi, Maryanne," said Jeff. He looked up as I dropped my purse down near his feet and glared at him. I didn't say a word. I was furious. How dare he speak to me after talking behind my back? We were supposed to be professionals around here, and therapists, for God's sake. We were supposed to be a team.

'What is wrong with these sick people?' I thought. I flung my head back, exasperated, and walked away from the nurse's station. As I turned the corner I ran smack into . . . guess who?

"Hello, my lovely," said Giancarlo, as we collided.

"Giancarlo, don't," I snapped.

"What's the problem? You are not happy to see me?" he said, offended.

"No, it's not that. I *am* happy to see you." He stared at me with his gorgeous green eyes and long, black eyelashes. A lock of his wavy blonde hair fell in his eye. "I'm always happy to see you. It's just . . . you scared me," I lied. He looked like a big puppy that had just been scolded. I felt bad; in fact, he was the only thing lately that did make me happy.

"Come to play volleyball with us, come. Come on," he coaxed.

"Giancarlo, I'm in a skirt, I can't." He grabbed my hand and led me down the hall. How could I resist? So I didn't.

I played volleyball with the kids, ran group, and participated in the kids' occupational therapy, and when it came time for our team meeting, no one said word one to me about getting the axe. That's because it was a shovel and the shit was just about to hit the . . . van.

"Okay, you guys in? Where's Pilar?" I asked, as the kids piled in the hospital van for their weekly outing.

"She's coming. I saw her," said one of the other patients.

"Here she is," I said. "Okay, is that everybody?"

The group hollered a collective "yeah!"

"Wagon, ho," said Dean, the therapist accompanying me on our little excursion. I was relieved too, because Dean was cool. He wasn't the kind of person to say a bad thing about anyone.

"Come here and sit," commanded Giancarlo, as I climbed into the van. I was already vigilant around him, but under the circumstances I was hypervigilant. I thought everyone could tell that he had feelings for me, and worse, that I liked him too. I nestled in between two of the kids in the back seat. Giancarlo sat behind me on the bench that faced the rear window.

"I want to kiss your lips," he leaned back and whispered into my ear. I brushed him away like a mosquito.

'Oh my God, is he crazy? I know someone heard him.' My heart was beating, pounding. I was filled with desire and fear.

"I must kiss you," he said, again. This time I pushed him so hard he fell off the seat and slammed into the back door of the van.

"Hey, what's going on back there?" asked Dean, scolding what he thought were the kids for acting out.

"It's okay. It's fine. He was just . . . he fell," I said, giving Giancarlo a warning look.

'What the hell . . . now I *know* someone heard him say that. The kids are totally staring at me,' I thought.

I rested my arm on the top of the vinyl bench that separated us, wishing we would hurry up and be where we were going.

"Hey, do we get to buy food there?" asked Jake, one of the newest kids. Giancarlo started to caress my arm.

"Knock it off," I blurted out.

"I was just asking," said Jake.

"Not you, Jake, sorry . . . yes." I angrily pulled my arm off the top of the seat. "Yes, you guys can buy food, but you have to stay with your partner," I reminded them firmly. "No wandering off on your own or we're outta there, okay?" Dean pulled the van up to the front of the bookstore where I used to work and we all piled out. "Back here in an hour?" I said.

"You got it," said Dean.

★★★★

"Nice jugs," said Dominick. He was just about to finish our program, and I couldn't wait.

"Give me that," I said, snatching the *Penthouse* magazine from him. "Did you not hear what I said? Huh?" He just looked at me like, 'What?'

"Do you want to leave tomorrow like a gentleman or do you want me to recommend that you stay for another month? And you too, Lawrence. Now go read something more . . . something else." I shooed them away from the magazine rack. "Go! And stay out of trouble, you two." I looked at my watch; only twenty more minutes.

Giancarlo came up behind me and picked me up. I screamed. "Jesus! You scared the crap out of me, Giancarlo."

"What is this—crap—mean?" he asked. I straightened myself out, still annoyed, but now jolted as well.

"Crap means like, shit, you know—stuff," I said, having to really think about what it meant.

"Oh, I get it," he laughed. "You shit on yourself because I scared you," he said, so proud of himself that he learned some slang.

"No, not like that. I didn't shit on myself. It's just an expression. It doesn't mean you really crapped . . . went to the bathr—forget it. Where's Jeremy? You're supposed to be with him."

"I gave him twenty dollars to go away from me so I could have you alone for myself."

"What?" I barked, then realized where I was. "What?" I whispered.

"Yes, I gave him moneys so he would leave me to be with you," he said.

"Look Giancarlo, I like you, really I do, but this is crazy. I'm going to get fired! You can't just tell. . . You can't just go around. . ." I knew I should have walked away. I should have *run* away.

"Come with me, Maryanne, to Italy. This is not your place. We belong with each others," he said.

"What are you saying? I can't just—" I started to say, but he grabbed me and kissed me. And at first I tried to resist. I was terrified someone would see us, but at the same time it was suddenly thrilling to be doing this very wrong thing. It was like approaching a waterfall, and instead of trying to fight it, you surrender, and just before you are about to plummet to your death, you let go.

In that moment I didn't care anymore. I mean, what else could happen? What else besides finding out your fiancé is a psychotic, seeing a young girl you cared so much about die right in front of your eyes, and then having an abortion? Everyone knows things happen in threes. No one was going to see us, and even if they did, I would just deny it or blame it on Giancarlo.

'Screw them. Who cares?' I thought. There was no possible way I could have cared less.

Well, Maybe on All Fours

"MARYANNE!" MY MOTHER SCREAMED into the phone.

"Mother? What is it? What happened? What time is it?"

I could hear the jostling sound of the phone being handed to someone else.

"Maryanne," said a man's voice, very calmly.

"Edward? Is that you? What's going on?" I said, now sitting up in bed.

"Maryanne, we need you to come down here. Larry's had a heart attack."

"Is he okay? I mean, is he going to be all right?

He paused for a second, "No sweetie, he's not. He's gone. So come down as fast as you can. Your mother needs you." Edward was my mother's best friend, and was not prone to exaggeration.

I didn't say good-bye. I didn't even hang up the phone. I flew out of bed, threw on my jogging suit, grabbed my keys, and was out the door. I screamed into the hospital parking lot at about sixty-five miles an hour and parked sideways in a parallel spot. I ran as fast as my feet would carry me into the emergency room.

"Mother!" I screamed, slamming my hands on the reception desk. "Mother!" I yelled.

"Miss, please. Can I help you?" said the reception nurse, trying to calm me down.

"Where's my mother?" I said, blinded by my tears and horror.

"Who is your mother, dear?" she said, calmly, trying to help.

"She's uhhh . . . he had a heart attack. Larry. I mean Lawrence Alexander." Just then my mother came around the corner. Edward was holding her up.

"Please . . . no. Tell me he's . . . Edward?" I looked at him, begging for him to tell me I was dreaming.

"He's gone, sweetie."

"Ohhhhhh, God, nooooo, please God, nooooo," I wailed, and fell at my mother's feet. Edward sat her down in a chair and my head tumbled into her lap.

"He loved me," I sobbed uncontrollably. "Why did God have to take him away from me?" How could this be? How could he take the only man who ever loved me like a father, who never ever tried to touch me or said one inappropriate thing to me? My grief about Larry pierced all the other places of sorrow I had hidden inside. My sobbing cascaded from one painful memory to the next.

"No, no, no, nooo," I whimpered while she stroked my hair. And my mother, oh my God, she had waited her entire life to be happy and finally she found her soul mate. They were like two peas in a pod, I used to say. In just a month they were to be married.

"What happened?" I asked, finally lifting my head up.

"He was swimming laps in the pool," she started to say, her eyes brimming with tears. "We had been talking about our honeymoon and he had just given me my engagement ring." She held out her hand to show me, and the tears were now spilling over. "He sat up on the side of the pool and lay back and the next thing I knew. . ." She couldn't finish. I looked at Edward.

"There was a doctor right there at the pool, Maryanne. There was nothing he could do," said Edward.

"What do we do now?" I said, my practicality taking over.

"I'm going to take her home," he said.

"I have to work. I am supposed to work. Let me call in and then I'll meet you at the house, okay?" I said. "Mother? Mother! I am going for a little bit, but I'll be over in just a while. Okay? Edward's going to take you back to the house, okay?" She was totally out of it. I looked at Edward. "I'll see you as soon as I can get there."

And Then Again, Fives?

"YEAH, HI, IT'S MARYANNE. Can I talk to Sharon or whoever's at the front desk?" One of the staff had picked up the call from the lunchroom. "Hold on, I'll transfer you," said a voice I didn't recognize.

"Maryanne, it's Sharon. Hang on just a minute. Dr. Thomas wants to speak with you."

"Okay," I said. I flushed with impending doom. Why did he want to talk to me; did someone see me and Giancarlo at the bookstore? No way. They would have said something that night. Besides, Dean would never have said anything.

"Maryanne? Good morning, it's Dr. Thomas," he said in his kind voice. He was such a nice man. As a matter of fact, he was the one who had hired me.

"Hi, Dr. Thomas, sorry to bother you. I mean, I know you want to talk to me, but I was calling to see if I could switch my shift because my mother's fiancé just had a heart attack and passed away this morning, and she's not doing well, as I'm sure you can imagine, so I was wondering if I could, you know, change my schedule a little bit. I know I took off that other time, but I had a medical emergency and, well, anyway, do you think I could take some time?" I rambled. I could feel the doom getting closer.

"Maryanne, you won't need to rearrange your schedule, because we're letting you go. You can come pick up your paycheck anytime tomorrow."

"What?" I responded in disbelief.

"I think we have incompatible philosophies. I think we're all better off this way."

I was floored. I mean, I thought somebody might say something about me and Giancarlo, but I never thought I would actually get fired—and I wasn't even sure that was the cause. Maybe it was something else. I really didn't think anyone had seen us.

"It wasn't only the bookstore incident, Maryanne, it was the staff difficulties and just an overall incompatibility." That bastard Dean, he told on me. I couldn't believe it. "So if there's nothing else, I wish you the best of luck, and if you need a personal reference you can always count on me."

"Thank you," was all I could say, and I hung up. 'Thank you? What the hell were you thanking him for, you doofus? He just fired you. Great, now I don't even have a job. Now what am I going to do?'

Do We Have Any Sixes?

"WHY DIDN'T JOHNNY AND TONY STAY?" I asked, not so innocently. I was packing up the last of my mother's kitchen. She was leaving the townhouse where she'd been living with Lawrence. My mother stared out the window into the yard.

"They had to get back to L.A.," was all she said.

'How convenient,' I thought. 'Of course they left. Why would they want to stay and pack up Mother and move her and spend every night holding her while she sobs herself to sleep, when they have Maryanne to do it for them? Selfish bastards,' I thought. 'Well, lucky for everyone I had the time.'

"Maryanne, there's a boy on the phone for you," said my mother.

"Who is it?" I yelled across the room. I was doing a last check in the bathroom.

"He says his name is Carlo."

"Giancarlo, Mother?" I said. Why could she never get the names right? She called Tim, Tom, and Rob, Bob. I think she did it on purpose, sometimes.

"Hello," I said, grabbing the phone.

"Hello, my beautiful flower," said Giancarlo. "I'm coming to take you for dinner somewhere."

"I can't. I have to finish packing."

"I don't mind."

"You don't mind what?"

"I don't care you have to do this thing, packing. I will wait for you."

"Well, then, you're going to have to wait all night because it's already five o'clock, and it's going to take at least another three or four hours. Anyway, I'm still pissed at you. I don't even want to talk to you," I said, remembering I was still mad.

"I don't care. I will wait into the night for your self."

"You do that," I said, and slammed down the phone. And he did.

✱✱✱✱

"Maryanne, why is that boy waiting in his car in the driveway?" my mother asked, looking out the blinds from the bedroom.

"Oh my God, it must be Giancarlo. What is he doing here?" I hopped off the bed and went over to the window. He saw me looking out through the curtains, jumped out of his car, and held up a bouquet of flowers.

"What is he doing?" asked my mother, who had returned to half-watching some old movie that was on.

"I don't know. Waving some flowers around, it looks like. What time is it anyway?"

"Almost ten thirty," she said, looking at the clock.

"I wonder how long he's been out there."

"I'm sure I don't know, dear," she said, with fading interest. "Why don't you go and talk to the poor boy?"

'Poor boy, my ass,' I thought. "Screw him. He can sit there all night for all I care." And so he did. I walked back over and lay back down on the bed.

✸✸✸✸

Ding-dong, ding-dong, ding-dong, ding-dong.

"Motherrrrrrrr!" I shouted from upstairs. "Someone's at the door. I just got out of the shower." *Ding-dong, ding-dong.* It didn't stop. "MOM!!?" I shouted even louder, grabbing my robe and storming out of the bathroom. "Where *is* she?" I said, storming down the stairs.

'Who the hell keeps ringing the—?'

"You? Are you still here?" I held open the door as I held my bathrobe closed with one of my hands.

"You are Arabian goddess, no?" he said, and shoved in my face the flowers he had apparently been sleeping with all night. And then I got it.

"Oh, the towel on my head," I said, and laughed despite myself. "Arabian, right, I get it. What are you still doing here?" I asked, resuming my anger.

"I told you, I will wait for all the night," he said, smiling and pushing the flowers for me to take. I snatched them out of his hand so I could get him to stop shoving them in my face.

"Did you sleep here . . . out there all night?"

"I did not zleep. I am waiting for you," he said, still smiling.

"Look, I don't know what you're trying to pull, but I hate you. I lost my job because of you. And anyway, this is not a good time for me, okay?" I said, and tried to shut the door on him. He held his hand out to stop it.

"I will not go away. I will wait and wait for you."

"Don't you, like, have a job or something?" I asked, surveying the area to see if anyone was watching.

"My job is you."

"That's not normal," I said. "And besides, you can't just stay here. Someone is going to call the police, all right, so just go home," I said, and tried to shut the door again. He stopped me again.

"Just let me love you. I don't need for you to love me back."

"Look, Giancarlo, you're very sweet, but I can't do this right now, okay?"

"What? What you have to do? I do it for you. We do it together." I knew he was never going to leave me alone if I didn't do something.

"Okay, okay. Come back later, and we'll go to lunch and celebrate your graduation from the program," I compromised, tired of trying to fend him off.

"I will wait here."

"No! Go home to your house and shower or whatever and then come back later. I'm doing something with my mother in about . . . what time is it?"

"It is eight forty-three," he said, looking at his watch.

"Fine, come back, like, at two," I ordered him, trying to close the door.

"I am be back at one o'clock," he said, as the door closed.

"Two," I said, from behind the door.

'A girl's got to eat,' I thought.

✸✸✸✸

"Mother, I'll only be gone for two weeks," I said.

"Keep your voice down," she snapped. I looked around the restaurant to see if anyone was staring.

"No one heard me, and who cares anyway?" I said, trying not to raise my voice again.

"And what about me?" she said, ignoring me. "You're only thinking about yourself." I wiggled my finger in my ear to simulate cleaning it out so I could hear her.

"Myself? What did you just say?" I said, furrowing my brow.

"You heard me."

"You have to be kidding, right?"

"No one can ever tell you anything. You're going to do what you're going to do."

"You must be confusing me with someone else. All I have done for the past six weeks is take care of you. I moved you. All by myself. I held you all night long—every single night, I might add—and I haven't made a move without checking with you first." I was seething.

"Do you want everyone to hear you?"

"You know what? I don't care if the whole restaurant hears me, 'cause I'm sick of this shit." I picked up my water glass, took a swallow, and then slammed it down on the table.

"Well, I never!" she gasped.

"Oh, stop your drama, Mother. Everything's always about you and your drama. Well, guess what? I'm going. That's right. I'm leaving and maybe I'm not coming back," I took another drink off my water and tipped it toward her. "So how do ya like that?" I said.

"You are cruel, you know that? Selfish and cruel, just like your father."

"Mother, if you think that was cruel, why don't you wake up and look around you? Your eldest son can't stand you and you fall all over yourself every time he decides to give you the time of day. But I'm cruel?" I shook my head in disbelief.

"That was low. How could you?"

Always melodrama.

"Oh please, whether you want to see it or not, it's not me who's selfish . . . and guess what?" I stood up from the table. "I've had it, I'm done—baked—fried—I can't take one more thing from you or anyone else. And you know what? Screw you."

I walked out of the restaurant and did what anyone in my situation might have—I sold everything I owned, dyed my hair blonder, and moved to Europe with Giancarlo.

But first I had to make a pit stop. And then I knew everything would be okay!

Lucky Seven?

OKAY, SO WE DIDN'T EXACTLY MOVE to Europe right away. Giancarlo's mother gave him a lump of money so he could go back to school and get a degree in something other than mixing music and playing tennis. She supported our relationship and thought I was his guardian angel. And because my AA friend Deborah had been bugging me to come live near her in Santa Barbara, Giancarlo and I took an apartment down there. Everything would have been okay, too, if Giancarlo hadn't taken his tuition money and snorted it up his left nostril, and then sold the car his mother bought us and snorted that up his right nostril. But now I'm getting ahead of myself.

"Maryanne, you can't just sit there all night waiting for Giancarlo," said my new friend Lena, who lived across the street from us in Santa Barbara.

"What if he doesn't come home again?" I cried.

"He's with Matt; don't worry, they'll be home like two puppies as soon as they run out of coke."

"It's been three days, Lena," I reminded her.

"I know, honey. They're just having a good time, that's all."

"We're supposed to get married tomorrow, Lena. Don't you think it's better if he's there?" I burst out crying.

"I know, sweetie. Don't worry. He'll be there. We'll all be there. Don't cry. You know what we need?"

"What?" I whimpered.

"A cocktail!" she said. "Get dressed. I'll be there to get you in two minutes." And she was.

I had spent the last three weeks housebound with anxiety. I couldn't drive, I couldn't sleep, I couldn't eat, my mouth tasted like metal, and I could barely breathe. At various times of the day the attacks were so bad that my hands would cramp up and parts of my body would literally become paralyzed. This thing that had secretly plagued me for going on four years was worse than it had ever been, even though I didn't know what "it" was yet. If there was any such thing as a "panic disorder" diagnosis at that time, I sure didn't know about it. I don't think that anxiety disorders were fully recognized as the crippling, debilitating psychological disaster, they can be.

"So this can be like your bachelorette party," announced Lena as we drove less than a half mile from our street to a favored watering hole for the bold and the beautiful.

"That's so nice," was all I could say. Literally.

"Look, I know you're upset with Giancarlo, but guys are like that, Maryanne. They're messed up! I mean, Matt has done this so many times. That's why I usually won't even let him get near that stuff anymore because this is what always happens."

"Uh-huh," I said, so she'd know I was listening.

"Come on, we're here! Let's forget about those guys. Let's go have some fun." It sounded good to me. I was up for anything that would make this abysmal thing get out of me. A drink, a sawed-off shotgun, whatever. Fortunately they were fresh out of shotguns, but had plenty to drink. And eventually, so did I. I threw AA out the window along with any other tools I had accumulated along the way that could have kept me sane and sober.

Halfway through my first top-shelf margarita, I could breathe again. I didn't even like margaritas, but for the first time in months I could relax. I didn't realize that I was about to throw out not only my sobriety but all the hard work that I had done for the past five years.

"Can we get a pitcher?" I asked the bartender, holding up my glass.

Lena broke into a great big smile and said, "What the hell, who knows when those assholes will be home. Let's get drunk." We clinked our glasses together. "Here's to getting drunk," she said. We clinked our glasses together again.

"No wait, here's to getting even," I said. We took another sip and clinked again.

"No, here's one. Here's to getting laid." That wasn't anything I would have normally clinked to, but I clinked anyway.

"No. Wait, wait. Here's to getting that good-looking guy over there to buy the next pitcher," I said. We drank, clinked once more, and then laughed uncontrollably.

"Here's to getting you two to move down so we can order a drink," said some dweeby little guy who was leaning on Lena's back, trying to get the bartender's attention. We looked at each other and burst out laughing again.

"Here's to being over five feet tall," said Lena, and sucked down the rest of her drink.

"I'll drink to that," I said, raising my glass to our new little friend who was suddenly struck with generosity and good cheer.

"And whatever they're having . . ." he said, reaching between us, handing the bartender a hundred-dollar bill. "Big things come in small packages," he whispered in my ear. "Drinks are on me, girls," he announced, and then disappeared into the crowded bar.

"Guh-ross," I said, out loud.

"What did he say to you?" she said, dying of curiosity.

"I don't even want to repeat it. Pig."

"Who cares. Let's get another pitcher."

"Good idea!"

"Here's to getting another pitcher," she said.

"Do you think cavemen laughed?" I said, trying not to fall off my barstool.

"What?" said Lena, emptying out what was left in our third pitcher into her glass.

"Cavemen? You know. Do you think they laughed?" I said, again trying not to slur my words.

"How the hell should I know?" she said, closing one eye, trying to keep me in focus.

"I mean, what was funny?" She stared at me through the bottom of her glass and shrugged her shoulders as she downed the last of her drink. "You see, that's exactly my point," I said. "Nothing was funny."

"Mmm," she said, holding up her finger. "I think I'm going to throw up."

"When will you be sure?"

"I wanna go home," was the last thing she said before she slid off her seat and hit the floor. It was definitely time to go.

★★★★

"Okay, all right, come on. Up. Stand up, Lena, I can't get you into the car unless you get off the ground," I said, trying to lift her.

"I don't feel so good," she said, lying in my arms like a one-hundred-thirty-pound rag doll.

"Come on, get up, we only have a little way to drive." I was having trouble standing up myself. "There we go, watch your feet," I said, stuffing her into the passenger seat of her convertible Porsche and closing the door.

"I'm going to throw up again," she said, squishing her face against the window.

"No you're not. We're going to be home in two seconds," I said, starting the car.

"Air. I need air," she panted, as I backed out of our spot.

"Here," I said, trying to find the button to open the windows. "There, zat better?" I asked triumphantly, trying to keep one of my eyes on the road. She was out.

"Okay, I can do this. Two exits and then we're home," I said to myself, out loud. The problem was there were too many lanes and I couldn't decide on which one to be in, and on top of that some butthead was right on my ass, totally making me nervous.

The butthead turned out to be two female highway patrol officers. Here's to drinking and driving. I was screwed.

"Can I see your driver's license and registration, miss?" asked the officer, shining a flashlight in my eyes.

"God, that's so bright. Do you have to—" I said, trying to block the light out of my eyes.

"Your driver's license, please," she said again. I reached around for my purse behind me.

"What's the matter, did I do something, officer?"

"We've been following you for the last half mile. You were weaving pretty recklessly in and out of lanes."

"I know. It's not my car . . . officer . . . ma'am. My friend was . . . is sick. So I drove and . . ." I replied, handing her my license. She directed her flashlight on it and then in my eyes again.

"Can you please step out of the car, miss?"

"Okay," I said, flinging the door open and trying to stand up without seeming too drunk. I figured I wasn't going to be able to hide the fact that I was drunk, but I didn't want to make a complete fool of myself. "I know I shouldn't be driving, officer, but my girlfriend was throwing up and she couldn't drive so, anyway, I did." I smiled, hoping she liked me, which seemed important at the time. "We only live, like, one second from . . . see, right there," I pointed over toward the beach.

"Could you step over away from the freeway please?"

"Okay," I said, trying hard to walk normally.

"Hold up your hand, please. I want you to count to five forward and backward, like this," she said, doing something with her fingers that I couldn't quite make out.

"I'm sorry, could you do that again. I didn't get . . . What? Like what?" I asked, totally confused.

"One, two, three, fo, fife, two, three, fo, one. Like this?" I smiled, hoping I got it right.

"Have you been drinking tonight, miss?"

"Oh, *yeah*. My God. So many. We had a lot of margaritas. Well, I mean not sooo many, but Lena threw up. She—we didn't eat dinner."

"Stay right here please, miss," said the lady officer, walking back to talk to the other officer. I stood there like a scarecrow, waiting for her to tell me what to do next. Cars that sounded like Jetsonmobiles were whizzing past like mini streams of light. The effect was starting to make me dizzy. "I'm sorry, miss, but you're under arrest for drunk driving," said the heftier of the two officers, slapping a handcuff on one of my wrists.

"Just a . . . no . . . I told you, I'm sorry. I know I shouldn't have been driving," I said, trying to wriggle away from the handcuff, "but she was barfing everywhere. I had to bring her home and . . . Please, if you could just take us home, we live right—"

"I'm sorry, miss. We'll get your friend home, but we're going to have to book you."

"Book me? What? Like a crime booking?" I said. "Ouch! Don't do that. Please, you're hurting me. I don't need these," I said, wriggling around like a dog trying to get free from his collar. The officer opened the back door of the patrol car and firmly guided me inside, pressing her hand on the top of my head so I wouldn't hurt myself. "Really, this is not my fault. I was driving her car. This is a mistake. If you just take me home I promise, I will never drink and drive again," I pleaded.

It was all so lovely, really—jail. They let me out of my handcuffs so that I could pose for my photo shoot. Turn to the left, turn to the right, stand up sit down, fight, fight, fight! Actually, there wasn't any cheering and, unfortunately, this wasn't a game. But more importantly, this was not my fault. Lena was the one who was drunk. I was just trying to help. She should have been in here instead of me. And I wasn't the only one who thought so.

"Got any smokes?" said the slight figure lying on the steel bunk on the other side of the cell.

"I don't smoke," I said, folding my arms tightly across my chest. I was at first pleasantly surprised. I'd thought I was alone. And under the circumstances I might have been comforted by some company. However, upon closer inspection of the figure strewn over the bed across from me, it was evident someone had made a terrible mistake. "Excuse me! Hello! Person! Yoohooo. I need to speak to someone, please," I called out down the dark hall. To no avail, I'm afraid. I lay back down, exasperated that no one was listening to me.

'How dare they! They can't just put me in here with some lunatic,' I fumed.

"You gonna eat that?" asked the craggy old woman, pointing at the bag lunch that I was using for a pillow. I lay there for a second, contemplating ignoring her, but I decided that I'd better answer her.

I'd seen what happened to Erica on *All My Children* when she was in jail, and it wasn't pretty.

"Here, have it," I said, sliding the bag over to her side of the room. I watched her out of morbid curiosity as she scavenged the contents of the brown paper sack, while I tried to decide exactly how scared I should be. Aside from the fact that she appeared to have no teeth (which only made me wonder how she was going to eat anything, particularly the apple she was now holding in her hand), she couldn't have weighed more than a hundred pounds soaking wet. So on a scary scale of one to ten, I wasn't very—scared, that is.

Clearly this woman had been raised in a cave; she had no manners. She didn't even say thank you. And she mashed rather than chewed—with her mouth open. I thought I was going to be sick. I sat up again, this time slipping my shoes off. I banged one against the bars.

"Helloo out there. People! I need to speak to someone. I don't feel well. Please, someone," I cried out with mild urgency.

'I cannot believe this. What the hell kind of place is this? I mean, what if I were really sick or something? Someone's going to hear about this,' I thought, spitefully.

"How long they gonna keep you here?" asked the woman as she smushed the sandwich with her gums into some sort of paste.

"Hopefully not long," I said, trying not to watch her eat so I wouldn't puke.

"Nice girl like you, why, they oughta let you go," she said, smacking her lips and rummaging through the rest of the bag.

"Yes, well, you happen to be right. I actually shouldn't even be here," I said. Just then a rotund Hispanic officer walked up to the cell.

"Miss DelRiccio?"

"Yes," I said, actually having sobered up. 'Finally,' I thought, quickly sitting up.

"You can make your phone call now," he offered, and opened the gate.

"Phone call? You mean you're not going to let me go?" I asked, with still a tiny bit of hope.

"I'm only here to take you to the phone."

"Oh," I said, terribly disappointed. "Do you know what time it is?" I asked, following almost on top of him.

"Uh-huh. It's just about three a.m."

"Do you know when they will let me go home?"

"Usually after eight hours, unless we're real busy."

"So if you're really busy, that means I can go earlier?"

"No, then it could be longer," he said. "Phone's right in here. You have five minutes," he said, and closed the gate.

"Uhmmm, excuse me, I'm sorry to bother you, but since it doesn't seem very busy and, well, the other cell rooms or whatever seem to be, you know, empty and everything, do you think I could have my own room? I'm not comfortable with that lady. I mean, she smells and it's making me sick, so if you wouldn't mind. . . ?" I asked, politely. He just chuckled and walked away.

'Why isn't anyone listening to me?' I thought. I was incensed. "I'm not kidding. I don't feel well," I shouted after him.

'I need to get out of here. I need to talk to someone who will listen to me,' I thought. Although it had been about a year, I knew exactly who to call.

"Hello," I heard faintly on the other end of the phone.

"Rob?" I said. "I'm so sorry to wake you. It's me, Maryanne. Are you awake?"

"Maryanne? What time is it?" he asked, yawning.

"It's three."

"Where are you? Are you okay?"

"No. I'm not okay," I said, still fuming. "I'm in jail!" I held the phone away from my head, expecting him to yell.

"Maryanne? Helllooo, Maryanne?" I could hear him saying something so I put the phone back to my head.

"Yes, I'm here, sorry. What did you say?"

"I said, what are you doing in jail?"

"It's a long story and I only have five minutes—well, probably four now."

"Well, what did you do?"

"I got pulled over for drunk driving."

"But you don't even drink."

"I know, I told you it's a long story. Anyway, they said they're going to let me go on my own recognizance after I've been here for eight hours." That was a big word; I don't know how I got that one out.

"That's not bad. How long have you been there?"

"Uhmmmm, about one minute." He laughed.

"It's not funny. There's some lady in my area—she's old and smells like urine and . . ." I began. He kept laughing. "Stop it. It's really not funny."

"I'm sorry, you're right."

"And anyway, she has no teeth and she ate my lunch and my pillow, and now this little man won't even let me have my own room. Can they do that? I mean, what if I really do get sick or something?"

"Maryanne, don't cause any trouble, just do what they say. You'll be out of there before you know it."

"Well, what happens when I have to go to the bathroom? I mean, there's no way I'm going in front of someone. What if someone walks by, Rob? Uh-oh, here comes the little guy. I think I have to go. Thank you, Rob. I'm so sorry for waking you up."

"Try and get some rest. You'll be fine. Call me if you need anything," he said.

"Thanks," I said, and hung up.

"Rest? Who could rest in a place like this?" I grumbled as I walked back to my cell. "Gee, thanks," I said, as the guard opened the door for me.

'I wish I were home in bed, curled up under my comforter,' I thought as I sat down on the steel plank of a bed. My eyes filled with tears. 'I just want to go home; I don't belong here,' I thought.

"They gonna let you out?" asked the old hag, interrupting my pity party.

"No," I whined. "Stupid place." I leaned back against the cold cement wall.

"Well, if you get outta here before I do, will you do me a favor?"

"What?" I asked, completely annoyed.

"Will you call my kids and tell them where I am?"

"Your kids?" I said, shocked by the notion.

"Oh, never mind, I forgot, they shut the phone off. Maybe you could go by and tell 'em yourself then, huh?"

"You have children?" She must have been at least sixty.

"I've got three—four, seven, and eleven. Two boys and a girl—she's the youngest."

"And they're yours?"

"That's right, 'cept they all got different daddies," she explained.

"And they don't know where you are right now?" I asked, reluctant to even be having this conversation.

"Nope, I didn't have a chance to tell 'em before I got picked up this time."

"Well, didn't the police tell them or go and get them?"

"Oh no, last time I told Terry—the oldest—to take the little ones and get out of the house so's they wouldn't have to go to no foster home."

"Well, how will they know what to do? They don't even know you're here," I said, now holding my stomach.

"That's right, and ain't none a my kids goin' to no foster home."

"That's awful. So where are they now?" I asked, not sure if I wanted to know.

"Oh, they'll be fine," she tossed at me.

"You know what? Never mind. This is none of my business. I'm sorry. I'm getting married tomorrow—today—and I wish I could help you, but . . ."

"That's good," she said. "My little girl's getting married next weekend."

"Wait. I thought you said your daughter was four."

"Oh yeah, that was the baby. Terry always called her his little baby."

'Okay, that's it,' I thought. 'This woman is totally wacko and I need to just breathe. Stay calm, Maryanne. There's no need to panic.

She's not going to hurt you; just close your eyes and pretend you're asleep. You're getting married in about twelve hours and next week you'll be on a plane to Europe. It will be as if this this whole place never existed. Everything is going to be okay.'

When Giancarlo said, "Marry me and I'll take you away from all this," I didn't flinch. I couldn't say yes fast enough. I didn't see that I was walking from the frying pan into the fire, from one horror to the next. And I certainly didn't stop long enough to figure that the one common denominator in my life was me. I just kept running, thinking that I was headed to some safe place.

And as far as Giancarlo's dogged pursuit of me, well, this was the only proof I had that I was worth anything. If he wanted me, I must be worth something, right? It was what I knew. My panic attacks were now so debilitating that there was no way you could have convinced me that there would be any other takers for such damaged goods. Jesus, I could barely leave the house. My mouth tasted of metal from grinding my teeth and not sleeping. I was a wreck. Survival mode took over, and I had all but forgotten about my connection with any power greater than myself. For me life had become black or white: I was either going to live or I was going to die.

How I made it to my wedding is a mystery to me. Luckily, the ceremony, across the street in our neighbors' backyard, was short and sweet. They were our only friends, so by default they became best man and matron of honor. Just for the record, he was Giancarlo's cocaine dealer. She was his wife—and, by the way, she was also the woman whose barfing her guts up was responsible for my being thrown in jail. The only other witness to the ceremony was their dog, who was blind in one eye.

★★★★

"Miss DelRiccio? Miss DelRiccio?" said the woman's voice.

"Huh, what?" I shot up out of a half-sleep. A normal person

would have been startled; I almost jumped out of my skin.

"I'm sorry to wake you, but we're about to land, so if you could put your seat in the upright position . . ."

'We're here! God, finally,' I thought.

"Giancarlo, wake up," I said, shaking him. "We're here!" Barely awake and totally sleep-deprived, we gathered our carry-ons and shuffled off the plane.

'Ohh, I am soo excited. I am in Europe,' I thought, as we made a beeline toward the baggage claim. My mind was swimming with romantic thoughts of decaf cappuccinos and the French Riviera and people named Angelo and Angelina. I was fantasizing about shopping for shoes in the piazza in Milan, when I was abruptly interrupted by a man wearing an automatic machine gun and green fatigues. He was holding a ferocious-looking German shepherd that was trying to sniff my crotch. Not quite the welcome I was expecting.

"*Ciao, Papá, ciao,*" Giancarlo hollered, flagging his father from across the baggage area.

"*Ciao, Ciccio, come va?*" said the austere, thick little man as he neared us. I put my bags down expectantly and smiled. I had heard so much about his father—Giancarlo made him out to be the Italian Superman. He walked right past me. The two of them hugged like lovers—which I thought was very strange—while I stood there, apparently invisible. They exchanged more kisses and then started yammering in Italian, still oblivious to my presence. They carried on—about what, I had no idea, because I couldn't understand what the hell they were saying.

"Uhhh, hello, people," I said, impatiently. "Aren't you going to introduce us?" I asked my new husband. The honeymoon was over and suddenly I was in no mood.

"Oh, *Dio,* I'm sorry. Maryanne. This is my father, Vincenzo," he said, putting our hands together.

"Hello," I said, trying to ignore his rudeness. After all, it was his only son and they hadn't seen each other in months.

His father handed me a box of unwrapped chocolates, kissed me on both cheeks, and then said something to Giancarlo in Italian. I knew by the way he was looking at me that what he said wasn't in my favor. I already didn't like him. I just wanted to go to bed.

"Come, we go and take a drink," he stammered, impressed by his own ability to utter something resembling English. I glared at Giancarlo. He meekly shrugged his shoulders and grabbed my bags, and threw them in the car.

Vincenzo had a brand-new M3 and Giancarlo explained, after he pulled my fingernails out of his arm, that in Europe, sports cars can go a lot faster because they are not required to have steel in the doors like in America. After which I mentioned that if his father drove any faster and didn't pick a lane, I was going to have to hurt someone.

Clearly what I wanted was of little importance to Vincenzo, because he decided we were all hungry and took us to a little restaurant called Camelot. Which would have been a good choice had I been at all hungry. Or if wearing sweats and tennis shoes to a five-star restaurant after not bathing for twenty-two hours were chic.

"You like the glamour in California?" asked Vincenzo in his very broken English, showing off his choice in restaurants.

"Yes, normally we do, Vincenzo, but we Americans are funny. We typically don't like to embarrass our new friends and visitors from far away by taking them to a fancy restaurant until they have had a chance to bathe," I said, indignantly. He looked at me, puzzled. Giancarlo looked as though he were holding his breath, and then his father let out an enormous laugh.

"You are funny girl," he said. "I'm sorry my English is not so good. I'm not understand what you said." I studied him suspiciously.

"Really? Your English sounds pretty good to me," I said, and then smiled at Giancarlo, who had gotten very quiet and was apparently trying to give me some kind of hand signal.

"So, tell me, Nicky . . ."

"That's Maryanne," I corrected him.

"Madonna," he attempted.

"Mar-y-anne," I repeated.

"No, I can't do it. I call you Nicky."

"Why is he calling me Nicky? Who's Nicky?" I looked at

Giancarlo. He shrugged his shoulders and started pounding his wine. "Look, Vinny, my name is Maryanne—M-A-R-Y-A-N-N-E."

"No, look," he said, pointing to my tennis shoes.

"What? This? Nike?"

"*Certo,* Nicky. *Si.* I mean, yes," he said. Now I officially hated him. He was renaming me after a shoe. That was undignified.

"That's not a name. Nike's a brand. Like Puma or Fila or Versace, you understand?"

"Okay! That's what I call you from-a now on—Nicky!" he said, and that was that.

Just as I was about to launch my finger into his father's face, further explaining why you don't rename individuals without their permission—unless of course you are my father or happen to be an Apache chief—Giancarlo reached over and intercepted my finger.

"Are you hungry, 'oney?" he asked, changing the subject.

"I don't care. I'll have what everyone else is having—'oney. So get whatever," I said, folding my arms and crossing my legs away from both of them.

"So, Nicky, Giancarlo says you are a model, eh? You look so big for to be a model," he said, stuffing a piece of bread in his mouth and taking a sip off his wine to wash it down. Okay, now I was going to have to kill him, one way or another.

"Really? Hmmm, I can see how you would feel that way. Gosh, compared to you, I must seem enormous." I wanted to wrap my hand around his throat and strangle him until his eyes bulged out of his head. "It's funny, too, because you're so much shorter and balder than I pictured you. You and Giancarlo are so different, almost opposite, in fact. I mean, he's so tall and handsome and all," I said, as I stuffed a piece of bread in my mouth, grabbed Giancarlo's glass out of his hand, and swallowed the rest of his wine down.

"I'm sorry, what is . . . bald-er?" asked Vincenzo, hanging on my every word, preparing for battle.

"Maybe you want drink some water?" asked Giancarlo. I stuck out my wine glass, signifying its emptiness, still staring at his father. Just then the food arrived.

"What's this?" I said, frightened to ask. It looked like it might still be alive.

"*Seppia*," was the only answer I got. His father put a nice large helping on my plate and smiled.

"Giancarlo said you having some problems with . . . how you call it? Alcohol," he said, taking a sip of his wine, savoring his retort. I pushed my plate away, disgusted by the gelatinous muck.

"Actually, Vinny—you don't mind if I call you Vinny? Good! My problem was more with drugs, like your son. But I don't do drugs anymore, so it's really not a problem," I said, shoving another piece of bread in my mouth and smiling. "So, I understand you're having some problems with gambling," I said, taking another swig off my wine. His father smiled politely and then said something to Giancarlo in Italian. "What? Did I say something to offend?" I asked, gloating, certain I had.

"My father, he wants to know if you like, uhhh, Chianti," said Giancarlo, who had turned about as white as the tablecloth.

"Sure, Chianti, Spumante, I'll have whatever he's having," I said, flippantly. His father nudged him and again they exchanged Italian sentiments.

"My father says we will stay with him for a while until we get our own apartment." I about fell off my chair. Vincenzo looked over at me and held up his glass.

"*Salute,*" he said, with a wicked smile on his face.

'Why, that fat little . . .'

"Touché," I said, and guzzled down the rest of my wine. I couldn't have been happier if I'd have poked my own eyes out.

It was bad enough I was now related to him, but having to live with an Italian Yosemite Sam was more than I could bear. Somehow I managed to find a job at a ladies health club that was a bus ride away from our flat. It was that or take up smoking while I watched ten-year-old reruns of *Days of Our Lives* dubbed in Italian, or soccer. Both were about as appealing as discussing the relative merits of crushing grapes with clean feet or dirty feet. Besides, I wanted to learn to speak Italian, and how was I going to learn if I sat home by myself? It's true, I did speak some Italian already. I had learned how to swear fluently, my father's cultural contribution to his progeny. As for the proper vernacular, I had made a deal with the girls at the club, who wanted to learn to speak better English as much as I wanted to learn to speak Italian, that they would only speak to me in English and I could only speak to them in Italian.

Just inside of a month I was amazed by my progress. I had learned enough directives to be an air traffic controller at Malpensa Airport. *Su, giú, su giú. A sinistra, a destra, a sinistra, a destra.* Up down, up down, left right, left right. How cool was that, Italian aerobics? Wait, can you say, "Colombian drug lord"?

★★★★

"Giancarlo? *Ciccio? Chi sono?"* I said, looking around as I walked through the front door of our penthouse flat. Every time I walked through the door my heart sang "Joy to the World." Finally, after months of matrimonial reprimand, at last we had our own sanctuary in Lugano, Switzerland. A three-thousand-square-foot reprieve from his horrid little monster of a father. Our flat was the only one in the building. Across the hall was a dentist's office, and beneath us were a furrier, two jewelers, a movie theatre, and a nightclub. What else did anyone need? I couldn't think of anything.

'Hmm, I wonder where he is,' I thought, setting the groceries down in our pristine little kitchen. I started to unpack and the phone rang. I ran over to pick it up.

"*Pronto,*" I said.

"*Ce,* Giancarlo?" said a man with a gravelly voice.

"*No, mi dispiace, Giancarlo non ce,*" I said, trying to disguise my obviously American accent.

"Do you know where is Giancarlo?" asked the man, recognizing I spoke English.

"No, I'm sorry, I just arrived myself and he isn't home."

"*Grazie,*" he said, and hung up.

'That was strange,' I thought. I didn't recognize his voice. We had only lived there a few weeks and hardly anybody had our number— mostly family and a few friends, like his best friends, Giorgio and Andrea. The latter who I adored, the former who I abhorred. And the feelings were definitely mutual.

No sooner had I put the phone back on the receiver than it rang again with that funny European chirp. I spun around, doing a one-eighty, and headed back toward the phone.

"*Pronto,*" I said.

"'Oney? *Sono io.* How are you?" asked Giancarlo.

"Where are you?" I said, my voice harsh. "I thought you were going to be home when I got here."

"I know, I know, 'oney; you can't believe the problems we having down . . . over here. I am home this night," he promised. I noticed his English was getting progressively worse and that he rarely spoke English to me at all anymore.

"Your mother is coming tomorrow from Leno; she couldn't come back with me. Your grandfather wasn't feeling well."

"*Tutto a posto?*" he asked, out of breath.

"He's fine, don't worry, he's just got a bad cold. Are you okay? You sound strange, Cheech."

"*Va bene,* I am okay."

"You sure? You sound like you've been drinking or something. You didn't drink, did you?" I asked, worried as usual that he had fallen off the wagon.

Our relationship was based more on pure need than on love. I needed him in order to escape the madness of my life, and he needed me to run interference in his. Giancarlo had lost his last job as an international trader due to drugs and alcohol. Oh, and for embezzling money from one of his clients. Now he was working with his father doing some sales thing. I didn't really know too much about it.

"Non worry. Why you don't go shopping, get something beautiful like you, and we go out to celebrate, *si?*" he said. That always put me in a good mood. Shopping. Even the sound of it . . . Now I was sufficiently placated.

"What time will you be in?"

"*Otto e mezzo.* I say to Adrienne we meet him for something to drink at Morandis."

"Good, that will be fun, okay. I'll see you in a little . . . Oh, wait. Some guy called for you just now. He said he would call back."

"*Come ti chiami?*" he asked, now very serious.

"I don't know; he didn't say and I didn't ask, but he sounded older, if that helps."

"It's okay, it's nothing," he said. "*Ciao bella, Ciao. Ciao, ci vediamo,*" he said, and hung up.

"*Ciao, ciao,*" I said, although he was already gone.

'What's nothing?' I thought. 'And why does everyone here have to say *ciao* ten times before we hang up? I start to hang up and then I hear something so I put the phone back to my head, and it's only them saying *ciao* again, so I have to say *ciao* again. Whatever . . . I'm going shopping. But first I need to make room.'

I decided to unpack from my trip down to see his mom and grandparents, who I absolutely adored, and then went downstairs to the cellar to put away my bags. I saw something sticking out of another suitcase that was lying on the floor, so I bent down to get a closer look. It looked like a plastic pouch of some sort. I pulled it out. Actually, it was a small, clear bundle filled with what looked like— powder. I reached inside the suitcase to see if anything else was in there, and sure enough, more bundles of white stuff. So I unzipped the whole suitcase. Yep, the whole darn thing was brimming with little bundles of white powdery stuff.

'This isn't baking soda, Maryanne. It isn't laundry soap either.' "Oh shit," I said, out loud. The largest quantity of coke I had ever seen was about an ounce, and it was stored in clear sandwich baggies—nothing compared to this pro job.

Then I spun around, totally spooked, and shut the door of our storage area. Not that I'd ever seen anyone down in that dank, gloomy space. No one ever used it but us. Still, I wasn't taking any chances. Then I heard something. It sounded like a door opening.

In two seconds flat I took the package of powder I was holding and chucked it back in the suitcase like a hot potato, closed the cover, and zipped it up. Then I shoved it with my foot back where I'd found it and stood perfectly still, waiting to see if someone was there. My head was racing with possibilities. Maybe it was Giancarlo, or maybe it was the police, or someone saw me come down here, or it was the cellar monster—like Freddy Krueger.

I waited a few more minutes before I dared to stick my head out to make sure the coast was clear. I quickly shut the door behind me and then tried to act normal, like nothing was unusual, as I walked over to the elevator, which everyone here called a lift. It was in use, which only amplified my suspicions. Who would be in the building on a Friday evening? I mean, who buys jewelry on a Friday night in Switzerland? Nobody, unless you were, like, desperate for a fifty-thousand-dollar cocktail ring before you caught the show. My stream of semi-delusional rationalization was interrupted by the lift door opening painfully slowly.

'Oh God, what if someone's in there and they have a gun and they're going to kill me?' That's all I had time to think before the door started to close. When no one lunged out I figured the coast was clear. Unless they were on top of the lift and were going to jump off through the top of the cage and attack me that way.

'Hurry. Hurry,' I thought. 'I just want to get upstairs. Wait, though. What if whoever took the lift before me is waiting for me in the apartment? No one will be able to hear me scream. They wouldn't even be able to hear the gunshot.' The lift jolted up and then down, signaling the end of the line. As the door opened I half expected to be greeted by a couple of thugs strapped with semiautomatics. But I wasn't, so I got out of the lift and cautiously crept down the hall. When I arrived at my front door, I grabbed the handle to make sure it was locked. It was.

'Whew,' I thought. 'Okay, they wouldn't lock me out if they wanted to kill me, but maybe they're right behind me. Hurry, hurry. Maryanne, unlock the door. Oh my God, the key won't go in. Hurry up!' I finally shoved the key in the lock, slipped inside, slammed the enormous wood door shut, and leaned my back against it, breathing hard. 'There, I'm in.'

Just when it seemed safe, I heard a knock. I jumped away from the door. I knew it! One of my worst fears was about to come true. Someone was going to get me. They had been waiting in the dark until I was alone and no one would see anything.

ZZZZZZZZZZZ, the doorbell insisted.

I panicked. 'Who was that? No one can get in here unless someone from inside the building buzzed them up, or they have a key. And no one really knows me anyway—okay, except the jewelers—but I'm sure they're gone.'

'Oh, wait a minute. Maybe Giancarlo lost his key,' I thought as I pressed against the door like Spiderman, poised to leap off my perch. I braved a shout. "Giancarlo?"

No one answered.

'Good, this is good; maybe they went away,' I thought. I let go of my breath.

"Is anybody there?" I asked, hoping against hope that no one was. 'Perhaps they didn't hear me.' I pressed my ear against the door to see if I could hear something, for any clue to whether they were still lurking outside my door.

Just when I had convinced myself that I could finally relax, I heard a man's deep, gruff voice reply in a delayed reaction to my inquiry: "Gino?"

'Oh my God, someone *is* there and he's going to kill me,' was all I could think. 'Okay, what do I do, what do I do? Uhhhhh, think . . . think, Maryanne.'

"Uhhhmmm, sorry. I think you have the wrong apartment," I said, off the top of my head, hoping to God it was true.

Then after another long pause, "*Che* Giancarlo?" said the husky voice.

'Oh *Madonna*,' I thought, stressing out in Italian now. 'Okay, shit.'
"Uhhh, Giancarlo's not here right now," I said, trying not to fully freak out.

"Can you please open the door?" he said with a heavy accent.

'Open the door? What does he think, I'm crazy? Wait a minute. I recognize that voice. It sounds like the man who called earlier. Maybe he's the pickup guy for the drugs in the cellar and is supposed to meet Giancarlo here. Or maybe Giancarlo stole the drugs from him and he's come to get them back and he's going to torture me until I tell him where they are and then kill me.'

"Please, open the door, I want only to speak with you for one moment."

'But he doesn't sound like a killer. Wait, what am I saying?'

"Uhhh, just a minute please, I have to get . . ." My eyes darted around the room for anything that looked like a weapon. "Here I come," I said, grabbing one of the silver candlesticks Giancarlo's mother gave us as a housewarming gift. I took a deep breath and slowly unbolted the door, carefully opening it, ducking my head in case he shoved his automatic in the door. I held the candlestick behind my back—in case I had a sudden stroke of bravery.

"Do you know where is Giancarlo?" asked the stout man with a tightly groomed beard and black leather jacket. His tone and manner were surprisingly pleasant. Still, I was too afraid to look into his eyes.

"I'm sorry, he's not home right now. He should be back about eight thirty or so. He is on his way home from a trip and he's late so . . . I mean, he was supposed to. . . Can I tell him . . . leave him a message?" I said, offering way too much information. I was grateful I wasn't lying dead on the floor in a pool of my own blood yet.

"Thank you, yes. Only this—that Gino would like to speak to him as soon as possible." He smiled, exposing his espresso-stained teeth, and held out his hand for mine and kissed it. "Giancarlo, he's a lucky man," he said. I was taken completely off guard.

"Uhh, oh, thank you." I blushed. He stared at me for a second and then brushed his hands through his slick, dark hair. I smiled, not knowing what else to say, hoping he was going to leave now, when I noticed something black and shiny tucked in the front of his pants. I knew guns, and that was a .357 Magnum. I knew because I'd had one. "Okay, so I'll tell Giancarlo to call you as soon as he gets here. Okay?" I said, starting to close the door as he turned to walk away. He didn't say anything, he just slowly disappeared into a silhouette in the dark hallway. I could see him studying my face in the dusky light inside the lift just before the gate closed. I will never forget the way he stared right at me. It chilled me to the bone.

I waited until I heard the lift stop at the bottom, and still longer until I heard the faint *clank* of the front door carry up into the building. I had to make sure he had really gone. Then I collapsed. I was too exhausted to cry and not even sure what had just happened. At this point everything seemed blurry. Until it occurred to me to be pissed off.

'That bastard! He lied to me—again. He promised he wouldn't bring any of that shit near our house. Goddammit, I knew it. When he gets home . . .'

✦✦✦✦

"Melissa? It's Maryanne. I'm sorry to be calling at this hour. Are you guys eating?" I asked, trying to be polite. I knew her fiancé was very old fashioned and didn't like to be interrupted at dinner.

"No, we're done. Alex is reading the paper," she said, with the faintest Southern drawl. Melissa was originally from Dallas. She had moved to Switzerland eight years before and worked as a dental hygienist. She had met Allessandro a few months after she arrived and they had been together ever since. Melissa and I, on the other hand, had only known each other for a little over a year.

"Melissa, remember when I told you I thought something weird was going on with Giancarlo?"

"Which time?" she said, sarcastically.

"I'm serious!"

"I'm sorry, sweetie. It's just that you already know what I think about him."

"I know you hate when I talk about him . . . but this is different."

"Hang on, Maryanne. Let me go in the other room. Alex is waving me out of here. He's trying to watch the game," she said. "Okay, that's better. Now I can talk."

"Anyway, Giancarlo said he was going out of town to some sales convention in Bari. He was supposed to be back yesterday," I started to explain.

"So, what's so weird about that?" I could hear her doing the dishes in the background.

"Bari? Come on Melissa, who has a convention in Bari?"

"I see your point, but still, maybe he just mixed up his words. English is his . . . what? Fourth language?"

"Okay, maybe. But then who is Gino, and what are all the bags of white powder doing down in our cellar?"

"I don't know what you're talking about—what bags?" she said, crunching on something.

"I went downstairs to put away my luggage from my trip and found my big suitcase stuffed with bags of white stuff, and then some guy named Gino shows up, who somehow gets inside our building and . . ." I said, now ranting.

"Maryanne? Maryanne. Stop. I don't want to know about this," she said, firmly.

"Great, so what am I supposed to do?"

"I told you about that family, and if I were you I would get on the first plane and get out of here. I have to hang up now," she said, and did.

I knew Melissa was right. I was in danger. But where was I going to go? Back home? I had come here for the express purpose of getting away from home. But this had turned out to be just as bad—the only difference was, my life here had subtitles.

I had an idea. I would talk to Andrea. He was French. French people always know how to handle situations like these and still look good.

"Halloo, Maryanne, how are you?" said Andrea, warmly, when he heard it was me on the phone.

"Great, fine," I lied. How are things going at work?" Andrea had been Giancarlo's partner at the bank where Giancarlo no longer worked.

"Super, things are going well here," he replied. I still couldn't get used to the European formality of small talk. It was tedious and seemed a giant waste of time. Still, out of respect and so as not to frighten off my potential comrade, I indulged. "How's your mother?"

"She's actually doing much better. My aunt is here and will probably stay on now that they are both alone."

"Well, that's nice for them."

"Yes, but my mother can be difficult. She is very bossy, you know," he said, and chuckled.

"How did you get to be so sweet then?" I teased. "You must take after your father."

"Oh, I don't know," he said, with a hint of embarrassment.

"So, anyway. I was wondering if I could talk to you."

"Talk? Sure, of course."

"No, I mean later tonight. Actually I was hoping we could meet before Giancarlo arrives."

"Yes, absolute. Would you like me to come to your home or what?"

"No, that's okay. Why don't we meet at the club downstairs from our flat, like, in half an hour."

"*Très bien,* I will see you then."

★★★★

"*Ecco,* Maryanna, what can I give for you?" asked the owner of the club.

"I would love a glass of champagne, if you don't mind."

"Of course," she replied, in her usual gracious manner. I was treated like royalty everywhere. We never waited in lines, always had the best tables, the finest champagne—and until now it didn't make me suspicious. "Were you looking for your husband?"

she asked, setting down a crystal-stemmed glass streaming with delicate bubbles.

"Is he here?" I replied, surprised.

"He was. He left only a short time ago."

I was flabbergasted. I'm sure I looked piqued.

"Oh, that's fine. Yeah, I, uhh, must be late, I guess. What time do you have?" I said, trying to stay calm.

"It's half past seven."

"See? I'm late, yep. Oh well, I'll have to call him. Uhmm, thanks," I said. "Wait. Could I . . . may I have another one of these?" I asked, holding up my glass, which I was about to down in one swallow.

★★★★

"I am sorry, Maryanne. I am late. Please forgive me. I was on the telephone with a client in Brussels," Andrea said, kissing me— *mmmmma, mmmma, mmmma*—three times. (European kissing etiquette: Italians twice, French three times, and the Swiss Germans—well, they didn't kiss.)

"No problem. Don't even worry," I said, grateful he had agreed to come.

"You cut your hair. It is great. You know, you look like . . ." he tried to think.

"Brigitte Nielsen," I said, finishing his thought.

"Yes, absolute, I was going to say this," he said, smiling from ear to ear. "Wait one minute, please. I would like to take something to drink." He reached into his jacket for his wallet.

"No, no, let me get it."

"Don't be silly," he said, looking for a waitress.

"Would you excuse me for one minute, Andrea? I'll be right back," I said, almost falling over myself trying to get out from my seat.

"*Dové* Giancarlo?" I said, walking up behind two guys I recognized sitting at the bar. They both turned and looked at me, stunned. "I said, where's Giancarlo?" They looked at each other, not sure what to say. "Look, I know you were just with him. He told me you went to Bari together; so where is he, huh?" I demanded, my adrenaline really starting to pump now.

"Quiet, please. Don't make a fool of yourself," said the tall one with a strange part-Swiss-German, part-Italian accent.

"Oh, so you want me to be quiet," I shouted. He turned his back away from me and took a drink from his glass. "Don't ignore me," I said, reaching around and pulling the glass away from his mouth.

"Are you crazy?" he said, wiping the spilled drink off his jacket and chin.

"Yes, as a matter of fact I am, but you're in luck, because I'm going to give you until the count of three to tell me where he is before I totally freak. One. . ." I started to count.

"*Sei pazza americana.* Come outside, everybody is watching at us," he said.

"Fine," I said. "I don't care where you tell me." We walked past Andrea, who was busy talking with the waitress. "So?" I said, folding my arms. "Where is he?"

"He went to see Giorgio. He's coming back at nine o'clock," he replied, and started to walk back inside. I stood there for a moment, trying to make sense of it all.

'Okay, if he's here, then where was he when he called? Here? Maybe he didn't even go,' I thought. And then I got a funny feeling in my stomach. I needed to go home, now.

"Andrea? Stay here, please. I have to run upstairs for two seconds, okay? I'll be back in one minute. Wait for me!" I said, and dashed out of the club.

I threw open the apartment door and began to survey the place like a human dowsing rod. I didn't know what I was looking for, but whatever it was, I knew I would find it. The intensity of feeling in my stomach was the ultimate litmus test. And sure enough, there it was, just the clue I was looking for to back up my intuition. I bent down and picked up a rolled-up one-hundred-franc bill that was barely peeking out from underneath the couch. As I was inspecting the makeshift straw, out of the corner of my eye I noticed some rather large streaks across my glass coffee table. I knew these were new, because I cleaned that table sometimes twice a day, even though we had a maid. I hated dirt, especially dust.

So I put two and two together. The still-damp straw and the streaks were evidence that they had been snorting cocaine off the glass. Which equaled, "I'm gonna f—ing kill him!" which I announced at the top of my lungs as I marched out of the flat.

I stormed into the club and strode right past Andrea. He started to get out of his seat, being the gentleman that he was. I held up my hand for him to stop and kept on walking toward my target.

"*Tu, sei morto,*" I said, grabbing the tall guy by the back of his shirt.

"*Ah, cosa facciamo?*" he said, pulling my hand away.

"*Fare la droga in casa mia?*" I shouted.

"Go outside, you crazy American," he said, pushing me away. I came right back, moving up close to his face.

"What did I tell you guys? Huh? All I asked you to do was to keep that crap away from my house. That's it. That's all I asked and you couldn't even do that," I said, starting to cry.

By now the entire club was silent, except for the throbbing house music in the background. It wasn't every day a woman called a man out in downtown Lugano. As a matter of fact, I would venture a guess this was a first. For the most part, if a woman went into a bar alone or with just one other woman, she was considered to be a prostitute. So I don't think they were quite ready for Maryanne, Ninja Warrior.

"Please, go outside," he said, getting up and pulling my arm, dragging me outside with him.

"So, did you guys have a good drug deal in Bari, huh? Is that it? And you just couldn't wait to snort up, you son of a bitch," I said, slapping his chest.

"Calm down before you are hurt yourself," he said, holding me back. He looked like a gorilla and actually smelled like one as well.

"Don't you touch me. Take your . . . hands . . . off . . . me," I said, trying to squirm away. And then something caught my attention in the distance. Across the street, in the distance, I could see a pack of guys walking toward the club.

"It's Giancarlo," I said, shaking loose from the gorilla's grip. He was with Giorgio and some other men I didn't know. The tall guy tried to grab me again as I walked toward the pack. I pulled away from him. "Let go of me," I said, gnashing my teeth together.

I walked off the curb and crossed the street toward the group, moving faster and faster. The closer I got, the clearer Giancarlo came into view. It was definitely him, only he didn't recognize me. He hadn't yet seen my new haircut, which was pretty dramatic. It was now two inches long and platinum. On top of which, he was most probably thoroughly high.

"So *there* you are," I yelled out. I had on a full-length, black cashmere overcoat, black leather gloves, and black biker boots. He stopped in his tracks when he realized it was me. I could tell he wanted to turn around and run. And he should have. But he knew better.

"Maryanne," he said, continuing toward me. Only now he was walking alone. His friends disbanded as soon as they saw it was me. "What are you doing here?" he called out.

"What do you mean, what am I doing here? We were supposed to meet here! Remember? Eight thirty?" He kept getting closer. Now he was crossing the street to get away from me. I followed him. We stopped in front of one of my favorite jewelry stores.

"How could you?" I said, as he tried to walk around me. "How many times did I ask you not to do drugs in our home? What about that do you not get? My home is my only sacred place. If you need to do drugs or snort heroin or whatever you do, why do you have to do it in my house?"

"I don't know what you're talking about. You're going crazy, no?"

"You liar. I know you were there. Don't lie to me! I have your little straw right here," I waved it in front of him. "You were just there, I know. I talked to Ferren, or whatever his name is. He told me everything. So don't even try and lie to me. And what is all that stuff down in the cellar, Giancarlo?" I said, moving toward him.

"It's not what you thinking, 'oney," he said, treading water, moving farther away from me.

"It's not what I think, 'oney?" I replied, making my fist into a ball. "Oh, I think it's exactly what I think."

"It's not mine."

"Really? It's not yours?" We were now nose to nose.

"I swear on my mother's life. It belongs to Gino, this guy . . . we were doing a deal in Bari," he said, finally telling the truth. Only because he was so busted.

"You know what?" I said, pressing my nose into his face. "You make me sick. I have done everything for you, taken care of you, tried to help you, spent night after night waiting for you to come home, thinking you were dead, and what do you do? And another thing. I can't stand that your father knows every move I make and that everywhere I go someone is taking my picture or that every time the phone rings now I think someone's calling to tell me you've been arrested. I want to go in the front door of clubs like everyone else. I don't want to be so afraid everywhere we go. "I only asked for one thing—one thing—to not do drugs in my house." My rage blew out of me like a nuclear explosion. I cocked back my fist and punched him smack in the face. He actually flew back and hit the jewelry store window from the force of it. "Shhhhit," I said, grabbing my fist in pain.

"Ohhhh," he moaned, grabbing his jaw, and slumped over in a pile on the sidewalk.

"I don't ever want to see you again, so don't bother coming home," I said, and walked away.

As I walked back to the nightclub, hoping Andrea was still there, I noticed that a crowd had gathered in front of the place to watch the whole scene. I didn't care. I was glad they saw me punch him. He deserved it.

'That'll teach him to mess with me,' I thought. It hurt so good!

"Are you fine?" said Andrea, greeting me at the entrance to the club.

"I'm okay," I said, shaking out my fist.

"Here, come and sit . . . take off your glove and put some ice on it," he said.

"Will you please just take me out of here? Please?" I asked, looking up at him, completely drained.

"Yes, of course. Wherever you want."

"Anywhere, just away from here."

He paid the bill and we left. He pulled around front to pick me up in his flawless Mercedes coupe. It looked like a black panther. I opened the door and climbed in. We drove to Campione, a small town about forty minutes from Lugano. It was like a mini Monte Carlo and was open all night. We went gambling, dancing, and then had a snack at a little café—there was one on every corner. It was the perfect distraction. We stayed until about three in the morning and then headed back for town.

"Do you want me to make you a fire?" he asked. I rolled my head to the left and smiled.

"I would like that very much."

"Perfect. I will take you to my home."

I was asleep by the time we pulled up to his house, and when I opened my eyes I thought we were at a museum.

"Where are we?" I asked, trying to focus.

"We are at my home."

"You live in a museum?"

"No," he laughed. "My mother gave this house to me when I was in school. My family lives mostly in Paris," he explained.

"Oh my God, it's huge. And it's just you?"

"No, the people who care for the house live in part of it," he said, fumbling for his keys.

"Ohhh," I said, as my eyes took in the mansion from top to bottom and across its vast expanse. "Is it like a historical landmark?" I was serious.

"No," he laughed. "At least I don't think so. Come inside." I was completely awestruck by the sheer enormity of the structure.

"So she just gave it to you?" I asked, walking around slowly behind him, looking at the art and drinking in the elaborate decor.

"Yes. I also have a lovely flat in Milan. You should see it some time."

"Sure," I said, mesmerized.

"You want some champagne?"

"Sure, why not. Who needs sleep? There's plenty time to sleep when you're dead." 'Jesus. Look where I am,' I thought to myself.

"Why don't you take off your coat. I'll go and get some glasses." I could hear the echo of his footsteps as he walked across the beautiful marble floor. I held my hands above my head and reached them as high as they could go and spun around and around deliriously, like a little girl.

'Yes,' I thought. 'This is how my life is supposed to be.'

I didn't go home until very late the next night.

✷✷✷✷

"Giancarlo," I said, as I crept through the door, undoing my coat. There was no answer. Then I remembered I was pissed and had banished him from my life. He must have taken me seriously.

'Whew,' I thought, 'he's not here.' I was exhausted, but I was too tired to sleep, and the truth was, I was frightened to sleep alone. So, for the next best thing, I flipped on the tube and flopped down on the bed. Then the phone rang, shattering my semihypnotic state.

"Pronto," I said, picking it up.

"What were you doing in Campione?" asked the voice.

"Giancarlo?"

"I know you were there," he continued, breathlessly.

"You know what—it's none of your business where I was, okay?" I said.

"You were with some ug-ally guy," he said.

"How do you know who I was with? And he was not ug-ally. Anyway, I'm busy right now."

"Is someone there with you?" he asked, sounding particularly strange.

"Yes, as a matter of fact, there is. He's lying here next to me and we're very busy, so why don't you go and screw yourself," I said, and slammed the phone down—twice.

'He's got some nerve,' I thought, and started to get undressed. Our flat was fairly big, but from the bedroom I could see the foyer if the door was open, and I happened to be standing right there when the front door flew open.

"You bitch," he screamed, running into the bedroom, wild-eyed. I had never seen him this way before. He was usually fairly passive. Now he was a raving lunatic. He pushed past me, shouting so loud that I had to cover my ears. "Where is he?" he yelled, and started running around the flat like a maniac, looking under the bed and in cupboards and behind doors. "Come out, coward!" he hollered. When I realized what he was doing, I started to laugh at him.

"There's no one here, you fool. I only said that to get a reaction."

"No, I know you were with someone. I saw him drop you off," he said, still frantically looking.

"What? Were you following me, you stalker?"

"My uncle told me you were in Campione. He saw you there kissing some—guy." He could barely get the words out of his mouth. "And now I will kill you." He reached up over my head and pulled something out from underneath a blanket I kept on top of the armoire. He slammed me back against the armoire, and next thing I knew, he had forced a pistol into my clenched mouth.

"'ancarlo!" I tried to speak, but the gun was shoved so far in that it was almost impossible to. I didn't know whether to laugh or pee in my pants. Having this wacked-out, gangly cocaine addict posing as a tough guy was hard for me to grasp. He was the kid I took care of and cleaned up after. It was like Scooby-Doo with a .357 Magnum. It wasn't him that scared me, it was the gun. I grabbed hold of the shaft, trying to pull it out of my mouth. He kept shoving it back in.

"I'm going to blow you all over the place," he shouted in my face. I looked into his eyes and saw that he wasn't playing around.

"Oh-kay," I choked, still hanging on to the shaft, trying to pull it out of my mouth. "'ancarlo, wait," I gurgled, gagging on the metal barrel.

"You think you are so tough to throw me out of my house, eh?" he demanded. "This my house. I will do drugs . . . what I want. You will not tell me what I can do."

I had two choices. Get the gun away from him or get the gun away from him. I pulled on the shaft hard enough so that I could speak what could have been my last words: "Okay, motherf—er, if you're gonna shoot me, do it! Don't just talk about it!" I let go of the gun and stood there with my eyes twitching. After about two seconds he pulled the pistol out of my mouth, and I opened my eyes to see what happened. I didn't hear anything, so I knew I wasn't hurt, unless I was dead and didn't know it. He put the gun down the front of his pants and slapped me on the side of the head.

"You are crazy, you know," he said. For the first time, I didn't argue with him.

To set the record straight, I made a phone call to the police department right before I was escorted out of the country two days later. I told them they might be interested in some classified *informazione* concerning one nineteen-year-old Swiss-Italian drug lord. I loved the idea that when they got to the bottom of Giancarlo, they would find Vincenzo.

"I think his first name is Giancarlo and his last name is . . . I don't know—Sclafani, something like that, and oh, he was forced against his will by his father to work for him, so please go easy on him."

What can I say? He was my husband, wasn't he?

When I arrived back in the United States, I weighed about one hundred ten pounds, my mother said my skin looked gray, and I was not doing so well upstairs. I thought someone was after me, and that everywhere I went people were watching me. And not just anyone, but "them." And they knew who they were. I had violated the family code. You don't ever rat on your family. And now I was going to have to pay. I called one of my mother's friends who I remembered had an extra room in her house, thinking no one would look for me there. She made an open invitation for me to stay with her. So that's where I went.

Peggy was a socialite and lived with a man named Carl, who was supposedly psychic or a trance channeler—I couldn't remember which. From what she told me, they slept in separate rooms because he apparently needed "his own space." And frankly I didn't give a shit. All I wanted to know was that I was safe.

I had been back in the States for only a couple of weeks when I ended up at the emergency room. Turned out I had a 104-degree fever and was diagnosed with pneumonia and mononucleosis. My lungs were filled with fluid, but I didn't have any health insurance so they sent me home the next day. They said there was nothing they could do for me. I spent the next three months in bed. I was so weak and frail that I had to crawl to the bathroom. I couldn't eat, and slept between my panic attacks, which were coming about every hour on the hour. Now I was terrified I was really going to die. Peggy and Carl would check in on me every once and a while, and instead of crying out and asking if they could hold my hand for one minute because I was scared to death, I assured them I didn't need anything. My mother, who knew I was ill and lived in the same condominium complex, never even called to say hello.

I slowly started to get my strength back. I even began watching TV, something I prided myself that I rarely did. One evening, a motivational speaker named Les Brown was giving a seminar on channel 9, and as much as I could be, I was glued to the set. Here was this striking black man with a mile-wide smile, sincerely sharing his success story, and telling me that if a mentally uneducable orphan like him could make it, so could I. The strange thing is that, for whatever reason, I believed him. And he wasn't even selling anything. Next thing I know, I'm watching a series of programs by John Bradshaw on the alcoholic family. Then I realize my problem: I'm a codependent. So between Les and John, I got it. It was simple. I was a codependent with no purpose in life, who didn't believe in herself. I had accessed my fundamental flaw—and I told myself if I could fix this, surely everything would finally be okay!

Over the next month I had a lot of time to put things in perspective as I regained my health. At first I thought I needed to toss out my Good Girl Handbook and start over. I saw that I had spent my life trying to take care of everybody else, focusing on what they needed or on what was wrong with them. Now it was time to decide what I really wanted.

Even though I could identify the problem, I still couldn't make the connection between my mind and my body—that I was sick and panicked because I hadn't taken care of myself for a long time and continued to put myself in danger. As a result, my body was overburdened. I was driven by fear and survival.

Clearly, I wasn't recognizing my part in all of this. What I was starting to understand was that although the faces were changing, the story was pretty much the same. What I couldn't see was why I made the choices that drew those situations to me like a magnet. I didn't understand the Law of Attraction.

By now God was a useless notion to me; I was too busy collecting psychological diagnoses in my attempt to make sense of all these catastrophes. So I made the necessary revisions in my Good Girl Handbook and then did what any warm-blooded, Italian-Irish, recovering Catholic girl with no self-esteem, who was sick of taking care of people, would do. I got married—again. But not before I burned a few bridges.

Now, About Those Penises . . .

"WHAT AM I, THE MAID? Put your dishes in the dishwasher," I said, half teasing my girlfriend Nina, who had come from Nigeria to spend the summer with me in Tiburon. I had been invited to a party in Marin County one Saturday night and never left. Nina and I had met at the Lancôme counter when I lived in Santa Barbara, and we had remained close friends.

"I don't know how," she said, staring at me doe-eyed. I thought she was kidding.

"What are you, retarded?" I said, pushing her aside, grabbing a dish from the sink and exaggerating the procedure. "You take the dish, and then you rinse it like so, and then, here . . . you put it in between these little white post things, like that, and then you shut the door," I explained.

"I have never cleaned a dish in my life." I looked at her expectantly. "I told you my father was the ambassador to France and at one time the treasurer of Nigeria," she explained.

"So, what, you don't have plates in Nigeria?"

"No, my family has always had servants for that kind of stuff," she said, casually.

"Really? Cool! I love that idea. Actually I think people should just throw their dishes out the window like the Romans did—you know, in the gutters—when they're done eating. What else didn't you have to do?" I asked.

"They pretty much did everything—bathe me, dress me . . . I think that's why I travel so much, because I get sick of being treated like a child."

"What? Are you crazy?"

"Seriously, I wasn't even allowed to date until I was twenty."

"Bummer. Okay, your highness, I'm over you. Let's get ready. And you can wash your own . . . self."

We headed into the city that night to go dancing, dressed to kill—or be killed, I suppose. That's when I met Ahmed.

"Hey, that guy over there keeps staring at you," said Nina, leaning into my ear while we were dancing to a Michael Jackson song at Harry Denton's Southside Club.

"Who?" I said, trying to get a look without looking like I was looking. "Is he cute?"

"He's beautiful."

'Right,' I thought. 'Usually people's definition of "beautiful" is "scary."'

"He's right over there. See him? He's got a white linen

shirt and slacks on. See him?" She was trying not to point.

"You mean the guy leaning up against the wall with the groovy gaucho pants?" I said, trying to keep to the rhythm of the song.

"Nooo, not him. Him." She pointed at the guy, who was looking right at us.

"Oh my God, he totally saw you," I said, slapping her hand.

"He's coming over here. Ohhh. Do your British accent," she said, and then danced away on her own. One of the ways I entertained myself of late was by accumulating an arsenal of names and accents to mess with guys' heads. My mother always told me I would never meet a real man in a bar (although she met my father in one), so this made sense to me. All men were pigs and dogs, so I figured I could do whatever I wanted, whenever I wanted—gee, who does this sound like?—including pretending to be somebody else. There were no rules. I was suddenly feeling very Sophia Loren.

"Helloo, would you like to dance?" said the truly beautiful-looking man with the white linen shirt. I wasn't sure where he was from, but he sounded Persian.

"Ehh, sure," I said, selecting my Italian accent.

The linen-shirt guy and I didn't exchange too many words the rest of the night, we only danced. He didn't even ask my name. And I was glad. There was nothing I hated more than some guy trying to get the stats on you when you could barely hear yourself think. You spend half the dance saying, "What? I can't hear you," and the other half trying to ditch the guy. So I was spared my usual departure speech: "If you want to dance, dance; if you want to talk, beat it."

"I would like to see you again. My name is Ahmed," he said, taking my hand and leading me off the dance floor.

"Ahmed," I repeated. "Yes, this would be nice. You can call me. I write my number for you." But this guy, he was no average Joe Buckethead. He was a real man, I could tell. He wore a Rolex and drove a Mercedes. And I actually liked him. That is, until he almost choked me to death.

Ahmed called me the next morning and every morning, afternoon, and evening after that for three weeks. He took me to the movies, to the theater, to dinner, and eventually to bed. It wasn't easy faking orgasms with an Italian accent, but it was necessary. I think it was when we started looking at houses and he began asking me questions like, "Do you like doing laundry?" and "How many children would you like to have?" that I started getting nervous. First of all, I could never marry a man who wanted me to do the laundry, and second . . . It didn't matter what second was. The laundry thing was enough—definitely a deal breaker.

★★★★

"What are you going to tell him?" asked Nina.

"I don't know. Maybe I could tell him I started taking English lessons because I want to sound more American, and then, like, over time I could just talk normal." Sounded good to me.

"Maryanne, he wants to marry you."

"So what's that supposed to mean?"

"You'll have to meet his family—never mind *your* family—with an Italian accent," she reminded me.

"I didn't think about that. You're right. It's ridiculous. I could never get away with marrying a Persian guy. My father would kill me."

"What are you talking about?"

"Just drop it; you don't know my father. Besides, the guy is starting to give me the creeps anyway. But he wants to take me out for my birthday. So I'll go out with him one more time. But you're coming with us."

That was fine with her. She had the same entry in her Handbook: If he wants to play, he has to pay.

"Screw guys," I said.

"Totally," she said. And she did. Several to be exact. Including Ahmed.

★★★★

"Hello," I said in my normal voice when I picked up the phone.

"So why haven't you returned my calls?" said Ahmed. I hadn't spoken to him for a couple of weeks, since Nina and I ditched him for some other guys the night of my twenty-fifth birthday.

"Well, maybe that's because I have nothing to say to you," I said, in one hundred percent American.

"And when were you planning on telling me you aren't really Italian?"

"What are you, a private investigator? I don't have to tell you anything. You screw my girlfriend, game over. That's it," I said.

"We didn't sleep together," he lied.

"Whatever you need to tell yourself, pal. I don't have anything to say to you," I said, but I didn't hang up, because I was curious about what he had to say.

"You know, you are a liar and you're fat. You are not even that pretty without makeup," he said.

"Okay, is that supposed to hurt my feelings? You know what's funny? Nina said the same thing to me before I threw her out. You guys must have been really bored if you had nothing better to do than talk about how pretty I'm not."

"What—do you think you can go through life doing what you want to people?"

"You know what? You don't know me, you don't know the first thing about me, so why don't you just shut up! And why are you calling me anyway?"

"I want you to pay me back for all the money I spent on you."

"Screw you. It doesn't work that way, buddy. You don't get the milk for free. Maybe in Persia, you get to screw your cows, but over here, it doesn't work that way."

"Screwing cows? What are you saying? Just give me the money." He sounded like an al-Qaeda terrorist.

"Look, you offered to pay. I didn't ask you," I said.

"How else were you going to pay for it?" he countered.

"Pay for what? What do you think . . . you have a pink slip for me now just because you bought me some cheap champagne and paid a couple of my parking tickets? What is it with you guys who think you can screw a woman over and then ask for your money back? So you can just bend over, Ahmed!"

"You bitch. I could kill you!" he screamed into the phone.

"I'm hanging up now. Don't ever call me again. Loser," I said, and hung up.

'I wonder if Nina was there when he called. I probably shouldn't have called her Kunta Kinte either,' I thought. I felt bad about that. 'But she slept with him. It wasn't that I minded it so much; it was the principle of the thing. He smelled, anyway. I could never be with a man who smells,' I told myself.

"Who were you screaming at?" asked Bryan, looking up from the basketball game he was watching as he lay on my bed.

"No one. Some guy," I said, and snuggled up next to him. "How's your ankle?" I said, inquiring about his new cast.

"It's okay, I guess. It kinda hurts, but I'm fine." Bryan was a boy I had met working at my first job at Marin General. He was sixteen at the time, I was twenty-one, and we were just friends. He tracked me down when I got back from Europe and came and took care of me the last month when I was so sick with pneumonia and mono. When he showed up again at my door, he was twenty years old, six feet four inches and looked like a blonde god. The only problem for him was all the other guys I was dating.

"I wonder who that is?" I said, jumping off the bed to go answer the door. "Who's there?" I called. No one answered.

'Hmmm, maybe it's the postman,' I thought naïvely, and opened the door.

"You f—. I have never met a bigger bitch!" Ahmed yelled. In one uninterrupted move, he grabbed my throat, yanked me out the door, and then slammed me up the side of it, lifting me off the ground.

He was choking me so hard that no sound could come out. My feet were kicking beneath me.

"I want my money, you f—ing bitch," he said. I kicked at him and finally got him in the balls, but he was so mad he barely winced and choked me even harder. "You're going to pay me back or I'll kill you." I was about to pass out.

"Is there a problem?" Bryan asked, as he hobbled out to the front porch to see where I had gone. He was about a foot taller than Ahmed

and outweighed him by about a hundred pounds. Ahmed immediately let me go. "I think you'd better hit it, buddy, or I'm going to
have to hurt you," said Bryan. Ahmed didn't think twice. He scrambled away like a greasy little cockroach.

'My hero,' I thought to myself. That totally turned me on. I
wanted to jump him right there.

"Are you okay, Bun?" he asked (that was my nickname because I
ate so much salad).

"I'm fine," I said, already over what had happened. I was feeling
frisky now. When you're used to trauma, you can shake it off like
water off a duck's back. When you're in the front lines, you toughen
up. So now, instead of calling intimacy "making love," I called it "sex."
And instead of feeling sorry for my victims, I convinced myself it
was their fault for being a guy. Bottom line: If you have a penis, I'm
going to eat you up and spit you out. The only God that had been
imprinted in me had a penis, so this scenario included him too.

"What was that all about?" Bryan wanted to know as we walked
back into the house.

"Oh, nothing. Just some guy who was tripping."

"He must have been tripping pretty hard."

"Yeah, whatever. I don't really want to talk about it," I said, and
jumped on him, knocking him over onto the bed. I forgot about his
cast—and so did he.

★★★★

Bryan was Beaver Cleaver and I had become the evil twin sister
in I Dream of Jeannie. Life had dictated that I be heavily armed and
ready to do battle. Bryan was the only place left for me to be truly
vulnerable. This wounded warrior could rest safely in his arms. I
trusted him completely. And his was the family I had always dreamed
of. So when he asked me to marry him, it wasn't that I didn't want to.
I really did. I thought that if I could enter their world, the beauty of
their lives could wash away the ugliness of mine. This was my chance
at happily ever after—where nobody swears and people drink hot

cocoa and wear footsie pajamas on Sunday mornings. Only one problem: I was already married.

"Why don't you just go and see him?" said Bryan, not fully understanding the scope of my dilemma.

"I can't just show up after three years like nothing."

"Why not?" he said. "He's your father."

"I know. You don't understand, Bryan. It's not like that," I said, starting to cry.

"What's wrong, Bun? You can tell me," he coaxed, giving me a hug and reaching for the shirt near the bed so I could wipe my nose. I hesitated.

"Okay, do you remember that movie we watched where the little girl was freaking out because she had to go and visit her dad? It was like an after-school special, and I told you to change the channel because I didn't want to watch it."

"You mean when you yelled at me and then ran into the bathroom crying?"

"Yeah," I said. "Well, do you remember why that girl didn't want to go?" I asked him, reluctantly.

"Uh, because her father was touchin' her, I think," he said, trying to remember.

"Yeah."

"Okay," he said, still not getting the connection.

"So, that's why," I said. He looked at me, still confused.

"That's why what?"

"The little girl. Get it? Helloooo," I said. "She doesn't want to be with her dad because . . . you know . . . the touching thing," I said, not wanting him to make me have to spell it out.

"Oh God, Bunny. I'm sorry. I'm so stupid," he said, grabbing me up in his arms.

"It's okay. It's just that I am so sick of having this thing in me, you know, and maybe if I could just say something to him . . . maybe it would go away." He just held me and rocked me back and forth.

Watching that television show had opened up all of the sexual abuse memories that had hidden themselves from me. Over the past few months, my panic attacks had subsided. I didn't know why, and I was afraid to ask; I was just glad they were gone. But now they were coming back, and I suspected they had something to do with what had happened with my father. I had seen a couple of therapists, and finally one of them gave me a hint about what might be wrong with me, explaining that anxiety is often linked with molestation.

"Let's just go down to see your father," Bryan said.

"You mean right now?"

"Yeah, why not, Bun? I hate seein' you like this, and if you think it will help, let's just do it. I'll be right there with you."

"You mean you would come with me?" I asked, starting to cry again.

"Of course I will, Bunny. I love you."

"Oh my God, that's the nicest thing I remember anyone saying to me. Thank you," I said, squeezing onto him like a little barnacle.

"Let's do it, let's go," he said. So we did.

Something had been growing inside me, welling up in the calm before the storm. Well, let's be honest, my life was like El Niño, so of course a storm was coming. Let's just say that now I was starting to see them when they were on their way. I think they call this growth. So I decided I needed to kill Zeus.

I felt like I finally had the courage to go and avenge myself, and now I knew what I was avenging. Now I finally knew what was wrong with me, and once I confronted my father about it, everything would be okay . . .

Excuse Me, Is This 666 Lucifer Road?

"I THINK YOU'D BETTER WAIT HERE," I said, changing my mind at the last second.

"Are you sure, Bun? I can wait outside the door if you want."

"No, I can do this. But thank you," I said, and smooched him on the lips. "I'll be back." I didn't feel exactly attached to my body as I floated through the door. I almost felt high. Like I was mainlining adrenaline, but in nice, steady doses. Nothing was going to get in my way.

"Can I help you, Maryanne?" said my father's longtime secretary, Margaret, who spoke to me as though we had just seen each other the day before. Her tone bore a disdain that forewarned me that my name was mud in them thar hills.

"As a matter of fact, Margaret, no, you may not," I said, happy to put her in her very little place.

"You can't go in there. He's in a—" I didn't hear the rest of her warning because I was hell-bent for his office.

"Hang up the phone," I said, slamming the door behind me so hard that the walls shook. He didn't even flinch. He looked up at me and smiled with this wicked grin on his face, like he'd been expecting me. I walked over to the foot of his desk, put both hands down, leaned in, and raised my eyebrows, indicating I wasn't leaving until I had my day in court.

"Okay. Charlie boy, my daughter just walked in, so I'm gonna hit it," he said into the phone, and then hung up, as though he wasn't being commanded.

"Bruno," I said.

"Maryanne," he parroted my tone, and then leaned back in his chair, curious, like he was about to watch a presentation. I stood there and studied him for just a minute, hovering over his enormous desk.

"Nice office," I said. "What do you actually do here?"

"A little of this, a little of that," he said, not missing a beat. I looked at his face, reacquainting myself with it. Looking to see any of myself in his features, his gestures, his posture, his attitude, the way he sounded—anything. I had never really done that before. He didn't seem to mind. He sat there unflinchingly while I visually interrogated him. I looked at the shape of his fingernails and the texture of the skin on his arms. (He almost always wore short-sleeved shirts to show off his perfectly sculpted body.) I noticed the outline of his lips, the shape of his eyes. I even looked to see if his eyebrows were arched the same as mine.

"You have, like, cow eyes," I said. "Mine aren't like that, they're more like Mom's, like almonds, she says," I blurted out randomly. He didn't say anything. He just stared at me, totally present, completely solid. I had had enough. I saw what I needed to see.

"So here's the deal, Bruno," I said, leaning over his desk even farther this time. "I know what you did to me and you know what you did to me, and I'm not leaving here until you admit it. I am not going to let you take one more breath of my life, got it?" I looked him dead in the eyes, letting him know I wasn't scared, that I had never felt more sure of myself. He met my gaze with equal penetration and then relented. I was stunned. He almost looked vulnerable. His expression seemed so unnatural, it was a strange sight to see.

"I didn't know how else to love you," he said, as I watched his eyes fill with tears. One even spilled over and streamed down his left cheek. I didn't know what to say. I was mesmerized by the fact that my father felt anything remotely resembling remorse. It was like watching Frankenstein cry.

Somehow it seemed wrong, but nonetheless he had my attention. "Maryanne, I just wanted you to love me and I didn't know any other way." Now he was weeping, I guess you could say. I had only seen him cry once before, when my grandfather died. Either this was a dream come true or I was imagining it. If I wasn't mistaken, my father was actually apologizing to me. Something I'd never heard him do before.

"Weak people apologize. Never ask permission, never say you're sorry," was one of his entries in my Good Girl Handbook.

"Maryanne, I want to make it all up to you. Come work with me, with the family. I'm building a dynasty. You can have everything you've ever wanted, but it will all be yours, so you won't ever have to take any bullshit from anyone again. No man will ever own you." It was like he'd been rehearsing it for months.

I could barely believe it. It seemed too good to be true. It was perfect. He made me an offer I couldn't refuse, and I didn't.

You might be asking why I would accept an offer from this man so easily and quickly after all he had done to me. That's simple. I had been waiting my whole life to hear the words "I am sorry," coupled with "Oh, and by the way, let me give you everything else you've ever wanted." What was there to think about? I also knew on some level that this offer was time-sensitive. That if I didn't act now it would be rescinded.

He stood up and said, "I want to hug you." I melted. My body had craved that for so long. This was the invitation I had never received, that I had been waiting my life for, the offer that represented the kind of love I never got—the kind of love that doesn't turn into a demand for sex. I was so deficient, so deprived, that my healthy desire to be held by my father propelled me over to him. I said nothing; my coming toward him was my yes.

I let myself fall into his arms. It felt like the most natural thing for my body to let go and be embraced by my own father. A warmth that started from the tips of my toes lapped up in successive waves—filling up my most private parts, filling up my belly, and overflowing out my heart. I surrendered fully into my father.

And then, the wave swelled up into my head. Instantly, my body recoiled; an alarm sounded and foot-thick impenetrable doors slammed shut, one after another, in the reverse order that they had opened, cutting off the flow of that warmth that only moments before had filled me. My mind had been distorted to believe that feeling good physically would inevitably lead to sex, which meant that feeling good had to be bad, especially when it came to my father. This was the only deduction I was capable of making.

I pulled away, gathered myself together. I made sense of what had happened by telling myself that we had simply shaken hands and struck a deal. That was the best I could manage. This was the first and only time in my adult life that my father ever held me. I didn't know that it would be the last. I had to believe that my father truly loved me and would never do anything again to hurt me. Any other truth would have been too much to bear. But the desolation would come soon enough.

I quit school—again—packed up everything I owned, including Bryan, and moved to Sacramento. The last place on earth I ever wanted to live. It was 103 degrees and counting. I found out where the most expensive apartments in the whole county were and we moved there—hoping this was enough of a barrier between me and bad taste—and then went to work. Which is basically all we did for the next eight and a half months solid. Fourteen to sixteen hours a day, seven days a week. But I didn't care, because this time it was mine. I had power of attorney, rule of the roost, and I was the boss. This was my dynasty, and I could do whatever I wanted. The best part was that my brother Tony had come to work for my father just a few months before I did. Over the years, he and I had become very close. I trusted my brother—he never lied, even when he should have.

Anyway, listen to this. I start making a lot of money, and I mean a lot of money, selling . . . insurance. I asked my father when I wrote myself checks if I needed to withhold any money for taxes, you know, like Social Security or unemployment, that kind of thing.

And he said, "Don't worry about it." So I didn't.

"Martha, did you make that deposit yet?" I called out from my office.

"I haven't heard from your father yet," she yelled back.

"Well, do we have enough for me to take my bonus?"

"Uhhh, let me see, wait . . . Yeah, looks okay. We should be fine. The rest will go in tonight, so take it," she said. Martha was my father's bookkeeper. She came along with my new office and every-thing else. She was a few years younger than me, single, dumb, and attractive, which meant my father was probably boinking her too.

A few moments later: "Maryanne, your father's on line two."

"Hey Bruno, I was just about to—" I started to say. "I know Dad, I just walked through the . . . I had to pick up the . . . I was on my lunch . . . I know, don't worry, I did it. Yes, I told him yesterday. Yes, I did. Yep, we got everything . . . uh-huh . . . that too. It's done. He said he'd get the rest of the cash to us by Friday," I said.

I had to pull the phone away from my ear—his response almost shattered my eardrum. "Would you stop yelling! Jeez. Just wait a sec-ond . . . I told him he could bring the rest of it Friday and that I would hold his Mercedes until he brought it back. Relax. I know what I'm doing here, so why don't you let me do it? Jesus. What? . . . Nothing . . . I didn't say anything! Just forget it. Go," I said. "Okay, I'll tell Jamie to take care of the rest of whatever when he gets over here. After we get the money . . . okay . . . good-bye." I hung up, walked out of my office, and stood near Martha's desk.

"Jeez, he goes on and on. It's not like we're dealing with nuclear explosives here. I mean . . . well, you know what I mean." Everyone in the office stared at me briefly and then went back to work. "Anyway, did Tony call? He said he was coming up today or tomorrow. Have you heard from him?"

"Oh yeah, he called earlier and said he would be here around seven, and not to make any plans," Martha replied, handing me a stack of messages an inch thick.

"When were you planning on giving these to me? Anytime soon? Are any of these since I got back from lunch?"

"Yeah, sorry. I, uh, forgot to put them in your box," she said, scratching her head.

"Thanks," I said, and walked back into my office and sat down behind my desk. I heard a knock at the door. "Yeah, it's open," I said. It was one of my salespeople. "Hey Maria, what's up?"

"Maryanne, do you think you could sign these for me? I have to go pick up my daughter from her piano lesson."

"No problem; here, let me do that for you right now."

"Have you lost more weight? You look so thin."

"I don't know. I don't think so. Why, do I look bad?" I asked, self-consciously.

"No, you could never look bad; you just look a little thin is all," she said, gracefully.

"Here you go . . . I mean, I've been totally stressed. Bryan and I haven't taken a day off in . . . what—four months?"

"You should go do something, have some fun."

"Thanks, Maria. Have a nice evening," I said. I loved her. She was such a nice lady. She always had something nice to say.

Fun? I thought about it and I couldn't come up with much. Wait, shopping is fun and sex is fun—well, not lately, we've been so tired all the time. Whatever . . . I'm too busy to have fun. But it stuck in the back of my mind and rattled around anyway.

★★★★

"Hey, let's go out tonight. I mean get all dressed up and go somewhere really nice," said Bryan.

"You must be reading my mind."

"Let's go into Old Town."

"Sure, wherever; I want to have some champagne. I haven't had anything to drink since, whoa, my birthday. That was over a year ago."

"All right, champagne it is," he said. This would be the first time since I'd known Bryan that we'd be drinking alcohol. We drove into Old Town and had dinner at a charming little Italian restaurant he'd picked out.

We had just ordered dessert. Bryan got out of his chair, walked over to me and knelt down. "Bunny, I love you," he declared. "I want to spend the rest of my life with you and I don't want to wait another minute." I was shocked at first. And then I thought he might be joking. I sat there in freeze-frame.

"Bunny?"

"Yes?"

"I just asked you if you'll marry me." He waited.

"No offense, but isn't this the part where you give me a ring or something?" I tried to be delicate, but I totally missed the mark.

Okay, I didn't wear much jewelry anymore. I had sold most of it to live off of after I came home from Europe. I was over the Mr. T thing. Even so, I thought the ring thing was part of the engagement deal, right? I continued to smile, hoping it had just slipped his mind and that my not-so-gentle reminder would stimulate his memory. He stayed on his knee, nodding his head again.

"Bun?"

"Bryan?"

"Will you marry me?" he said again. And then I realized he was waiting for me to answer.

"Oh God, Bryan, yes! Oh my God, yes, of course I would love to marry you. I mean, I *will* marry you. I love you, Pooh Bear," I cried, tilting out of my chair to reach him and hug onto him.

"I didn't get you a ring yet, Bun, because I know how picky you are." I glared at him. "And, I didn't want to take a chance and get something you weren't going to like," he quickly added, totally redeeming himself. I loved this guy. I felt like the luckiest girl in the whole world.

"Oh Bryan," I swooned. "That is about the sweetest thing I've ever heard. You didn't get me a ring because you wanted me to have what I wanted. Ohhhh, I love you . . . Shit!"

"What? What's wrong?" he asked, startled.

"Oh my God, Bryan. I just remembered. I can't marry you. I mean, I *can* marry you, I just can't marry you right now," I backtracked, totally embarrassed.

"It's okay, Bunny, relax. We don't have to get married tonight. We can wait a couple weeks or—"

"You don't understand. I mean I really can't marry you right now, or even next week," I said, frantically.

"What do you mean, Bun? Is it your anxiety? Are you scared? 'Cause we can wait, Bunny."

"No, no, it's not that. It's that I . . . I forgot to tell you something." Actually there were a lot of things I had conveniently forgotten to tell Bryan, like what my father really did for a living. But never mind that for now.

"Honey, there's something I have to tell you. And I don't want you to get mad at me, okay?" Stiff from being down on his knee, he took my words as a cue to get up and sit back down on his chair. "'Cause it's kind of a big deal," I continued, "and, well, I know I should have told you before, but I sort of forgot, and now, well, it's probably a really good time—not that there's a really good time, per se, to tell you this, or tell anyone this kind of thing—but you know, under the circumstances . . . I mean, I think I should tell you this thing because, well, it will just be a bigger mess than it already is and—"

"Bun?" He held up his hand, signifying I should halt. "Why don't you just tell me?" I nodded in agreement and started slowly. "Okay," I said, taking a deep breath. "You know when I told you I was in Europe traveling around and stuff?"

"Uh-huh," he said, leaning back in his chair.

"Right, well, uhhmm, my friend . . . that I was with—the girl?"

"Yeah."

"She's a guy," I said, and took a sip off my champagne. My mouth was bone dry.

"Okay," he said, now leaning forward, waiting for the rest.

"Okay," I said, taking another breath. "So the guy? He wasn't a guy. I mean he was a guy—is a guy," I stammered. Bryan stared at me, suspicious, raising his left eyebrow.

"Anyway, he's my husband," I said, and powered down the rest of my drink.

★★★★

"Dad. Bruno! Stop yelling at me for one minute and let me. . . would you just let me explain?" I said. "I can't remember the man's name who married us. He was some minister guy we hired. He said he would file the paper with the city after the ceremony and that was it," I explained. "No, I told you, we found him in the phone book . . . oh God! No—under 'Ministers,'" I said. "Dad! No . . . I don't want you to hurt the guy. He didn't do anything. I just need to get a copy of my marriage certificate because that's where we got . . . I know . . . you told me . . . I don't need to talk to the mayor, Dad, I just need you to call Dennis. I need to find out from him if, because I'm a Swiss resident now, I can file for divorce here or if I have to go back to Switzerland," I said, by now exhausted. "Fine . . . okay . . . break his legs, Dad . . . that's great. That's exactly what I need you to do. That should solve my problem absolutely . . . good. Thanks . . . I'm hanging up now, Pop. I have work to do. *Ciao*."

"Maryanne? Your brother, on one," said Martha over the intercom.

I pressed the button and said, "Thanks, got it . . . Hey Tony, what's up?"

"Dad just said you wanted him to do a number on some minister guy in Switzerland," he said, chewing food in my ear.

"Are you eating?"

"Yeah! Why?"

"You've been hanging around Bruno way too much."

"Whatever . . . so what's the deal?

"I told Dad I needed him to call Dennis for me to see if I have to go back to Europe to get a divorce because of my U.S./Swiss dual citizenship."

"Dennis? What's he gonna do? He's a criminal defense . . . Oh, I get it, so what's up with the minister?"

"I don't know. I'm just glad I didn't tell Dad his name."

"Yeah," he said. "Okay, I'll be up there tomorrow morning early."

★★★★

"Maryanne? Psst, Maryanne,'" whispered Maria.

"Come in here and shut the door. What's going on?" I asked.

"There's something you should know," she said, looking around the office.

"Pull the shades," I said. "Sit down, what's happening?"

"Last night late, I heard Martha talking on the phone to your father."

"Yeah, so what? She talks to him every night."

"'So what' is that she told him you are ripping him off, writing checks and not entering them in the books."

"What?" I exploded, jumping out of my seat.

"I'm telling you—that girl, she has it out for you, Maryanne. Why do you think your brother came back so soon?"

"Tony? Does he know?"

"Sure, your father told him to come and audit the books. They already took your name off the accounts. That's why they had you leave the office for that meeting this morning."

"Why wouldn't Tony just tell me? I don't get it! What else did she say to him, Maria?" I asked, feeling totally betrayed.

"She told him you were writing checks to Bryan too."

"Unbelievable, unf—ing believable," I said. "Thanks, Maria, you're a doll. I won't forget this. You can go now."

"It's not a problem, Maryanne. I just thought you should know."

"Do you know where my brother is now?"

"He's in the conference room."

"Thanks. Oh Maria? Would you tell Martha . . . Never mind, I'll do it. Close the door, would you?"

'Okay, you little rat. You want to play with me?' I thought. 'Let's play.' I got up out of my chair and walked out into the office and directly up to Martha's desk. She was talking on the phone.

"Absolutely, Mr. Carter, you can drop it off . . . Hello . . . hello? Hey! You hung up on him!" I held down the receiver of the phone while she spun around in her chair.

"Get up. Now," I said, standing over her.

"What are you doing?" she asked, nervously.

"Do you need some help getting up?"

"I don't . . . what are you . . . ?" she stammered.

"I said get . . . up . . . now," as I poked her in the shoulder with each word. By the time she stood up everyone in the office had stopped what they were doing. I was too pissed off to care. "Outside," I said, pushing her along.

"I don't want to go. Where are we going?" she whined. I pushed her and she lurched forward. Anytime she'd stop, I'd push her forward again. When we got outside the office she turned around defiantly and folded her arms.

"What's the big idea, hanging up on that client? You know your father—"

"Shut up," I said, half an inch from her face. I could feel the veins in my forehead throbbing. "Thank you," I said, straightening my blouse. "Do you have any idea why we're standing out here, Martha?" I said, calm as ice. She shook her head. "Oh, see, but I think you do. As a matter of fact, you know exactly why. The thing you don't know is that I am about to make your life miserable because of it. You're going to wish you never met me, Martha, I promise you. And just so you don't forget. . ." I started poking her in the chest, about to mow her down as she started backing up. "Just so it's perfectly clear, let me say that you have made a very big mistake coming between me and my family, Martha. Very big. And if you ever try to get between me and my family again, you will be permanently sorry. Do you understand?" She nodded her head. "I said, 'Do . . . you . . . understand?'" poking her in the chest again.

"Yes," she gulped. "Yes."

"That's good," I said, getting ready to backhand her. "'Cause I would hate to have to *really* hurt you." And then I popped her in the chops. Blood spurted out of her nose. Her hands sprung to her face. I watched the blood drip between her fingers. I wasn't the type of person who likes scary or violent movies, but this didn't seem to bother me. I started to walk away. I looked back at her, now crumpled on the ground. "Oh, Martha, clean that up, would you? We wouldn't want people to get the wrong idea," I said, and walked back into the office.

Everyone had scurried back to their desks, trying to act like they hadn't been watching through the window. All eyes were on me when I walked in. "What?" I said out loud as I barreled through the door. "Mind your own f—ing business," I snarled, as I stormed into my office.

"Yes, hello, can I speak to Ellen Henley, please? Sure, I'll hold." I looked up at the clock. It was after five. I hoped she was still in. "Oh, hi, Ellen? This is Maryanne DelRiccio. We spoke last week? Right. One of my employees is financing a car with you guys . . . Right. Martha Saunders . . . right . . . well, that's the reason I'm calling. I'm not sure if this makes a difference, but when I gave you her monthly income, I made a terrible mistake. She makes thirteen hundred a month, not three thousand. Right . . . oh, really? . . . gosh, I'm sorry for the trouble. I hope this isn't going to be a problem for her now. Oh . . . I see . . . well . . . hmmmm . . . maybe she can find someone to cosign for her. Right . . . I understand. Well, she's going to be so upset. She just loves her new car. Of course . . . it's no problem . . . I'll fax it over right away. Thank you for your time . . . you too. Bye-

bye." I smiled and leaned all the way back in my chair.

'Hmphhh! That takes care of that. One down.'

"Maryanne? We need to talk," my brother said as he walked into my office, interrupting my temporary triumph.

"Is everyone gone?" I said.

"Yeah, Terry just left. I asked Bryan to run out and grab us some Chinese food so we could be alone."

"So what's going on, Tony?" I asked, as if I didn't know.

"Look, Maryanne, I don't even want to know what went on out there with Martha—"

I interrupted him. "She told Bruno—"

"I don't want to know. Bruno sent me out here because he told me you're on drugs again. So I need you to take a test for me, Maryannie," he said, standing there with his hands in his pockets.

"What? He thinks I'm on drugs? Why? Did someone tell him that?" I asked, totally blown away.

"Have you looked in the mirror lately? Look at yourself, Maryanne. You look like a stick and you're freaking out all the time, at least that's what I'm hearing—and the whole thing with Martha this afternoon. . . I don't care what she did, you don't do that. You know that," he said, looking so disappointed.

"So I've lost some weight. I'm stressed out of my mind over here. I'm working seven days a week. Tony, I haven't taken a day off since we've been here," I said, raising my voice.

"Relax, Maryanne. I'm just telling you what's happening."

"Don't tell me to relax. I hate when people tell me to calm down. I'm not calm. You just accused me of being on drugs and you want me to calm down? I'm not on drugs, Tony. I haven't done cocaine since I was a teenager!" I shrieked.

"Look, all you have to do is take a drug test and everyone will be happy, Maryanne."

"I won't do it. Not for you—not for anybody. Why should I? I didn't do anything!" I screamed.

"Quit yelling. Jeez, sit down. Dad took your name off the accounts today. He's serious about this."

"I can't believe this, really! I can't believe this is happening to me. Why is he doing this, Tony?" I felt like I was losing my mind.

"I know . . . I don't know what his problem is, Maryanne, but let's just do this thing and get it over with," he said.

"What a goddamned hypocrite. He does drugs every day, Tony. He's a junkie. He shoots steroids two or three times week, he smokes pot every day. Drugs are his whole life, and he has the nerve . . ." I broke down. "Tony, you know I love you, right?" I said, looking straight at him.

"Yes, of course."

"If you want me to take this test I'll do it. But I want you to know that it is going to do irreparable damage. Which you realize is exactly what Bruno wants."

"What do you mean?"

"Don't you see what he's doing?" He shook his head. "He's pitting us against each other, Tony. Why do you think he had you come here instead of coming himself? If he really thought I took money from him, do you think we'd be having this conversation right now? I'd be dead. Remember what happened to the last guy who stole money from him?"

"I didn't think of that."

"Why would you, Tony? That's not your nature, and he knows it. It's me he wants. I've become too powerful, and instead of just dealing with that, he has to put me in my place, the sick f—," I said. Tony sat down in the chair, for the first time considering what I'd said. "So, if you want to believe him, fine. But just know what you're doing. You will have made your choice. Maybe we didn't realize that this was inevitable, but now . . . Look, it's not too late. We can still walk away."

"Right," he said, half convinced.

"I'm out, Tony. Seriously. This is it! There's nothing else he can do to hurt me. Just walk away with me." So we both did.

Did somebody mention the IRS? Who said that?

****

Bryan and I packed up, moved out, and were gone the next day in our U-Haul. We moved back to Marin, got pregnant, got married. My father wasn't invited to the wedding. In fact we were married on his birthday.

Turns out, my first marriage never really happened. The minister was a fake. At least that's what Dennis, the family attorney, told me. Apparently, no one could find any documentation substantiating the marriage. It had mysteriously disappeared, and evidently so had the minister. I didn't ask. All I knew was I had a green light to move on. The wreckage of my past had been swept aside long enough for me to make my escape and cross the border into another version of happily ever after.

At least now someone was there to hold space for me so that I could take a look at which battles I wanted to fight. Until now, I'd mostly run from one thing to another. But when I walked away from my father this time, I had my self-respect with me. Armed with that, and with nothing to lose, I threw myself into Reverse, hit the pedal to the metal, and backed up over the skeletons that were heading toward my closet. Then I pushed in the clutch, shifted into fifth, and took off flying. Instead of being driven by life, now I was in the driver's seat.

★★★★

"Mother, you're not listening to me. No matter what happened in the business, he promised he was going to set us up, and now he's screwed me. I'm not going to let him do that one more time," I said, tears streaming down my face as I sat across from my mother in her living room. I watched her rotate her tiered diamond ring with her thumb while she looked right through me. "Say something . . . please . . . don't just sit there and stare at me. Mother, he wouldn't give me a dime. How are we supposed to live?" I demanded.

My mother and I had made up after she heard that I was pregnant. We hadn't spoken since I'd been back from Europe. I never could keep a grudge, which in some cases was truly unfortunate.

"I'm going to do it, Mother, and you can't stop me. He can't just keep f—ing people over. Who does he think he is? I mean, look at what he did to you and Isabella, and what's-her-face, Belinda, and whoever he's with now. Jesus, Mother. Why is everyone so afraid of him? He's just a man. All I have to do is make one phone call and he's totally . . ." I almost finished my sentence.

My mother set her tea down, slowly got up from the couch, and walked over and sat down next to me. It made me nervous. It wasn't like her to be so quiet, so calm and collected. She was a drama queen, for God's sake. I thought I could get her going at least a little bit, although she rarely spoke about Bruno in any context. Something was definitely going on.

"Sweetheart? You know I love you," she said, an obvious disclaimer.

"Yes, Mother, I know you love me. What does that have to do with anything here?" I asked, annoyed by her contemplative posture. She grabbed my hands in hers.

'What, does she want to pray all of a sudden?' I thought. "Mother? What?"

"You can't," she said, and then squeezed my hands.

"I can't what?" I said. "I can't call the IRS? Yeah, hah—watch me," I said out of the side of my mouth. Looking away, she squeezed my hands harder.

"No, Maryanne. You can't," she insisted, holding my attention to the dead serious look on her face. I had never seen my mother look this way before, and let me tell you, I have seen her look many different ways. The hair on the back of my neck stood up and a slight chill ran down my spine.

"Mother, what are you talking about?" And then came the longest pause my mother and I had ever shared. Like right when someone grabs your hand before you're about to jump off a cliff.

"He'll hurt you, Maryanne," she said, tucking her lips together, pained to have ever had to utter such a thing.

My stomach dropped and my heart plummeted to the bottom of it, crashing into the shallow pool. I knew by the look in her eyes that she was telling me the truth. That my own father would have me taken out if I ever crossed that line. We sat together saying nothing, lingering in the horror and ugliness of what she had just revealed. No tears sprang into my eyes, no waves of sadness or contempt. Only the blankest place you can ever imagine, wiping out everything I'd ever known.

Something completely shifted for me that day. Realizing that my life was so disposable in his eyes took me over the top. The ability to interpret what I was actually feeling disappeared. Most of what was left was anxiety or a mild form of depression. All I could do was shut down and turn off. Everything else was like a blank space with no expectancy that it would be filled.

My body, however, was keenly aware of what it needed—to stop. I had fifteen years of running under my belt. My body had stored all that trauma and something had to give. My panic attacks were as bad as ever. I couldn't even drive to the grocery store without an escort. I didn't know what my anxiety and panic attacks were trying to tell me, so I just made my world smaller and smaller in an attempt to stay in control. It seemed like the only thing I could do.

The thing that saved me was that I was going to have this baby. This baby was conceived in absolute love. When I found out I was pregant, I knew I wanted that. I also was aware of the awesome responsibility that faced me, and how easy it would be to damage this innocent being. I was going to do anything in my power to make sure that my child wouldn't have to go through what I had. Now I was no longer fighting for my own survival; I had been bestowed with the incredible honor of protecting and serving this precious being. My job was to take care of him and teach him how to care for himself. Suddenly my life wasn't about me anymore. I am sure that's what saved me.

Welcome to the Jungle

I WAS TWENTY-EIGHT YEARS OLD when my son, Warren, was born the seventeenth of November, 1991. I left his father six months later. We had been scraping the money together to buy a house. I even shopped at Payless Shoe Stores—that's how willing I was to do without so we could build our dreams together. And then one day I pulled our credit report and found five credit cards I didn't know about, with astronomical balances. I called my husband at work, twice, and he wouldn't talk to me. Hours later, from a hotel room in Roseville, he finally called and admitted that he had been cheating on me. I had the itemized charges to prove it.

Any hope I'd managed to cloister over the years collapsed. The only chance it had had to grow was in my marriage. Now it was gone, along with any hope I had in trusting any man again. It had always been bad guys that I trusted. But Bryan was supposed to be one of the good guys people were always telling me about. As far as I was concerned, his betrayal lumped all members of the opposite sex into the same category. My father said it best: "All men want to do is f— you." When Bryan left, I never shed a tear.

Being with my son gave my life meaning. I loved him. I loved being a mother. But something critical was missing. I had read somewhere that we all have a life purpose, and if you "follow your bliss" you will ultimately be happy. I wasn't going to take a chance and ask myself what that would consist of. I knew that my mind couldn't be trusted to come up with the answer. So I went straight to the top.

But not before I reflexively apologized to the God I used to know for not having talked to him for so long. It was like not seeing one of your best friends in seven years, and as soon as you do, it's as though they had never left. Just because you've lived underground for seven years doesn't mean the sun hasn't been there all along. So I decided to pray. But my understanding of who God was had broadened into something much more vast than the God I was first introduced to. Thus I turned to what I was currently experiencing as the Universal Divine for an answer.

I sat in my study every day for three months, vowing not to leave until some manifestation of the Divine saw me and responded clearly to my question: "What is my life purpose?" That's all I wanted. It seemed like a reasonable request. And I wasn't going anywhere until I got an answer. But I didn't know how to listen. So my mind leapt into the gap and reminded me of everything I had told myself over the years that was supposed to make everything okay.

If I could get away from my father, then everything would be okay . . . if my mother loved me more, everything would be okay . . . if the kids at school didn't reject me, everything would be okay . . . if we didn't live on the other side of the tracks . . . if my mother stopped drinking . . . if I were a famous model . . . if I lived in another country . . . if my boyfriend didn't leave me . . . if my father built me a dynasty . . . if I married into the Beaver Cleaver family . . . if I were Skinnier, Tanner, and Richer . . .

When I ran through all those lies I told myself, what was left was enough silence inside so I could hear the answer to my question. Two months into this waiting, waiting, waiting, I sat in the study, my legs up on my mahogany desk, my hands resting gently in my lap, as I prepared to go deep inside for my afternoon meditation. By now I had read practically every self-help book known to man and my metaphysical repertoire ranged from the most basic to the bizarre. I was no stranger to the notion of life unseen, though not a fan of any particular spiritual bent. So I wouldn't necessarily characterize what happened next as a bona fide vision. I would have said it was more like an isolated psychotic episode—at least at first. *Conversations with God* hadn't been written yet, and no one I knew talked to the Divine directly.

'What is my life purpose? Come on, what is my life purpose?' And I waited, and then waited some more. And then I slipped into the sanctity of a placid silence that normally I had no access to.

"Bridge the gap!" said a very loud, distinctive voice inside me.

"What the—?" I opened my eyes and looked around the room. 'What was that?' I thought and closed my eyes again. As I was about to slip away again, this incredibly brilliant picture of a bridge with a gap in it flashed in front of my eyes long enough for me to make it out. Then—*blip*—it was gone. 'Whoa, what was that all about?'

"Bridge the gap!" said the booming voice again. It was like someone was holding a megaphone inside my belly. This time I almost fell out of my chair.

"Jesus Christ! Who the hell was that?" I blurted out, looking around the room. I wouldn't have been surprised if someone actually appeared. Of course no one did, at least not that I noticed. So I did what anyone would when some loud voice without a body attached to it talks to them. I politely asked, "Is anybody there?"

No response. I was partially relieved.

"Okay, I've heard about this stuff before. People hear voices all the time, right?" I said aloud. "But those people usually are on medication, Maryanne, and I've never heard about God screaming spiritual messages to anyone except that Jewish guy you met at that party who was arrested for walking naked down Center Street because he thought he was Martin Luther King.

'No, just relax, close your eyes, see if it happens again,' I thought, trying to convince myself this was normal.

"Okay, I'm closing my eyes now. What is my life purpose? What is my life purpose? That's good . . . now breathe, Maryanne. Big breath in. *What* is my life purpose? And out . . ." I started to relax. And then—*bam*—there it was again, the golden bridge with a big gap in it, only this time it stayed in my mind. So I started asking questions—quickly—like in charades. "A bridge? The Golden Gate Bridge? Uhhhh, the Bay Bridge? Uhmmm, the Brooklyn Bridge?"

'No . . . oh yeah, Bridge the Gap, right . . . the bridge had a gap so . . . I know . . . oh . . . we're going to have an earthquake and I should tell everyone! No . . . What is this? Bridge the gap? What gap?' I said inside my head, and then I heard it again.

"Bridge the gap! Write it down!" said a deliberate voice.

"What? Write it down? Like I'm going to forget that, right?" I laughed.

"Write it down!" boomed the voice.

"Jeez, okay, okay, I'll write it down," I said. I opened my eyes and looked for something to write on. The only thing within reach was a book I was reading, so I opened the back cover and wrote inside,

BRIDGE THE GAP. "Okay," I said, to whoever. I didn't hear anything, so I sat back down and closed my eyes again, waiting to see if the voice would make contact again.

After I sat for a few minutes, I got another picture. It looked like an ear with a lantern hanging from it.

"Hmmm?" I said. 'An ear with a lantern. I wonder what that means.'

"Listen and you will hear. See and you will know!" said the voice.

"*Okay*," I said, still not quite comfortable with the decibel level of the transmission, not to mention the transmission itself. "Listen and you will hear . . ." I started to repeat, but was again interrupted.

"Listen and you will hear. See and you will know. Write it down!" said the voice.

"All right, I'll write it down." I hated being bossed around. I drew a picture of an ear with a lantern, which looked more like a duck, and then wrote underneath it, "Listen and you will hear. See and you will know." And then went back up to the top of the page and drew a picture of a bridge with a gap. Well, I'm no artist, so I would have to remind myself that the picture was not of a training bra.

"All right, so now what?" I asked, leaning back, more comfortable with the drill. "Close my eyes, get trippy pictures, some voice screams for you write it down. Got it. Let's go. I'm ready for some more." I closed my eyes again and waited and waited. Nothing happened. And then, just as I was about to doze off, I saw one last picture, but this time there were no words. It was of a huge piece of thick glass covered with green felt on one side, being thumped against by piano keys. "No words, huh? Okay, fine. I'm not writing that one down then," I said, and then I heard the baby crying.

Like I said, I didn't tell anyone about what happened. I almost tried to forget about it myself. I put it in the same category as one of those dreams I'd had that I couldn't shake the residue of, sometimes for days.

That is, until I was driving home from work one evening. That's right, I got a J-O-B; until I got some answers I had to go back to work. (I even drove there by myself because I refused to let my anxiety get the best of me.) I had answered an ad for a real estate assistant, and since I knew the business, it seemed like a cinch. When I called, the guy told me he had already hired someone, but I told him I knew he would call me back and that he would hire me. And he did.

Things like that were starting to happen more frequently. Either that, or I was starting to pay attention. What I used to think was just coincidence was starting to feel like synchronicity, though there was no way prove it. Nonetheless, I was intrigued.

So I was driving home one Friday night in the middle of rush hour, and I hated traffic; I had some of my worst panic attacks in it. Out of nowhere, flashing in front of my eyes, was a giant movie screen with a red velvet curtain pulled to the sides, revealing a big gold block that read: BTG Productions. I was lucky I didn't crash into the embankment. The thing filled my entire field of vision.

'What the hell is this?' I said to myself, swerving sharply to the right and then correcting the wheel to regain control. 'BTG Productions? What is that? BTG Productions,' I said, again and again, hoping it would finally ring a bell. Then I got it.

"BTG. Bridge the gap . . . Bridge the Gap Publishing!" I said, excitedly, and then I remembered I still didn't know what the heck "bridge the gap" meant.

As I said before, I wasn't particularly interested in getting any feedback that I might be crazy. I had heard enough of that in this lifetime. So, unfortunately, this profound encounter with the Divine was entombed in that private space I reserved for miracles and possibility. That was where I kept any hopes and dreams that hadn't been decimated—or desecrated.

My day-to-day survival issues drowned out the voice. It was like trying to hear a whisper in the middle of a rock concert. All my attention was on making it to work without having a panic attack, or not having to run out of my office because I thought I was going to die of heart failure.

Over the years, in my quest to survive, I had freeze-dried my idea of God, thinking I could just add water whenever I wanted and he'd be there again for me. What I didn't realize is that God isn't the guy in the sky with a beard and a staff; he isn't an idea or a concept either. The power of the Universal Being is undeniably something so big and so real . . . which is why I kept coming back. Its spiritual gravity was gradually pulling me toward recognizing the distinction between God as a concept and that God that lives inside of me. But that was yet to come.

For now, Bridge the Gap would be the name of the production company I was about to create so I could produce my own television shows. The name symbolized me starting to wake up.

✸✸✸✸

About six months after Bryan and I split, I was sitting in my living room one Saturday morning. Warren was taking a nap and I was surfing through the cesspool that people called television, trying to find a cooking show. I loved to cook and enjoyed learning new recipes. I had just written a cookbook for my family. I flipped to a channel where this Italian woman had her own cooking show. She was teaching us all how to make a soufflé.

"So, you take de egg-shella like-a dis and-a you putta de yoke like-a dis, and you make eet back and a fort-a like-a dis and-a then-a you, and then-a you . . ." she stammered.

"Yes, and then you . . ." I said, trying to help her from my couch.

"And-a then you—" she put the eggshells down and scratched her head and started laughing. "Huh? I can't remember, so forget it!" she said. I got off the couch and walked up to the set.

"What? What do you mean, 'Forget it?' You can't say that! This is critical information here. You can't just forget it," I said, talking to the television. I grabbed the remote control unit and changed the channel, exasperated, and then just flipped it off.

'She can't do that,' I thought. 'Who does that? God, I could do better than that. At least I speak English,' I thought, and then it hit me. 'Then why don't you?' I thought. 'Why don't you? You could do that. You could have your own cooking show. Why not you? You could do at least as well as she can. Besides, what have you got to lose, Maryanne? I mean, just look at all the crap on TV. You can't do any worse than what's already on.' So I went for it.

★★★★

Warren was eighteen months old when I finally quit my job, determined to carve a name for myself in the media. For a little over a year I had been working in real estate, the last real job I would ever have. The fact that Jack was my boss and my boyfriend made it easy for me to quit; he had already started paying my bills. The fact that Jack was married was his wife's problem. I couldn't be bothered with that. I was a train coming down the track, and unless you were getting on board, you needed to get the hell out of my way.

My ex-husband Bryan worked with someone named Martin, who directed commercials. Our children went to the same preschool, which made him, in theory, more easily accessible. Supposedly he was hip and always looking for new projects, and I had just the ticket. All I needed him to do was see me on camera for two seconds and I knew he would listen to my idea.

I had signed up for a class at our local cable station where they taught me the nuts and bolts of technical production. I learned how to use a camera, set up lighting, how to edit—you name it. And in less than six months I had produced a ninety-minute tape packed with footage of me interviewing people, asking the question, "How long does it take to hard boil an egg?" That question would change my life forever.

★★★★

"Martin? Yeah, hi. Excuse me. Martin . . . Sorry, I'm just trying to get . . . excuse me. Hi, my name is Maryanne and . . ." I said, bumping people out of the way so I could get his direct attention, as a varied assortment of parents moved out of the school with children in tow. I had come at two thirty on the dot because I had seen him there at early pickup one day.

"Hi." I held out my elbow to shake, because my hands were full with Warren and I had the videotape in his diaper bag in my other hand. Martin just kept walking. "You're Martin, right? You know my ex, Bryan Wells? He works with you at . . ." I stammered a bit, totally jacked that I finally got near him.

"Yeah, I know him," he said, and kept walking.

"Well, see the thing is, I have this tape . . ." I held it out. He didn't even look at it. "And I was wondering . . . I mean, if you could just look at it, it would only take, like, two seconds for you to look at because I have this great idea and . . ." I spoke as fast as I could because he was now opening the door of his car and putting his son in his car seat. "So, I mean, I wouldn't bother you under normal circumstances, and I'm sorry, but really, my idea is stellar and I know if you . . ." I tried to smush it all in there, but it was too late.

"Sorry, I'm really not interested," he said, closing his car door. And that was it. Until the next day.

"Martin! Hi, remember me? Maryanne? Bryan's ex," I said, leaping out in front of him. This time I had put the tape in Warren's diaper bag and flung it over the same shoulder I was carrying him on so I could shake his hand. "It's really nice to meet you," I said, sticking out my hand and pumping his enthusiastically.

"Nice to meet you too," he said politely, and started speeding up. I kept talking.

"Remember that tape I told you about? Well, if you could just take one minute and look at it, I promise you won't be sorry. I have this great idea for a show I want to tell you about and . . ." He didn't care.

He stuck his son in his seat and then said, "You know, now is not a good time," and opened his car door.

"Okay. So when is a good time?" I asked, standing there in my resolve.

"Uhhmm, let me think about it," he said, climbing in his car.

"Wait, why don't you take this," I said, flipping the cassette out of Warren's diaper bag like a gun from a holster, "so you can. . ."—he drove off—"watch it at home," I finished saying. It didn't matter; tomorrow was another day.

"Martin, hi . . . Maryanne," I said, catching up to him the next afternoon. "Wow, what are you, like Mr. Mom?" He actually laughed. "Look, Martin, I'm not going to give up. I have a feeling about this and I think you will agree with me if you will just look at this tape." I waved it in his face; this time I was ready and had it in my hand. "I promise, just two minutes—that's all I'm asking—and if you hate it I'll never bother you again," I said, handing him the tape. "I put my phone number on the little sticky thing on the cassette. Call me," I said, waving at him as he crossed the street and headed for his car.

About six thirty that night my phone rang. I thought it was going to be Jack saying he was on his way.

"Hey, Sexy, whatcha doin'?" I said. Caller ID didn't exist yet.

"Sorry, it's not Sexy. It's Martin."

"Oh God, I'm sorry. I thought you were . . . never mind," I said, fully embarrassed.

"No worries. Hey look, I watched your tape, Maryanne. It was hilarious. You're a real talent. No kidding," he said.

"Really?" I squealed with delight. "I mean, you're not just saying that?" I asked more calmly, trying to be serious.

"No, really, the camera loves you, you're funny, and your accents are awesome."

"Oh, I'm so glad. I was hoping you would like it. That means so much to me," I gushed.

"So yeah, let's get together and talk about your idea," he said. And we did.

When I pitched Martin my concept, he immediately went for it. He thought doing a show about food and sex was brilliant. There was no such thing. There was Dr. Ruth and, more recently, the Playboy Channel, but nothing in between. Our idea was unique and its time had definitely come. All we needed now was a network that thought so too!

Wanted: Bay Area Talk Show Host Seeks Interviews with Couples and Individuals for Sexy New Cooking Show

THAT'S WHAT THE AD READ, and we ran it for one week to see what would happen. To our surprise, the response was overwhelming. Returning all the calls took us almost two weeks. Hundreds upon hundreds of people were chomping at the bit to tell their tales. We initially ran the ad because the format we chose involved a studio audience. But based on the response, we decided to have the show be about real people, not celebrities that none of us could relate to or even cared about. And I chose a kitchen for the set, and cooking for the theme, because at every party I had ever been to everyone inevitably ended up in the kitchen, sitting around eating or drinking, talking about sex.

I was certain that this was the bridge I needed to gap, and come hell or high water, I had every intention of doing just that. The battle of the sexes had become a huge chip on my shoulder. All I had to do was look at my life and see that this was the cornerstone of all my ills, my heartaches, my trials and tribulations, my suffering, my tales of woe. And if I could settle this matter and show the world the truth about it all, I could help end all human suffering (particularly mine). It was then that I absolutely knew, without a shadow of a doubt, that if I could just do *this*, everything would be okay.

So Martin and I pressed on toward my latest goal—to end human suffering—and proceeded to produce a pilot for our new show, called *What's Cooking? with Maryanne*. To give you a flavor of the ordinary people we ended up attracting, I'll tell you about one person we interviewed.

"Good morning! Thank you so much for coming," I greeted the short, bald Indian man in the rent-an-office space we had reserved to conduct all our interviews.

"Hallooo," he shrilled with his sweet voice, and politely sat down. He placed a brown paper bag on the conference table that was big enough to seat twelve, and then folded his hands in his lap and waited patiently for his cue.

"Oh good, Martin's here now. We can get started in just a minute," I said to our little visitor. He looked so innocent and just sat there silently, like a well-behaved child waiting for his mommy. I could see Martin through the blinds as he hurried toward the room. He was notorious for being late.

"God . . . traffic . . . uhhh, sorry I'm late," he said. He slammed his coffee mug and briefcase on the table, brushed his hair back, and took a seat.

"Okay then, let's get started. Mr. Rajnem—I'm sorry, is that the correct pronunciation? Raj-nehmm," I said, trying to properly enunciate his last name.

"Don't worry, you may just call me Raji," he said, with a heavy Indian accent.

"Well, that's fine. Good, Mr. Raji. Let's talk first about why you responded to our ad, if you wouldn't mind," I said. He didn't speak. He only smiled. I looked over at Martin. He just shrugged his shoulders.

"Uhh, Mr. Raji? You can talk now, uh, if you want, about, you know, why you answered the ad." I said, and smiled back at him.

"Oh, I'm sorry, you want me to talk to you about why I telephoned?" he said.

"Uhmmm, yeah. That's the idea." Martin sat there looking at something he had just scraped out of his ear. "Okay, Mr. Raji."

"Yes. Well, one evening I was at home making honey-baked prawn, and it was very warm indeed, so I had the window open," he started.

"Honey-what?" asked Martin.

"Prawn," I said.

"Right," he said, and leaned back in his chair, inspecting the sole of one of his Tevas.

"Sorry, Mr. Raji. Go ahead."

"It's okay," he said. "So I was standing in the kitchen with the window open when suddenly a bee flew in."

"A what?" asked Martin.

"A bee," I said. The little man looked at me for approval. I nodded my head. "Go ahead, Mr. Raji."

"And as I was saying, it was very hot, so sometimes when it's this hot I like to cook in the nude." Martin and I shot each other that smile where your mouth doesn't actually change position but your nostrils flare and the muscles around your eyes widen into a grin. We both got the visual at the same time: this little guy cooking naked in his kitchen so all the neighbors could see. "And then the bee—it landed on my penis and stung me. I must have dripped some honey on it," he explained.

Just then, Jack blew through the door. I knew he was going to like this. Anything that spelled S-E-X Jack wouldn't want to miss for the world.

"Sorry I'm late, guys," he said, tiptoeing in and taking a chair.

"Mr. Raji is telling us about how he likes to cook in the nude," I said, filling him in. He nodded and then reached over and shook Martin's hand quickly.

"What's up, Martin?" he said.

"I'm sorry, Mr. Raji. Please continue. So the bee flew through the window and landed on your penis, and then what happened?" Jack looked over at me and then at Martin; he pulled his chair closer to the table, yanked up his belt a little, adjusting himself, and came to full attention.

"And so, yes, the bee flew through the window and stung me on my penis. And my penis swelled up to about three inches in diameter," he went on. The three of us looked at each other out of the corners of our eyes. "And then I noticed that the swelling was very arousing and so I began to masturbate. And now what I do is I capture the bees in a mayonnaise jar and place about three or four of them under my foreskin," he continued.

"Your what?" asked Martin, who was an amazing creative artist but a total space cadet.

"Foreskin," said Jack and I, simultaneously.

"That's right. And sometimes, I will insert ball bearings in my urethra, and when I ejaculate I hold a glass jar in front of my penis and let the balls crash into the jar. I enjoy the sound; it gives me pleasure," he said, and then smiled broadly at us, exposing teeth that looked like they were about to drop out.

"Insert what?" said Jack, wincing, grabbing his crotch underneath the table.

"Ball bearings," Martin and I said, in unison. I turned and looked at him. He winked at me and smiled.

And just when I thought I had heard everything, the little man added this little morsel to his already indigestible fare. "Sometimes when I am preparing dinner for a lady friend, I will lie on top of the dining table and place a bouquet of fresh flowers into my urethra, or perhaps a candle. It's really quite surprising!" he added.

"I'll bet," I said, looking at my watch, hoping the little brown paper bag he set on the table wasn't full of bees—or flowers. I tried to imagine what one would say in response to this unusual salutation.

★★★★

My feelings were stuffed almost completely in my head by now. I was sure I was working the proper vision, convinced I'd been given a glimpse of my life purpose directly from the Source.

'It's my turn now,' I told myself. 'And nothing is going to stop me. Why should I pray for further guidance? There's no need for further directives from the cosmos. Let's not confuse matters with the details. Just show me the money.'

★★★★

"What time is our appointment?" I asked as we racewalked from the parking lot to the convention center.

"Well, we don't actually have an appointment, Maryanne. That's what I was trying to tell you last night," said Jeff, the producer / director of our cooking show pilot.

"You didn't tell me that!" I said, suddenly miffed. "Great, that's fricking great, Jeff. What are we supposed to do, walk in there and just hope someone will talk to us?" I said, pissed that I was now in a bad mood.

"Well, like I was trying to tell you, we can spend most of today schmoozing and see if we can make some contacts. We only need one or two good ones."

"Jeff, this is your job. I hired you to produce results. I can't do it all," I said, showing my badge to the security guard as we walked through the doors. Jeff didn't even bother to respond; he knew he wasn't going to win with me. You couldn't. I had become the thing I hated most—my father. It was my way or the highway—and that was not up for negotiation.

I looked around the conference arena. It was so big I couldn't even see the other side. "Okay, look, I'm going to do a sweep, see what's what and then I'll meet you back here by. . . It's nine thirty now. Say, noonish. And then we'll go from there." It wasn't a question and I didn't wait for an answer, I simply rolled up my sleeves and walked off.

'Moron . . . I can't believe I came all the way here and . . . whatever . . . don't think about him. You can do this, you can totally do this. He would only embarrass you anyway. You made this show happen, Maryanne, so just forget about him,' I told myself. My version of a pep talk before I got in the ring. Because for me it was always a battle, a fight I had to win.

I walked around studying the booths, taking stock of all the different networks: Multi-Media Entertainment—who at the time produced Oprah and Phil Donohue—Disney, Garth Ancier, and Warner Brothers, just to name a few. And as I made my rounds, it became clear that to get in to see anyone who was anyone I was going to have to conjure up some magic. It was about eleven thirty and I felt like I didn't have much time. I always felt like the clock was ticking, like life was just about to run out and I didn't want to miss out.

"Excuse me?" I asked the receptionist, who stood behind the barrier separating me from my dream come true. "I have an appointment with David—oh God, forgive me . . . I'm so spacey this morning

. . . I can't even remember my own name," I said, and then laughed accordingly.

"I know what you mean," she said, commiserating with me.

"The Director of Original Programming? Duh, Oh God," I said, popping myself in the forehead like 'Wow, I shoulda had a V-8,' in this case 'Duh, I can't remember his name.'

"Terry Chambers?" she said, pointing to a handsome young guy in a double-breasted suit who was speaking to a group of Asian men.

"Terry Chambers! Thank you. I have an appointment with Terry this afternoon and I'm running a little behind and hoping you guys are too," I said, holding up and crossing my fingers.

"Way behind," she said. "Don't even worry about it."

"Great. I'll be back," I said, pretending to race off to somewhere important.

I met back with Jeff and told him I was on to something over at Casting House Entertainment and that all he needed to know was that they produced Geraldo. Which meant their venue was big enough for them to bend their minds around our show. I said I'd meet him back at the hotel later and I took off again.

I cruised around the conference for another hour or so, making notes and watching to catch clues of how this whole show business thing worked. I was a quick study and by one o'clock I figured I was as ready as I would ever be. I approached the booth slowly, careful not to let myself be noticed. I needed to move in gradually, so I could feel the water before I jumped in.

The first thing I had to do was get past the desk, and then it was downhill from there. I noticed there were two girls at the reception desk now and certain people were coming and going without checking in, so what I needed to do was clear.

"So, how's a girl supposed to get a drink around here?" I asked, grabbing onto the arm of the next guy who was walking into the booth area, tagging along, my face turned toward him so the receptionist couldn't see me. It worked like a charm.

"Wow, getting an early start?" said the shiny young man as he escorted me back to the bar. "Knock yourself out," he said, chival-rously, dropping me off.

"Yep, I can't make it through my day without knocking back a few OJ's," I said, tipping my proverbial hat to him, so to speak. He laughed and walked off.

Many of the booths were elaborately decorated, complete with full bars, red carpets, and hors d'oeuvres served by waitpeople cloaked in everything from tuxes to outrageous costumes. The bigger the company, the more decadent their presentation. Casting House was no slouch. Their presentation was clean, sophisticated, with just a little edge, as evidenced by the giant glossy poster of Geraldo hang-ing on the wall in the reception area. I thought it was perfect.

I lingered at the bar, drinking my OJ, waiting for my chance to pounce, and then. . .

"I am soo sorry I am late," I said, walking right up to Terry, kiss-ing him on the cheek and then grabbing his arm and standing flush to his side. He was being venerated in a group of four other people and was about to fall asleep. I could tell because I had been watching him. His arms were folded and he wasn't making eye contact. No one had succeeded in engaging him. But I was about to change all that.

"It's no problem, really, we were just finishing up," he said, excus-ing himself, grinning from ear to ear, relieved for the interruption.

"Thank you. Sorry," I said to the group of yawners that had just been booted. He grabbed my hand and led me over to the couches and sat me down. "First of all, thank you. I didn't know how else to get your attention," I said.

"Don't apologize." He laughed. "You probably did me a favor."

"All I need is five minutes of your time."

He looked me up and down, smiling, and said, "I don't know who you are, but whatever you've got, I want some of it." I wrapped my other hand around his and leaned in audaciously.

"The name is DelRiccio . . . Maryanne DelRiccio . . ."

Terry loved my idea, and as far as he was concerned, I was an absolute hit. He said I had everything it took, but there was just one problem. I assumed he meant that I was virtually unknown. The real problem turned out to be that he was a married man who wanted me to audition on the casting couch. Oblivious at first to the real motive for his interest, I reminded him that in a year's time, instead of having twenty channels, we would have two hundred, and that content would be the name of the game. He countered that no one, big network was going to bank on the future of an unknown. That's not the way it worked in Hollywood. You did what worked. He called it the winning formula. But the only winner in his scenario would be him.

So how did I not get that this guy just wanted to nail me in the sack? Was my head so far up . . . in the clouds that I would miss something so obvious? I assumed that the ring on his finger was insulation from any potential indiscretion, but I was wrong. Again. A year later, after he had baited me with the promise of being the newest talk show Whoozits on national television, I discovered he had not only taken leave of Casting House, but he had taken me. One night I was channel surfing, and there was *my* show in all its glory—except I wasn't on it.

Note to self: As my mother always said, if it walks like a duck and talks like a duck, it's probably not a fuzzy bunny. Lesson Not Learned: A duck is a duck is a duck.

I felt completely thwarted. I didn't know where I'd put my Good Girl Handbook, but I knew exactly where my shit list was. Right underneath "All Men Inhabiting Planet Earth" I wrote, "Terry Chambers and All of Bullshit Hollywood." I told myself that I didn't need anyone anyway. I didn't need anyone telling me what to wear, how to act, what I could and couldn't say. The whole point of doing my show was to expose the truth so we could all be free to say what we really wanted to. So we could stop living the fake, robotic lives that had us all bunged up in the first place. I was on a mission and all I needed was to find someone who would give me a huge wad of cash and not try to take something from me. How hard could that be? Milli Vanilli made it, and they couldn't even sing. So I went back once again to the Main Man and put in a request.

Someone had told me, "God doesn't pull you out of the pond to drop you in the ocean." I was banking on that. If he would just take two seconds off from running the Universe and tell someone to help me—I mean, how tough is that?—then, for sure, everything would be okay.

'Okay, God, I've been trying to turn my will and life over to you. The least you could do is cough up some cash . . . so I may better do thy will. I only need five hundred thousand dollars to get this thing off the ground. It's not like I haven't paid my dues—what else do you want from me? So if it's not a problem, now would be a good time. Amen.'

I shifted gears from my original concept of a food and sex show to take a more universal stab at disenchanting the world by debunking social myths such as: Men are more sexually driven than women. The new format went well with the chip on my shoulder.

★★★★

"Aren't you the gal who has that cable talk show . . . what's it called?" asked the handsome, well-groomed man as I finished out my last set on the bench press. He was easily six feet tall, and carried himself well.

"*From the Hip*," I said, as I looked up, pleased to be recognized.

"I'm sorry, my name is Dante. Dante McDonald," he said.

"Hello," I said, partly suspicious, as I was of most men who would approach me at my club. I wondered if he was a famous football player or something; he had that kind of aura.

"Look, I don't want you the get the wrong idea," he said, like he was reading my mind. "If you knew who I was—obviously you don't recognize me—you would know I don't go around . . . well . . . let's just say that there is something about you. . . I've seen you before and wanted to say I really admire what you are trying to do for people. Your show is good, and if there is anything at all I can do for you, know that I am in a position to help you." He reached out his hand.

"I don't know what to say." I settled for "Thank you," and shook his hand. I could tell by the way he closed his eyes and gently bowed, holding his hands together in prayer position, that we believed in the same kind of God. He had made a public display of his devotion; he had to be for real. Who does that, especially in a fitness meat market? Anyway, he didn't look like some jump-on-the-yoga-bandwagon kind of guy.

I had finally found the missing link! The problem with all my other plans of attack was that the other people in the equation didn't believe in any sort of God. And since I had given God a promotion to CEO, as of my last prayer, the Universe was obviously giving me a sign. I had been sent someone who was coming from the same place I was. What else did I need to know?

Even so, I knew better than to start future-tripping. My head reminded me—not to mention the voice of my mother, my brother, and the bird on the ledge—that I needed to stay in touch with reality here. People don't materialize out of nowhere and start offering to make your dreams come true. And since I had already been on plenty of roads that closely resembled this one, I didn't want to set myself up again. So I decided to just let it stand and say some extra prayers later.

I felt a tap on my shoulder. "Here's my card, Maryanne. God bless you," he said. I was sure he meant it—I had chills.

I ran into Dante two weeks later. I had propped his card up against my computer and looked at it every day. I was surprised to see him, but I really shouldn't have been. I had been reading a lot of books about the universal flow of energy and prosperity, so the concept of drawing people or things into one's life didn't seem overly fantastic anymore. Still, there is a subtle, yet almost surreal, astonishment when something actually manifests out of the force of one's desire.

"That is so weird. I was just thinking about you this morning," I said, and gave him a hug, not even thinking twice about it. We were standing in front of Whole Foods Market in downtown Mill Valley. I was about to grab some lunch.

"How's it going for you?' he asked, peeling his sunglasses away from his face.

"Really?" I said, looking deep into his eyes.

"Of course." .

"Well, I've thought about what you said to me. That if I need help, to let you know. The truth is, I do," I explained.

"Well, let's go talk about it," he said. "Do you have some time?"

"Actually, I do." We walked over to a restaurant nearby and sat out on the patio.

"See the thing is, this is my dream. I want to do this, not just for me, but so I can touch the lives of people who suffer. It's the biggest way I can think of to help—using television as a medium to reach as many people as possible versus as a tool of capitalism and sensationalism. Don't get me wrong, I don't think there is anything wrong with money; it's just that things seem so out of balance, you know what I mean?" And that's all I could get in, because for the next two hours Dante barraged me with all his dreams and goals, telling me how he was revolutionizing the world himself. He said he couldn't tell me too much because it was classified information, and apparently there were people who were willing to do dreadful things to get such information. I assured him I was not one of them. After he was finished dazzling, trying to impress me with his ten-digit status as a megaweight, he said, unexpectedly, "So what's your bottom line, Maryanne?"

"You mean, how much money do I need?" I said, taken offguard.

"Yes, to build your dream, how much would it take?"

"To do everything I want to do, and not have to cut corners? A million dollars," I said, as though I were being granted a wish, throwing out what seemed like an astronomical amount.

"Done," he said. He sounded like Richard Gere in *Pretty Woman*. Too bad he didn't look like him, but I'll tell you right then, I could definitely relate to how Julia Roberts felt. He took a gold Cross pen out of his breast pocket, slipped the cocktail napkin out from under his mineral water, wrote something down, and then flagged down a waiter who was passing by.

"Would you please read this and then sign it?" he asked, in an austere tone.

So the young man did, and then stayed by the table to watch for my reaction.

"Here," Dante said, handing me the napkin.

I, Dante McDonald, promise to pay
Maryanne DelRiccio the sum of $1,000,000
on or before December 1, 1996.
Dante McDonald

To capture my reaction to this hastily written inscription on this three-by-five-inch cocktail napkin, I would have to include a sound byte in the book. I screamed so loud that all the heads in the restaurant swiveled simultaneously in my direction. I laughed and cried and then I jumped up and down. I was hysterical. This man had just signed over to me what I had wanted for as long as I could remember—absolute immunity. I could write my own ticket now, call my own shots. I would never have to fake another orgasm again. Which reminded me . . .

"Let me get this straight. You're just going to *give* me this money?" I asked, waving the napkin in my hand—"clutching" is more accurate.

"Uh-huh."

"And I don't have to pay you back?"

"That's right."

"'Cause here's the thing, Dante. I'm not going to sleep with you. No offense, but if that's what this is about, you can have this back." But I was still gripping that napkin.

"Maryanne, I have a girlfriend and I'm very happy. I don't want anything from you—well, except one thing."

'Uh-oh,' I thought, 'here it comes.'

"When you make it," he said, leaning in so close I could see his nose hair, "I want you to do the same thing for someone else. That's all." Then he leaned back, waved his hand to ask for the check, and said he needed to go; he had an appointment in the city and was running late.

I was on cloud nine, maybe even cloud ten. Wherever I was, I never wanted to leave. I floated through most of the rest of that week.

Until it came time to collect.

"Hey Dante, it's Maryanne again. Do you think you could call me back? We need to talk about the money thing here because I'd like to start production as soon as possible."

The next day: "Hey Dante, it's me again, Maryanne, and I know you're probably real busy, but I need to talk to you. Please give me a call."

And the next: "Hey, Dante, it's me. I opened a trust account at First American Title. You can call and ask for Margie. I know you're super busy, but if you could transfer the money over, that would be great. Here's her number."

And then the next. "Look Dante, I don't know what's going on, but there's a whole crew of people waiting on you, and you said you would take care of this right away, that it was no problem. But it's starting to seem like a problem. Would you please call me?"

And then I got pissed.

★★★★

"Look Maryanne, call his office and talk to someone else who's there," my brother Tony said.

"I already did that. It goes right into voice mail," I said, frustrated.

"Well, maybe he's out of town."

"And he hasn't checked his messages for three weeks?"

"Well, did you check him out on the Internet?"

"Yeah, they have a site, but I can't find them on the NASDAQ, or anywhere. Like he told me, no one's ever heard of them."

"Well, are you sure he's legit?"

"I mean, I *say* yes. I know people who know him. They all tell me the same story, that he's some super-genius guy who's worth six billion, blah, blah, blah. And I've seen him around for a couple of years."

"Did you call your attorney?"

"Uh-huh, he's looking into it now."

"Well, then, we'll just have to wait."

"I know, it's just that it's so weird, Tony. I can't believe he would do this. He believes in God and everything, Tony. He's not like all those other assholes. But what if he is . . . I don't even want to say it . . . do you think he's a con artist? The weird thing is, he hasn't taken anything from me, and I haven't given him anything."

"Are you sure?"

"Yeah, I mean, empirically speaking, but I see what you're driving at. I'm just . . . I don't get it," I said. And I didn't get it—the money that is.

The whole time I was trying to reach Dante, he was sending me letters—often hand delivered to my post box. They were filled with advice about my son, random bits of philosophy, and declarations of his love for me (that hardly made sense for someone who swore he was in love with another woman and didn't want to sleep with me). He wrote about everything except about the money.

Dante finally called me a month later and told some outrageous story about how he'd had to hide out and that he would have been putting me in danger if he had contacted me. When I confronted him about the money he became belligerent, accusing me of calling him a liar. He said that he was glad he was finally seeing my true colors, since he had been about to profess his love for me—again. The only color I saw was red, and when I hung up that phone I completely flipped out.

What was I, part dog and color blind? Why did I not heed *this* red flag? The one that started to wave when I called the number on his flimsy business card—obviously printed on his own computer, with fresh perforated edges—and discovered the number was disconnected? Yeah, but he told me that was because he was back and forth from New York so much that his secretary forgot to pay the bill.

And I wanted to believe him.

Or the red flag that popped up when I drove past the address on his business card so I could get a look at his empire's headquarters? It happened to be the same address as Whole Foods, which as it turned out, was where his mother worked. I had been too afraid to ask about that one, so I simply told myself that he didn't want anyone to know how to find him because they all just wanted his money.

Or how about the time when he took me shopping in Union Square just because he could, and I picked out several items racking up to about the seven-thousand-dollar mark? Yet when it came time to pay, he said he had to phone his attorney to release more money on his credit card because he was in such heavy negotiations that his funds were being controlled by his executor. He promised he'd send me the clothes as soon as the money came through. But it never did, and when I asked, he accused me of not trusting him and hung up on me.

Or what about the red flag that flapped in the breeze any time he would leave and slink around some corner? I never did see him get into his car, or any car, for that matter. Of course I told myself that he had a limousine, and out of humility had arranged to be picked up and dropped off someplace out of sight. I never did ask about that.

Should I go on, or is here where I should say how much I needed to solidify my belief in some cosmic power greater than myself? I had prayed, he had answered, or so I thought—thus I wanted Dante to be for real because that would mean that God had heard me and answered my prayers. Otherwise I was going to have to rethink everything, and I wouldn't know where to start.

I spent the next year and a half almost completely housebound. The only thing I did with any modicum of success was take care of my son and breathe in and out. I was too depressed to go on, but too chicken to kill myself, and I hated myself for both reasons. Before, I could always figure out what to do next; I could fix the problem, get over the thing, or change the situation. I could become whoever or whatever I needed to. But this time there was no I, no me that even cared. When I looked in the mirror, I saw nothing that resembled anything I recognized.

★★★★

I dragged myself out of bed on no particular morning. My son was visiting his father and I was now living with Jack. We had a beautiful home with a spectacular view of the bay, but all I could see was gray. I picked up a book off my coffee table and decided to read instead of staring out the window like I had done for the past eighteen months. The book was called *The Bond Between Women* and I was reading about how girls as young as five years old were being sold by their parents and then prostituted out, made to service upward of thirty clients per day. I was moved to tears, which in the last year and a half was rare. I had stopped feeling anything at all, except to muster up my genuine love for my son.

In the middle of a paragraph, something inside me began to rumble. My body started to shake from this internal quake, and for no apparent reason, I blurted out, "Screw you, God. You motherf—er, what do you want from me? I barely asked you for anything, and I get this? Is this some kind of joke? Well, f— you. Do you hear me? F— you!"

I stormed over to the phone, picked it up, and called one of my stepmothers.

"Isabella? Yeah, hi. It's me. Yeah, good. Look, I need Bruno's pager number," I said, not having spoken to her in months. I wasn't up for any chitchat bullshit, and she could tell. She didn't even ask, gave me the number, and I hung up. I didn't say good-bye.

★★★★

Since, as I said, I hadn't spoken to my father more than twice in the prior ten years, when my telephone rang, I must say I was disturbed when I first heard his voice. But I quickly recovered.

"Hello, Maryanne," he said, with his unnerving even keel.

"Bruno, I must say I am surprised. I didn't think you'd call, but then again. . . Well, I'm sure you know that I'm not calling because I have anything nice to say to you," I said. He stayed silent. I went on. "It occurred to me that my birthday is next week and I decided I was going to give myself a birthday present I would never forget." Still not a peep. I couldn't even hear him breathe.

"So here's the deal, Bruno. I just want you to listen. You don't get to say anything. No arguing, no defending, no swearing, just listen to whatever I need to say. And you don't get to hang up either. You just have to take it. Because it occurs to me that I have saved up about thirty years of horror that I have stuffed inside of me and you need to stand there like a man and take responsibility for your part in it. And one more thing, Bruno. I don't have anything nice to say. I will probably yell and swear because I don't like you—as a matter of fact, you disgust me and I feel nothing but grave contempt for your existence, so there it is. Do you think you can handle that?"

"Lay it on me," he said. And I did.

"Let's see, first I have some rhetorical questions. That means you don't respond. For example, what did you tell yourself that made it okay to just walk out of our lives and not take care of us? What kind of selfish bastard just leaves his children? I wish I could say you did a shitty job at parenting, Bruno, but you did worse than that—you did so much damage that I find it hard to believe that God allowed you to reproduce.

"What's worse is, you knew. You knew what you were doing. You knew the difference between right and wrong and you brought me into this hell, this drug-infested place that reeked with death and destruction, and you didn't bat an eyelash, which makes you all the more disgusting. Just what kind of deal did you make with the devil, Bruno? It must have been very compelling.

"Incidentally, I have never approached you before to tell you how I felt because part of your punishment for being such a piece of shit is that you don't get to have me in your life. And that will continue to be true, because nothing you say or do will ever erase the suffering you have caused me. And I'm sure I speak on behalf of all the victims you have preyed on. You deliberately chose weak people that you could use and abuse, and siphoned the life right out of each and every one until there was nothing left. But the mistake you made with me is, I am you. I have all those gifts you have neglected, only I am stronger and smarter than you are. And I am the only one who is not afraid of you Bruno, because I see you for who you are—and now I will watch you as you decay.

"I hope that you suffer and die in pain. That will be the only pleasure you have ever given me, you evil f—.

"The pathetic thing is that there is a little part of me, a small piece, that feels the need to apologize to any part, however small, inside your ugly, hollow heart that is good. I'm sure you understand that on some level the child inside me is reluctant to hurt you in any way, but *I* am not—so f— you! I have spent countless days and hours, time I will never recoup, intellectualizing and rationalizing that, 'Oh, you were a sick man, an alcoholic, etcetera.' But the thing is, Bruno, I am tired of taking my rage out on everyone else—most of all myself. I can't even stand to be who I am, so f— you for that too. It's like I'm handicapped and you are the cancer that keeps eating me alive, and every time I cut it out it just grows back in another place.

"We are all ashamed of you, ashamed to use your name, embarrassed to even know you. The path you chose was weak and vulgar and the damage that you have done is irreparable.

"And oh, f— you for all the times that you invalidated my feelings and told me I was full of shit, so that later in life I couldn't trust what I felt. I can't even take care of myself, you f—. I'm too afraid to even drive my car. I can hardly take care of my son, you barbaric bastard, so f— you for that too. Now, I'm sure I'm leaving some important things out, but the idea of staying on the phone with you much longer makes my skin crawl. So let me just say this: F— you for everything I forgot to say!"

After a long, silent pause that marked the end of my tirade and left an obvious invitation for some feedback, he said, "You're right. Everything you said is right on. I agree with it all, and there is nothing I can say or do to change the past."

"Hey, Bruno, don't underestimate the power of a sincere apology, even under these circumstances."

"I am sorry, Maryanne, and of all the people's lives I have damaged, unfortunately I have done the most harm to you." His tone wasn't insincere, but it was flat.

"I hope you suffer somehow for it," I said. "I'm going to be thirty-three years old next week, no thanks to you, and the irony is, I wish I were dead. Anyway, thank you for not hanging up. Maybe if I'm lucky this will help," I said, in closing.

"Anytime, anytime at all," he replied. The weird thing was, he meant it.

"Good-bye, Bruno." There was a pause.

"Good-bye, Maryanne." I hung up first.

Payola

TWO WEEKS PASSED. I was in Manhattan celebrating the second week of my birthday month. Fourteen days and counting until the big three-three. I thought thirty-three was going to be one of my better birthdays, because, well, Jesus Christ died at thirty-three and, frankly, that was the story I was telling myself. Jesus made it and so can I. Whatever. It was working for me.

Anyhoo, my best friend Shakti and I had just walked into Patricia Fields on Eighth Street when I got the call on my cell phone. I was amidst Technicolor feathers, glitter, and sequined costumes, and surrounded by men in drag who were better looking than most supermodels. I was excited to hear Isabella's voice. We had remained close and spoke almost as often as I spoke to my own mother.

"Oh my God, Iz, you can't believe this place," I whispered into the phone. I rarely bothered with pleasantries. "I'm in this boutique called Patricia Fields. All the girls are guys here. I mean, they're all uuhhmm . . . you know, what do you call those guys who dress up like women?"

"Maryanne," Isabella said, interrupting my little *La Cage aux Folles* fantasy. "The little girl your father molested"—she paused, and

I could hear her swallow hard—"killed herself two days ago." My mouth dropped open. I stood there, not sure I had heard correctly. My father had been arrested several months earlier for molesting his current wife's—wife number four's—young niece, and his trial was pending. One of the bigger details of my life I tried to ignore.

My body broke out in a slight sweat. I pulled at the collar of my shirt as if I could get more air to breathe. I couldn't talk. I heard Isabella's voice as though it were far away, "Are you okay, honey?" Her words had sent me further back into the darkness that I had only imagined I had blanked out. I turned for the door. I couldn't breathe. I walked outside onto the sidewalk, smack into the middle of the oncoming pedestrian traffic. I wasn't aware that I was still holding the phone to my ear. The twenty-four-hour bustle of the Big Apple went on mute inside my head as people passed around me like a stream of ants on a mission. All I could see was a picture of this precious little girl, terrified and alone, and now dead. Isabella waited, silent, on the other end of the line.

"How'd she do it?" I wanted to know. A passerby bumped into me like a pinball and I reflexively moved back up against the building away from the crowds.

"I'm not sure. I mean, I don't know yet," she replied. I had been waiting for months to hear word about my father's sentence. I was not only prepared for that, I was looking forward to it. I'd been having many fantasies of him being raped in jail by his new peers, and at times savored the gory details and variety of ways he would be violated. But nothing could have prepared me for the horror and the resignation I felt about this young girl's suicide. In that moment I became the shoe I was always afraid would drop. And it crossed my mind, 'It should have been me.'

"How is it that God would let this creature roam the earth, Iz? How? Can't somebody stop him? I mean, what the hell, he can't just keep . . ." I realized the futility of my words. Bruno always managed to escape justice. It didn't matter what I thought or said. My only hope now was that he would die a gruesome death befitting such a monster—in prison, where he belonged.

I hung up with Isabella and walked with Shakti across town to the Mercer Hotel where we were staying. 'Happy Birthday, Maryanne,' I thought to myself. 'Happy frickin' Birthday, girl.'

Bruno was sentenced to prison and went to jail on the day of my thirty-third birthday. Somebody in my family said he told the authorities that the little girl was mentally unstable, which, apparently, was how he pleaded his case. He was only sentenced to nine months. I wondered whose payroll the judge was on. I wondered if my father would have the same luck in hell.

Mamma Mia

"TICK, TICK, TICK, MY LOVE," said my mother as I greeted her at the door one bleary Saturday morning.

"What is that supposed to mean?" I asked, moving out of her way as she traipsed in.

"It means that you're not getting any younger, my dear," she said, smiling, and then let out a mini cackle of a laugh. I stood in the foyer, crunched in her embrace. It was easier to acquiesce to her hug than resist. Her spirits were high. Mine were obviously on hiatus.

"You want some tea or juice?" I asked, untangling myself from her and heading into the kitchen, shrouded in my robe.

"Water's fine," she said. I knew her so well, I could hear her surveying the place with her subliminal white glove. "Thank you, sweetheart," she said, taking the cobalt-blue glass filled with water from my hand. "You know, Maryanne, you don't get this time back," she said, setting the water down on the counter without taking a sip.

"What are you talking about?" I asked. I was annoyed and too tired to try to understand her dissociated tirade. She didn't seem to notice.

"I didn't enjoy my life until it was too late, Maryanne. I don't want that to happen to you. You are in the prime of your life. You have everything anyone could want. You are smart, you are beautiful. . ." She gently reached out and held my chin. ". . . you are talented, you have an incredible little boy. You're with a man who loves you. You have it all." I stood there, listlessly. It just sounded like *wa, wa-wa, wa-wa . . .*

"Don't let it pass you by, honey. It's your turn, your time." I was so out of it, I just stared at her and wondered how it was that her eyeliner was closer to her cheekbone than her eyelid.

"Aren't you excited? You and I are going to Hawaii in two days, and you're engaged to a lovely man," she said, holding up my hand to remind me of the three-and-a-half-carat diamond ring that perched on my finger. "What is it, Maryanne? What?" she asked, sensing my distraction. She looked as though she could just shake me.

"I don't care about that stuff, Mom," I said, yanking my hand back. "Don't you get it? None of that is it." My hands clenched into fists and I hoisted them into the air. She stared at me, obviously confused. I sighed and then announced, "I can't feel my life. Everything feels the same—like blank, nothing. Not high, not low, just . . . nothing—do you know what I'm talking about?" I waited, hopelessly hoping she could understand. She sat down in a chair next to me in the breakfast nook and took my hands in hers. She looked adoringly into my eyes and then past me.

"I know I have never said this to you before. Maybe I wasn't ready. I don't know. God knows . . . but Maryannie . . . I am sorry. I am so sorry I wasn't there for you, honey. But I am here now, and even though it's taken me a long time, whatever we need to do, I am here."

My body reacted before I could. The ache in my heart was inexplicable. Those three words coming from her: "I am sorry . . ." Whoever was trapped inside of me had desperately longed not just to hear them but to *feel* them. I must have thought they would heal me, but as I stood there, what they did was release a tidal wave of old wounds and pain. I let it crash through me, around me, even knock me down. And instead of drowning, I floated and drifted . . . and then waded. After what may have been moments or seconds, I remember realizing I wasn't dead.

It was as though for my entire life, I had shoved all my pain and true feelings deeper and deeper until they sunk below sea level, but the rest of me had been barreling at sixty thousand feet through life like a Concorde jet. Then one day, while cruising along, hauling this toxic cargo, I was blindsided by my mother. She ripped me wide open. Whatever was inside me that hadn't hardened into emotional scar tissue was sucked out by the force of her words and was swirling around the kitchen. I only realized I was crying when she handed me a kitchen towel to sop up my face.

"Happy Birthday, my little girl," she said, folding her arms around me. I let her hug me, melting into her as we gently swayed back and forth.

"Happy Birthday to you too, Mommy," I said, my head buried in her silky blonde hair. At that moment, I remembered that she had been sober for eighteen years. Her rebirth, my death—my life. Wrap your mind around that, Darwin . . .

★★★★

The truth of my mother's words was like a heavy ball bearing being thrown into a sand-filled container. The weight of the ball and its downward momentum pushes the orb past the sand's attempt to stall it, until the bearing finally reaches the bottom. *Plunk,* there it is. All my hiding places—the lies I had told myself, my stories and excuses for why my life was the way it was—were exposed simultaneously, just long enough for me to get a good, healthy glimpse of it all. I had been given the gift of seeing the truth, where before I was blind.

It was the first time my mother had admitted any culpability at all, for anything. It didn't occur to me that she could have asked me for forgiveness; I knew that saying she was sorry was the best she could do. And the honest simplicity of her apology explained something I was never able to understand because I had been in so much of my own pain: It wasn't that my mother was bad, she was just human.

This wasn't a child standing before her, it was a thirty-three-year-old woman, and I was close to something. The filters that my past created—whatever had been tainting and distorting my view—had disappeared long enough for me to realize that there could be an end to my suffering. But I still had to contend with my mind's survival strategies, its need to control every move I made. So there I was—one foot on the boat, one foot on the dock.

The Beginning of the End

THE RESIDUE OF MY MOTHER'S unofficial inauguration to the rest of my life was tick-tocking inside my head like a grandfather clock. She had not only ripped open my guts and watched them spill out everywhere, she had also turned up the flame under whatever was left still brewing deep within me.

There I sat, at the edge of my bed in my fancy new house with its panoramic views and cherrywood floors. Beyond the sliding glass doors, the morning dew glistened like scattered diamonds dangling from the leaves of my prized Japanese maple. My three closets were filled to the gills with more clothes than I could ever wear. I spent my days making sure my son's life was the stuff of happy childhood memories. Other than that, I had resigned myself to playing tennis and working out so I could stay skinny, and making sure Jack took the necessary risks so we could get richer. I was already tan—I was half Italian.

Everything looked good on the outside, but in happily ever after, I wasn't supposed to feel the way I did about myself. I recognized that I had fallen back into what I was trying to escape—being unfeeling, angry, and mean. I treated myself even worse. For example, I would routinely inspect my body, starting first thing in the morning with a scrupulous flaw check. My whole day could be ruined based on my findings. On good days, thighs, when extended and flexed straight out in front of me, don't touch. The wider the gap, the better. On bad days, thighs are dangerously close to touching. That meant I was fat, which was unacceptable or—in other words, so was I. (Note to self: "hubris" is derived from the Greek word for a false sense of self-confidence.) This daily examination epitomizes how insipid my life had become.

My relationship with God over the years had run hot and cold and existed on a need-to-know basis: When I was in trouble I needed to know what God was going to do about it. My mask of spiritual arrogance as a self-appointed expert in the field of New Age rhetoric was suffocating me. Because the truth was, over the years I had dressed God up in every costume imaginable—as reincarnated prophets, high-class gurus, and an assortment of avatars, trance channelers, and psychic astrologers. Everyone who applied for the position got an audition from me. I really didn't know God at all.

And what's worse is: Everything I knew in my head, all the books I had read that promised to set me free, all the workshops that were supposed to give me everything I ever wanted in thirty days—some of which included a money-back guarantee ("Excuse me, who do I talk to about a refund? My life is still f—ed up)—all the well-intended therapists who said they could help me heal and love myself. All of that amounted to . . . what? I wanted to know.

A highly successful man I once met told me that his goal was to have his insides match his outsides. I remember thinking how marvelous yet how unachievable this sounded. Well, here I was, and after thirty-three years I could finally claim to have accomplished this goal—I now felt like shit inside and out. Before, I could always run to the next "When I get _____ (fill in the blank), then everything will be okay." But now I finally got it that that was a lie.

As I sat there on my bed, I don't remember feeling much except despondent. It seemed that my only alternative was to stop fighting and accept that trading up was the way of the world and that I had fooled myself into believing there was something more than that. Getting a bigger house, more diamonds, bigger boobs, being Skinnier, Tanner, and Richer—all of which were supposed to be the grand prize—was the booby prize. And that's the only kind that was being given out. There was no such thing as rich people who are truly spiritual, which had been my last hope. God may have created the Universe, but it seemed like this spiritual journey thing was just another sham. So for a girl like me, life as I was living it was about as good as it was going to get. Whoever is Skinny, Tan & Richest wins. Game Over.

I rolled up in a fetal position and squeezed my legs close to my body. I whimpered while tears streamed from my eyes onto my beautiful brocade bedspread. I didn't care that my tears would ruin the spread, that my mascara and lipstick might leave permanent stains on the silk and velvet fabric of the pillows. I sunk deeper into my bed, further into the blankness. I didn't give a damn about anything at all.

This was one of the few times in my life when my mind had no chance. No more clever thoughts, no more fancy metaphors, no rationalizations. There was just . . . nothingness. And I was too far gone into that place to be afraid. The me I had pretended to be could always come up with a plan, and I had simply run out of plans. I just wanted not to die.

I watched the shadows in the room change shape as the sun moved slowly toward the mountain where it would eventually set. I listened to the downstairs phone ring and ring. I heard the mail person drive up, open and then close the box, and then drive off. And occasionally I saw the silhouette of my dog, Brutus, spying me through my sliding glass windows, his head cocked in curiosity.

It was almost dusk when I unstuck my part-goopy, part-crusty face from the bed. I didn't actually have to go to the bathroom, and I can't tell you what posessed me to get up. What I know is that I dragged myself in there, put my hands on the rim of the sink, leaned toward the mirror that covered the entire wall and uttered, "God help me." The only part of me that was real barely squeaked out the words.

I looked down at the white tiles separating the basins as I watched my tears drip from my nose. I couldn't look at myself. I continued my most sincere, most desperate plea ever. "Are you there??? Please . . . if someone is there . . . somewhere . . . anywhere . . . please, talk to me."

And then I said, "I'm sorry . . ." I didn't know why I was apologizing, but somehow I knew I had failed. I should have been better, I should have been stronger—I don't know *what* I should have been. "Because if you're not there . . .

"I can't do this anymore!" I started to gasp. My chest was convulsing—in, out, in, out. My head fell back and my whole body wailed.

The commentator in my head evaporated. No more monitoring me, watching my every move, criticizing me for being theatrical or, worse, labeling me crazy. What I was left with was the sublime weightlessness of pure being. What I didn't know yet was what I needed to unbecome in order to sustain that. That would come later.

I could barely hold on to the counter, so I stumbled back into the bedroom. I stopped at the edge of the bed, got down on my knees, and then prayed these words. I remember them as clearly as I remember giving birth to my son. I turned my face up to the heavens: *"God, please show me the way."* That was it. I pleaded the words over and over: *"Please show me the way. God, please show me the way."*

For the first time I wasn't asking God to fix anything or rescue me from some crisis or grant another of the barter demands that punctuated our on-again, off-again relationship over the years. It had always been about trying to figure out what combination of Good Girl behaviors could get him to grant me his grace. Now I was offering my whole self—including all that was broken, all that was ugly . . . I withheld nothing.

I laid myself at his feet. I gave him all of me. And in return he gave me back himself.

My heart felt like the center of the sun, and the truth that God is there, is here, is in me, *is* me, radiated out of my entire being. It was the most real thing I'd ever felt in my life. And I knew it was never going to leave. I had finally found the thing I had been looking for my whole life. At exactly the point when I exhausted every effort to know God in my mind and simply gave up, God's true identity was revealed to my soul. And it filled in every blank—the entire abyss. I was home.

Epilogue

WITHIN A YEAR, I was graced with enough strength and guidance to leave Jack. This time it wasn't another escape tactic. I didn't make myself the victim; I just wanted to live. I'd been dead for so long.

Jack was the only security and identity I had known for years; we had been together since my son was a baby. So this was no small leap of faith. I had no idea how I was going to care for myself and Warren. And I had not slept alone in my entire adult life. For decades I had been living in a constricted world where my confidence and support came from the power behind my throne—which was always a man. One after another, I had made each one my safety net. I believed that I was too broken for it to be any other way. I had orchestrated a life-long puppet show so I could be taken care of. It was always an equal exchange. I gave everything I had—including my soul—in trade for a safe place to rest.

But now I was ready to go. For the first time I was no one's beautiful arm-charm, nor was I the poor adult child of alcoholic parents, or a terrified, abused object of desire or jealousy. I knew with complete certainty that I would never experience again the kind of suffering that had come with those roles and had plagued me my whole life. I realized that Jack hadn't done anything to me, that everything was perfect, including me.

All my old stories slipped away like a satin sheet off a bed. Finally, I was just me—what was left, who was here. I had been given Grace.

As for my happily ever after . . . my Good Girl Handbook has since been retired. I think I left it in the pocket of my mink coat, which, by the way, I sold some time ago to a woman from the burbs who was half my size. Her husband thought she looked great in it.

I didn't need that coat anymore. Since the day God came into my heart, I always know how to get back home. And that place has no dress code. There's just God, waiting patiently for me . . . whether I am a good girl or not.

A Letter To My Readers

MORE THAN FIVE YEARS HAVE PASSED since that day in my bedroom when I saw the truth. I had been given Grace, but I didn't know how to keep it or if it was even possible to do that. I didn't want to have to ever go back to where I came from. And in return for saving my life, I gave God my word that I would spend the rest of it trying to help end the suffering of others. But I was far from ready to do that, and didn't have a clue how.

Which is what my next book, *Fat, Pasty & Poor: The Lies I Tell Myself,* is about. It is about the battle that went on between will and Grace inside of me, as I fell off my path again and again—this time faster and harder because of what I knew was true. The villain in the next part of my journey is the subtle and sophisticated lies I told myself, masquerading as truth and God's guidance. The things I said and did in front of God—never mind in the name of God—will make your hair stand on end.

Just when I thought I was out of the woods I realized I had hurled myself headfirst into the abyss, the place where I had stuffed and hidden every single excruciating thing I had been incapable of feeling and had hoped would just go away. In each plummet and vista on my continuing roller-coaster ride, God revealed to me a safe way to go into this darkness so I wouldn't have to face it alone. I call this teaching *The Shomi Method: Six Steps for Successful Living,* which I based on the laws of physics.

A series of workshops and CDs is available to anyone who is looking to fill in their blank. This system works regardless of what you were planning to go to your grave with.

So, my brothers and sisters, as this part of my journey ends, and before we enter the next, I'd like to encourage you to ask yourself: How big is my blank?

Until then, many blessings.

Maryanne Comaroto

www.skinnytanandrich.com

BRIDGE THE GAP PUBLISHING
336 Bon Air Center, Suite 124
Greenbrae, CA 94904
www.skinnytanandrich.com

PLEASE SEND ME THE FOLLOWING:

QUAN.	ITEM	PRICE
_____	*Skinny, Tan & Rich* / Hardcover $24.95 ea. / $33.00 (Canada)	_____
	(Deduct 10% discount for five or more)	_____
	SUBTOTAL	_____
	(CA residents add 8.25% Sales Tax) SALES TAX	_____
	($3.50 for first book, then $.50 for each add'l book) SHIPPING	_____
	TOTAL	_____

_____
NAME

_____
COMPANY NAME

_____
ADDRESS

_____
MAILING ADDRESS *(IF DIFFERENT FROM ABOVE)*

_____
CITY   STATE   ZIP

_____
HOME TELEPHONE   FAX   EMAIL

PAYMENT:

❑ Checks payable to *Bridge the Gap Publishing.*
　 Mail to: 336 Bon Air Center, Suite 124 | Greenbrae, CA 94904

❑ VISA ❑ MasterCard ❑ AMEX ❑ Discover

Cardnumber:_____

Name on card:_____

Exp. Date: _____(mo) _____(year)

■ Toll free order phone 1-888-40-SHOMI (secure message machine).
　 Give mailing/shipping address, telephone number, MC/VISA
　 name & card number plus expiration date.
■ Online orders: www.skinnytanandrich.com
■ Email orders: orders@skinnytanandrich.com

www.skinnytanandrich.com